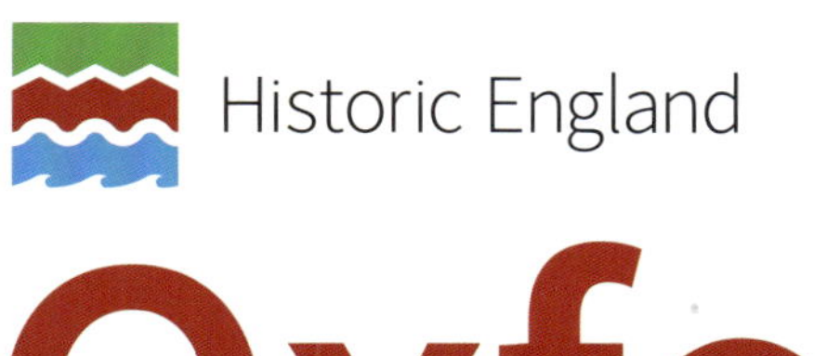

Oxford

Stanley C. Jenkins

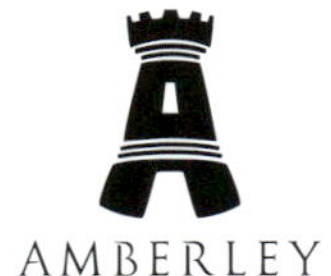

First published 2017

Amberley Publishing
The Hill, Stroud, Gloucestershire, GL5 4EP
www.amberley-books.com

Copyright © Stanley C. Jenkins, 2017

All colour images author's own except bottom image
page 30, bottom image page 39, and bottom image
page 79. Bottom image page 34, bottom image page 50
and sketch plan page 91 also author's own.
All other images reproduced by permission of Historic
England Archive.
© Historic England Archive: top and bottom image
page 18.
© Historic England Archive (Aerofilms Collections):
page 54-55.

The right of Stanley C. Jenkins to be identified as the
Author of this work has been asserted in accordance
with the Copyrights, Designs and Patents Act 1988.

ISBN 978 1 4456 7390 5 (print)
ISBN 978 1 4456 7391 2 (ebook)

British Library Cataloguing in Publication Data.
A catalogue record for this book is available from the
British Library.

Origination by Amberley Publishing.
Printed in Great Britain.

Contents

Introduction   5

The Oxford Colleges   7

University Buildings   49

Some Places of Worship   62

Miscellaneous   86

About the Archive   96

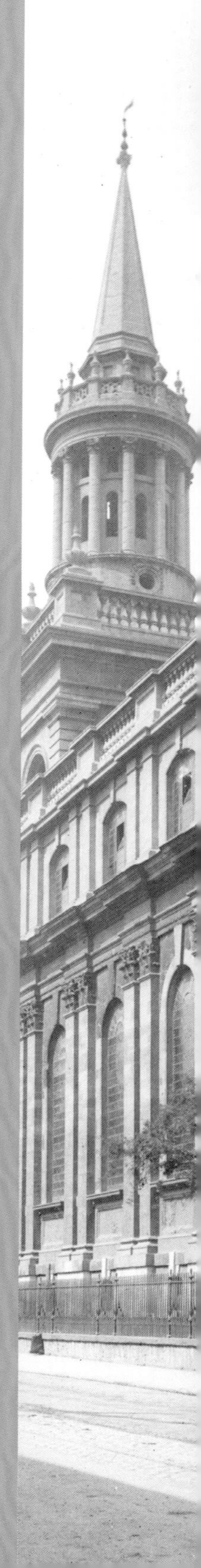

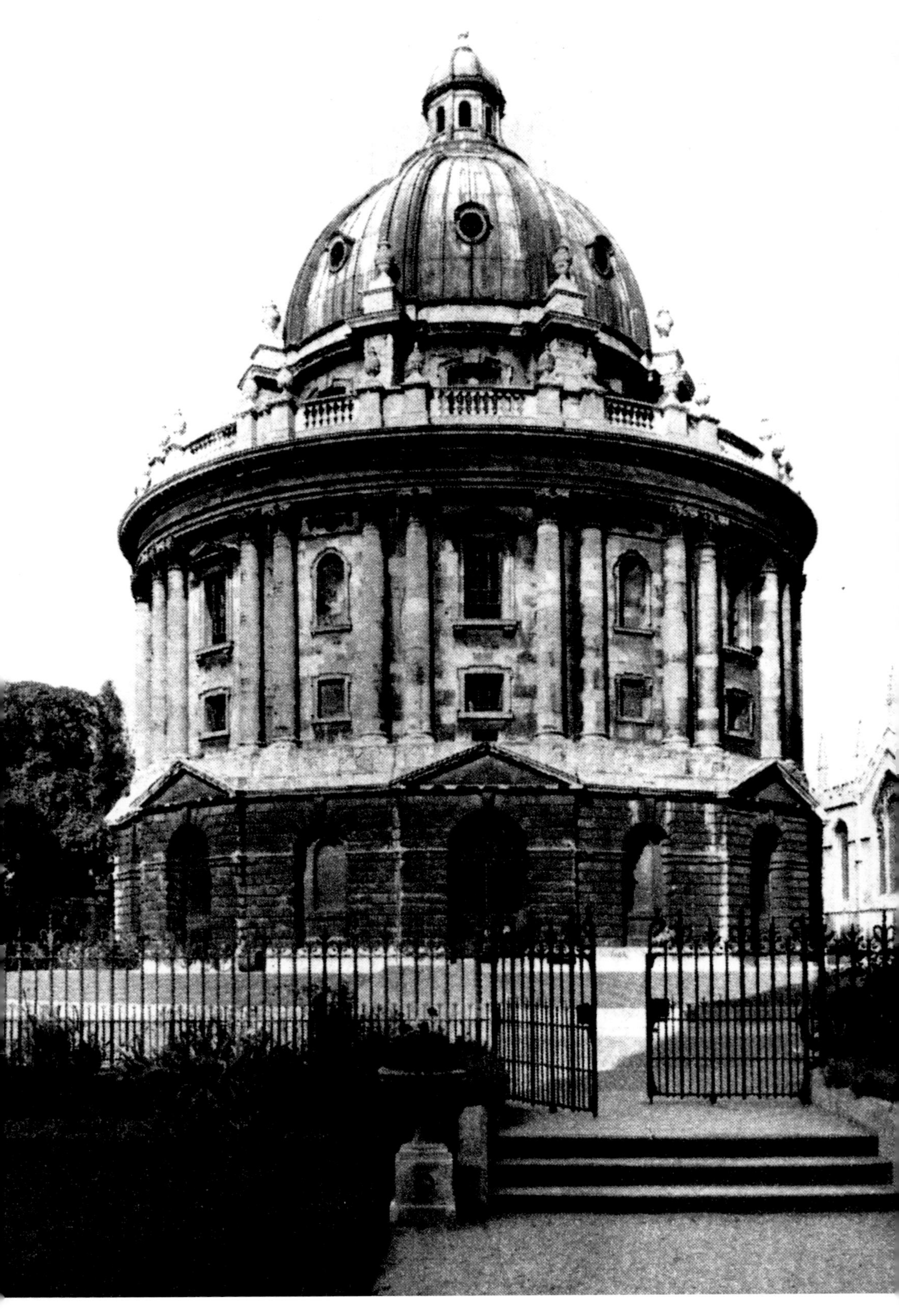

Introduction

Oxford is first mentioned by name in AD 912, the town being one of the 'burhs' or fortified places that King Alfred and his descendants had constructed to protect Wessex during the Viking wars. At that time Alfred's son Edward the Elder and his daughter Aethelflaed were slowly, but inexorably, recovering English territory from the Danes. Aethelflaed was the widow of a Mercian nobleman who had been entrusted with the defence of London, and it is likely that she would have employed her father's engineers to lay out the new burh at Oxford. Although there was already a minster church and a small pre-existing settlement in the vicinity, the new town was on an immeasurably greater scale, and for that reason Lady Aethelflaed can be seen as the founder of Oxford.

The burh at the Oxen-ford was built in a strategic position at a crossing point on the River Thames. It was well-sited for defensive purposes, and was laid out between the Thames and its many subsidiary channels, and the River Cherwell. The surrounding marshes and low-lying areas provided natural defensive features, while the burh itself was encircled by stockaded banks and stone-faced ramparts. To the west, a 'hythe' or wharf was constructed on the River Thames, which enabled the new settlement to be supplied from Reading and London. Despite a destructive Danish attack in 1002, this West Saxon stronghold soon developed into a prosperous and thriving town.

The Domesday Book records that, in 1086, Oxford contained 'as well within the wall as without ... 243 houses which pay geld, and besides these there are 500 houses less 22 so waste and destroyed that they cannot pay geld'. Additionally, there were 217 houses held by the king, bishops or other important people, together with a further eighty dwellings held by the priests of St Michael's or St Frideswide's. From this documentary evidence, late Saxon Oxford must have contained around 900 houses, and assuming an average figure of five people per household, this would suggest a population of approximately 4,000 people.

The streets of the Saxon burh were laid out in a cruciform arrangement within the protective wall, and this basic town plan has survived until the present day. The crossroads at the centre of the town became known as 'Carfax', or the Four Ways (*quatre voies*) – these four thoroughfares being Cornmarket, St Aldates, High Street and Queen Street, which extend north, south, east and west respectively towards the long-demolished city gates. In the eleventh century the town was enlarged to the east.

Oxford became a recognised centre of learning during the twelfth century. As the number of students increased, hostels or 'halls' were opened to accommodate them, while benefactors began to found autonomous colleges, which tended to be much larger than the halls, and were supported by endowments. It is estimated that there were, in the mid-fifteenth century, around seventy halls in Oxford, together with ten colleges, though in the fullness of time further colleges were founded – many of the earlier halls were absorbed or converted into the new collegiate foundations. By 1852 there were nineteen colleges and five halls (including Magdalen Hall, which became Hertford College in 1874, and St Edmund Hall, which was incorporated as a college in 1957).

Oxfordshire was heavily involved with the Civil War, which began on 22 August 1642. The first large battle took place at Edge Hill, near Banbury, on 23 October, and although this engagement was inconclusive, it enabled the king to set up his wartime capital in Oxford. The city was extensively fortified by a sophisticated system of earthwork bastions, while at the same time the Royalists created an outer ring of detached outposts at places such as Woodstock Palace and Bletchingdon House. For the next four years Oxford was in a state of semi-siege, though the Parliamentarians made no attempt to storm the city, and on 24 June 1646 the Royalists surrendered without bloodshed.

The population of Oxford in 1801 was 11,694, rising to 37,057 by 1901, by which time the urban area had extended well beyond the confines of the original settlement. However, the main period of growth took place during the early twentieth century, when the city expanded in all directions, absorbing once-rural communities such as Headington and Cowley; the population had reached 80,540 by 1931, while in 2011 Oxford had an estimated population of 151,900.

The Oxford Colleges

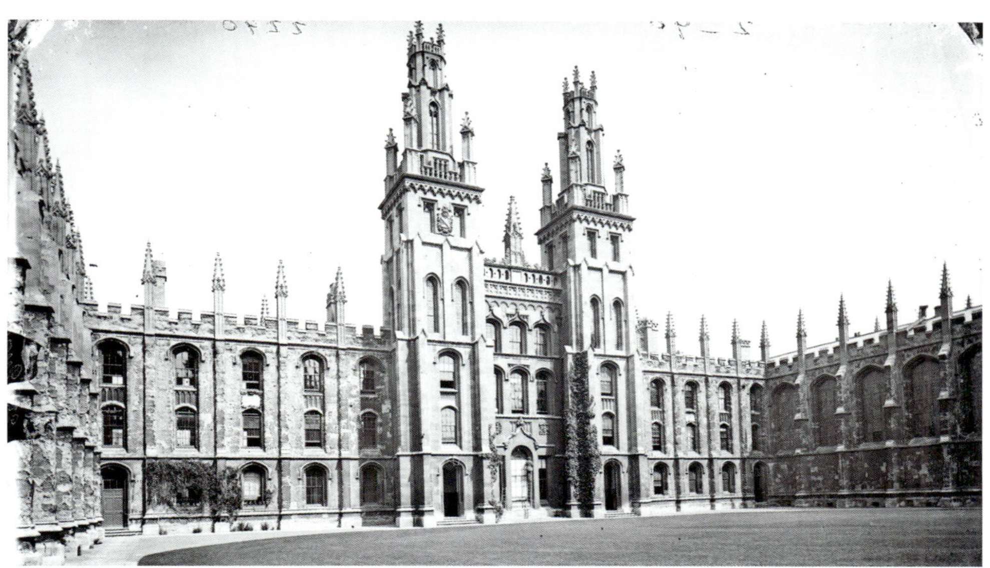

All Souls College

All Souls College was founded by Archbishop Henry Chichele (*c.* 1362–1443) in 1438 as a college and chantry in which masses would be said for the souls of those who had died during the Hundred Years' War – the college being, in effect, a medieval war memorial. The college has three quadrangles, the earliest being the fifteenth-century Front Quadrangle, while the largest is North Quad, designed by Nicholas Hawksmoor (*c.* 1662–1736). The accompanying photographs show Hawksmoor's distinctive 'twin towers', which dominate the eastern side of the North Quad.

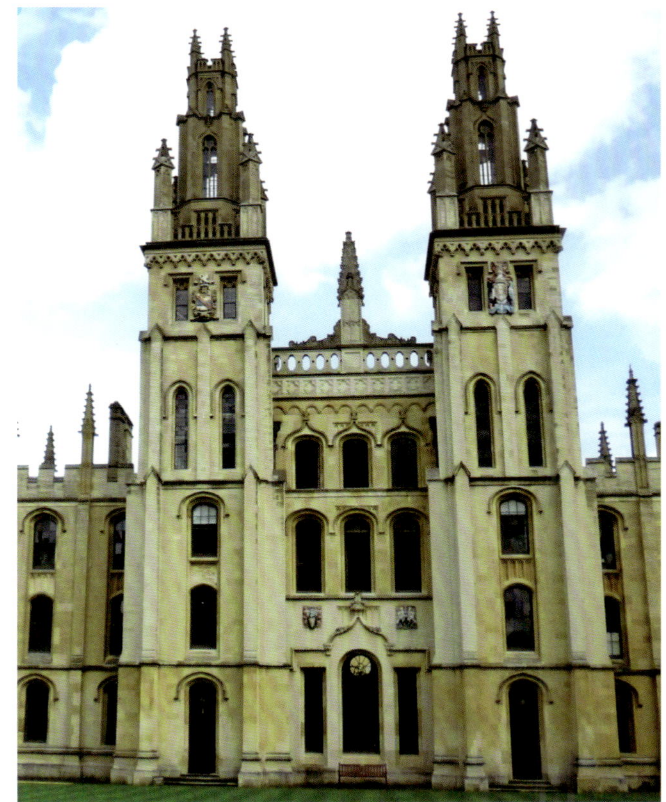

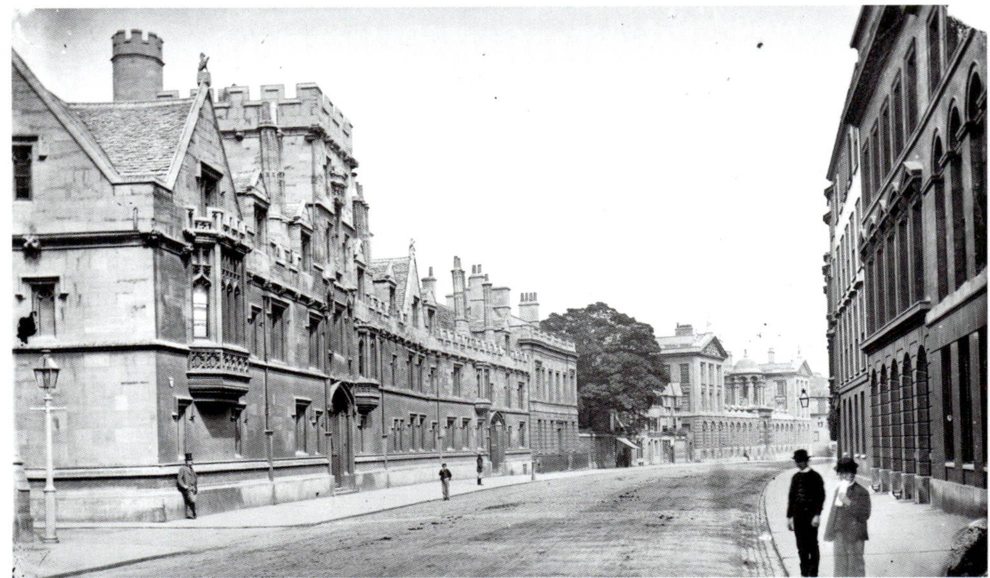

All Souls College

Above: This classic Oxford view, dating from 1870, is looking east along 'The High' towards Magdalen Bridge. Queen's College is visible in the distance, while the lengthy façade of All Souls College can be seen to the left of the picture. The gate tower, giving access to Front Quad, dates from the fifteenth century; a second gateway, which can be seen beyond the slight 'kink' in the façade, is part of a sixteenth-century extension.

Below: Looking westwards in the opposite direction towards Carfax.

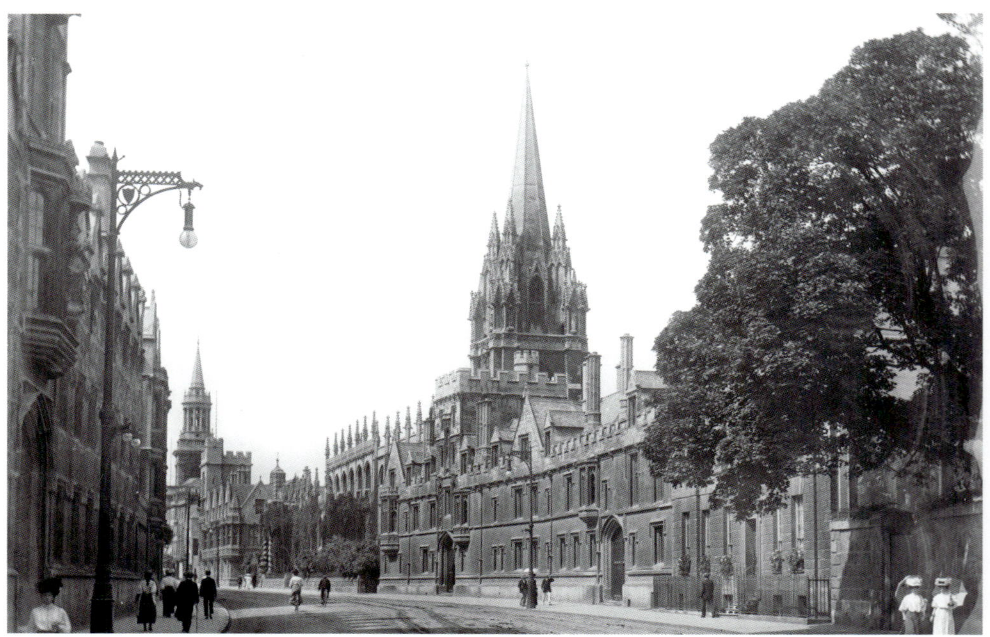

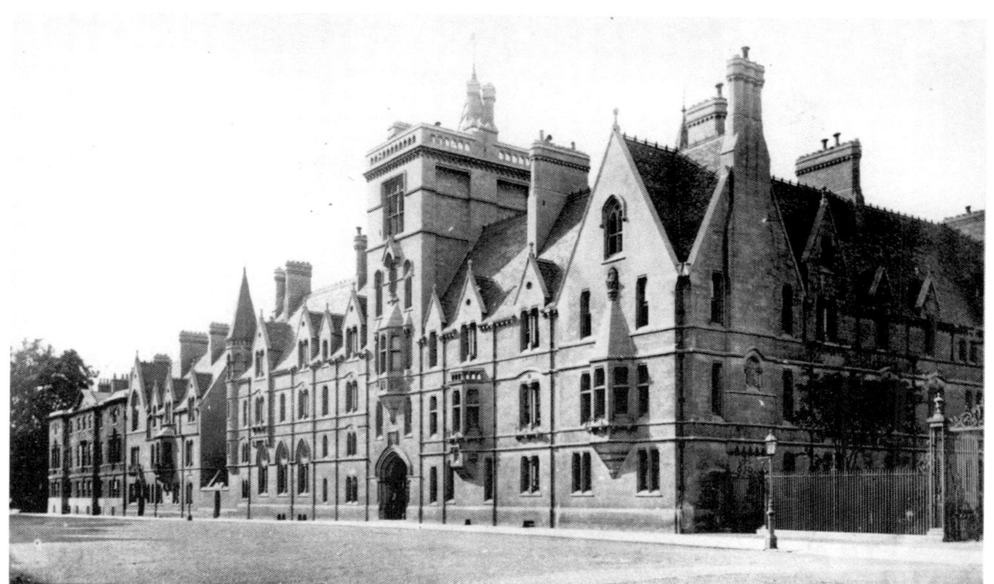

Balliol College

This famous college was founded around 1263 by John de Balliol (*c.* 1200–68) of Barnard Castle, the father of King John of Scotland, in penance for an attack on the Bishop of Durham. The college boasts an immensely long frontage that extends from St Giles', and around the corner into Broad Street – the main Broad Street façade, shown in the upper picture, being in the Gothic Revival style. The architect was Alfred Waterhouse (1830–1905). The college was originally intended to be a hostel for poor students, but it became a conventional college during the fourteenth century. There are two quadrangles, the largest being known as the Garden Quad. The lower photograph is a detailed view of the chapel, on the west side of the Front Quad, which was designed by the Victorian architect William Butterfield (1814–1900) and erected in 1856–57.

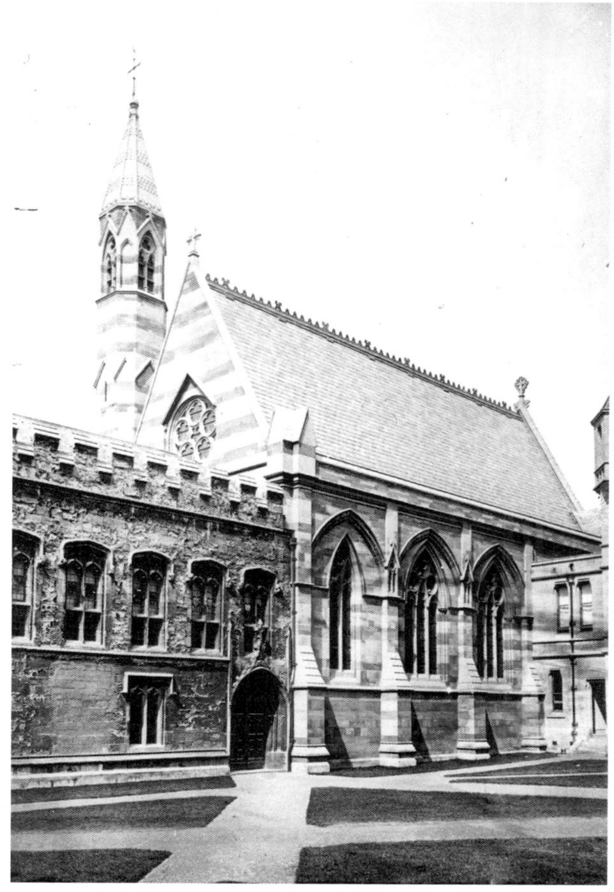

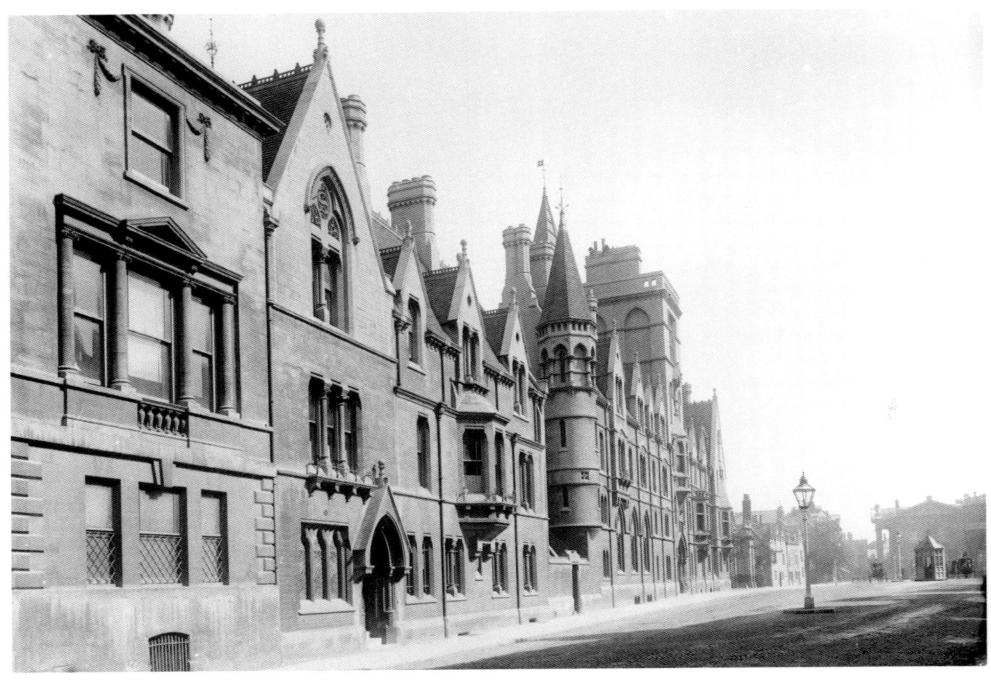

Balliol College

Above: A further view of the Broad Street frontage, looking eastwards. Famous alumni associated with this college include prime ministers Herbert Asquith (1852–1928), Harold Macmillan (1894–1986) and Edward Heath (1916–2005), together with the political economist Adam Smith (1723–90).

Below: A detailed view of the hall by Alfred Waterhouse, which is sited at the north end of the Garden Quad.

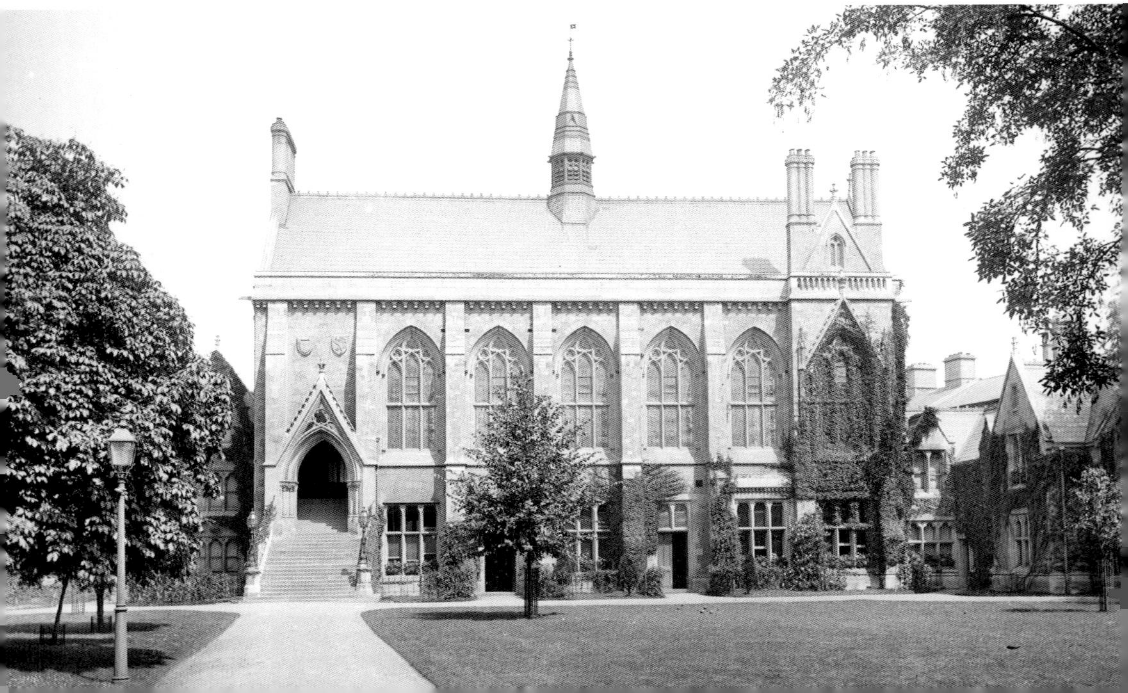

Brasenose College

Brasenose College was founded in 1509 by William Smith, Bishop of Lincoln (*c.* 1460–1514), and Sir Richard Sutton (*c.* 1460–1524), its name being derived from an old door knocker of Brasenose Hall, which had occupied part of the site. The original Brasenose College buildings, known as the Old Quad, are entered from Radcliffe Street, but the college was extended southwards to the High Street during the nineteenth century. The upper picture, taken by local photographer Henry Taunt (1842–1922) in 1875, depicts the main gate tower on the eastside of the Old Quad, which was built in 1512, while the colour view shows the High Street frontage in 2012.

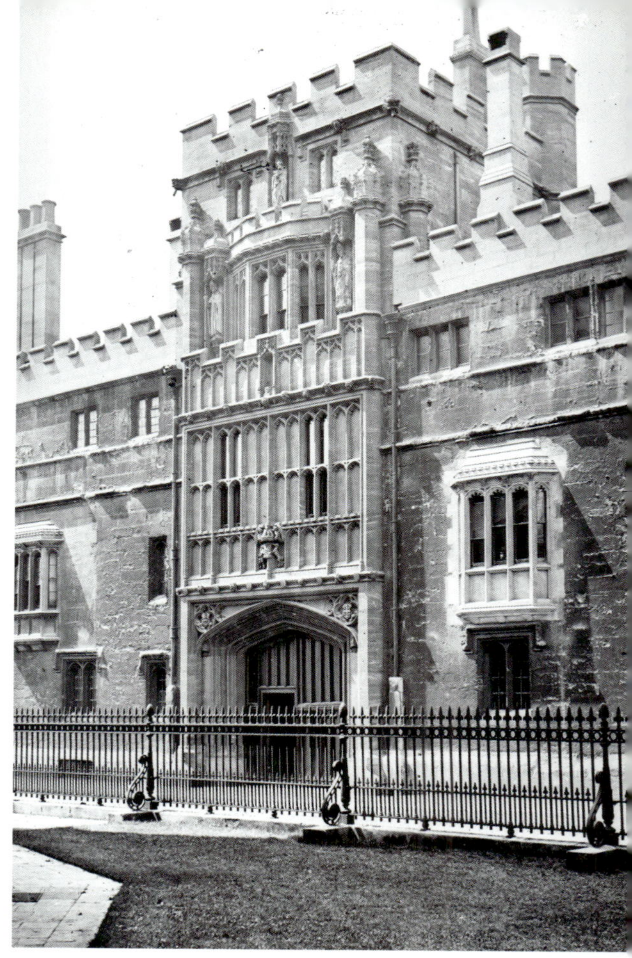

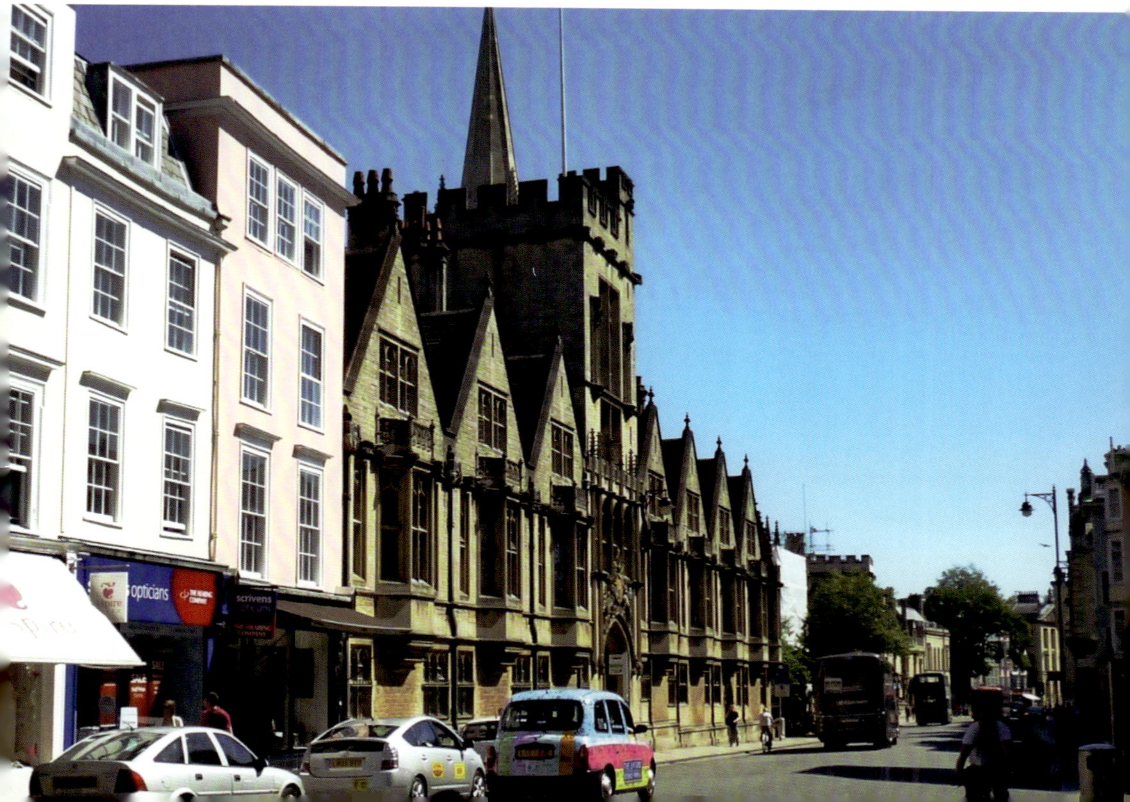

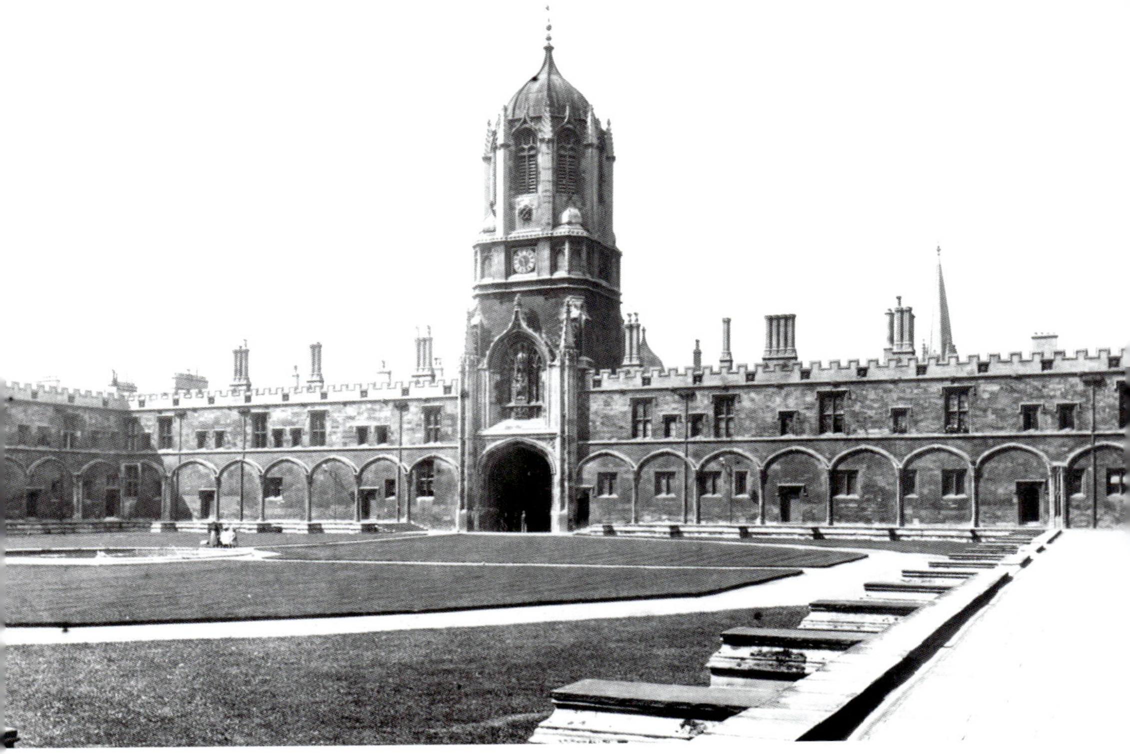

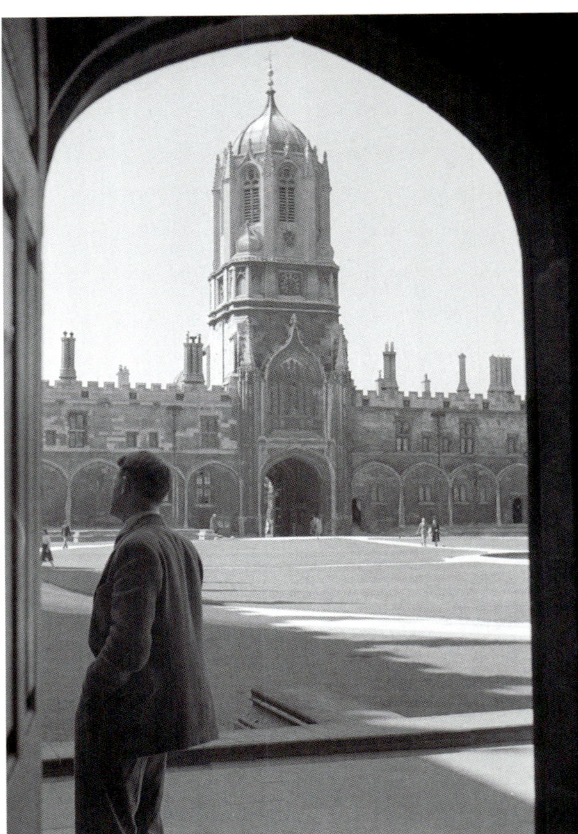

Christ Church

Christ Church was founded in 1525 by Cardinal Thomas Wolsey (1470–1530), who intended to build a magnificent new college on land that had formerly belonged to St Frideswide's Priory. Several monasteries were suppressed to provide funds for the new college, which was to have an establishment of 180 persons, including a dean, 100 canons and thirteen chaplains, together with professors, teachers and choristers. In the event, Cardinal Wolsey's grandiose building scheme was brought to an abrupt halt in 1529 when he fell from power; around three-quarters of the great quadrangle had been built by that time, together with the largest hall and kitchen in Oxford. These two photographs show the main quadrangle, known as Tom Quad, looking west towards Tom Tower.

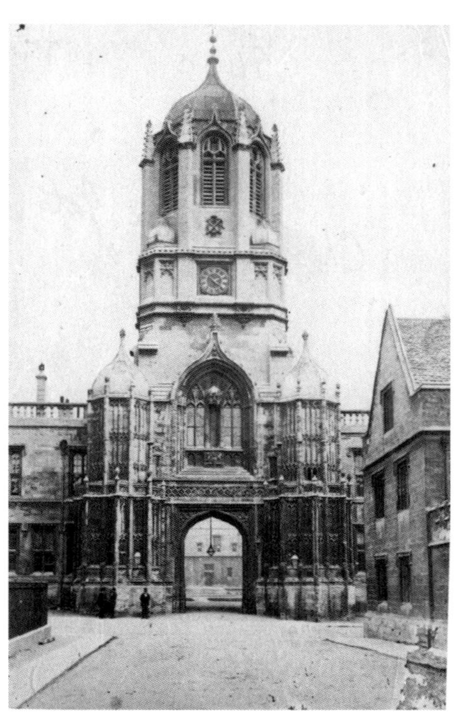

Christ Church
Right: Tom Tower, at the entrance to the college,
is something of a hybrid – the gatehouse having
been built by Cardinal Wolsey – whereas the
iconic tower, with its ogee cap, was added by
Sir Christopher Wren (1632–1723). Within
the tower is 'Great Tom', a 6.25-ton bell that
once hung in Osney Abbey. Tom Quad, which
measures 264 feet by 261 feet, is the largest
quadrangle in Oxford, but it has an unfinished
appearance insofar as the cloisters were never
roofed over as Wolsey had envisaged.

Below: The hall, with its hammer-beam roof,
measures 115 feet by 40 feet.

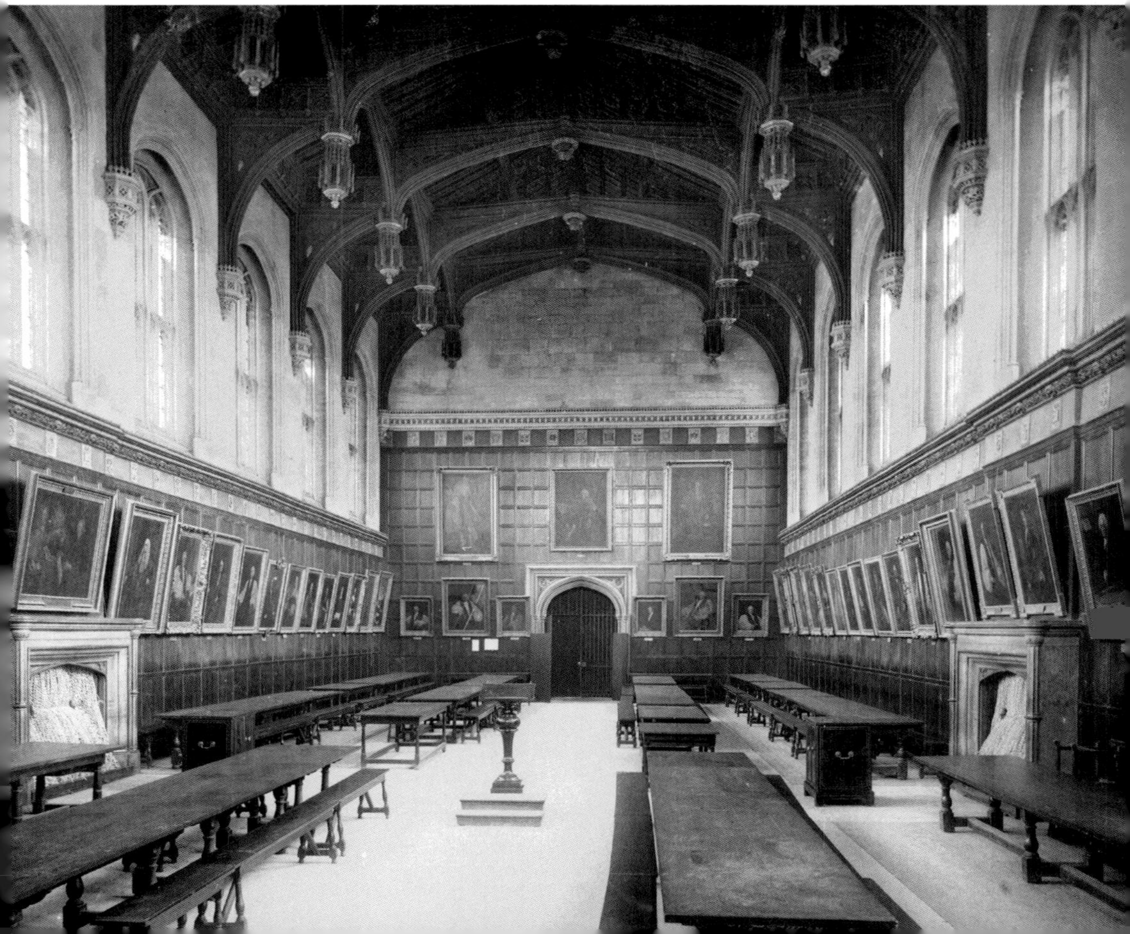

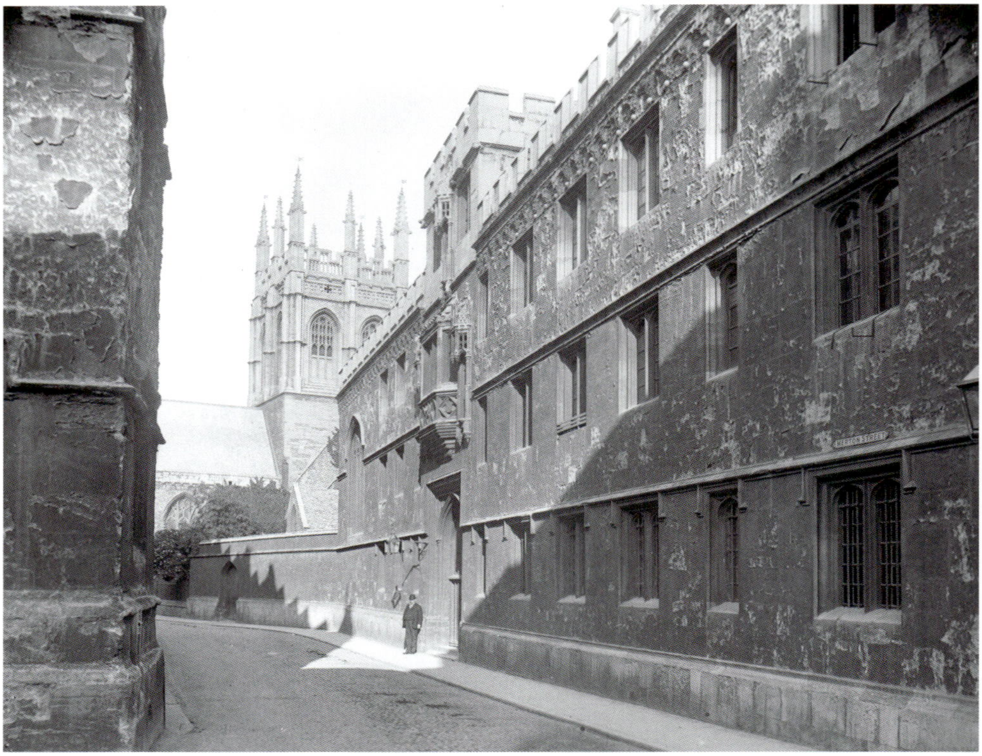

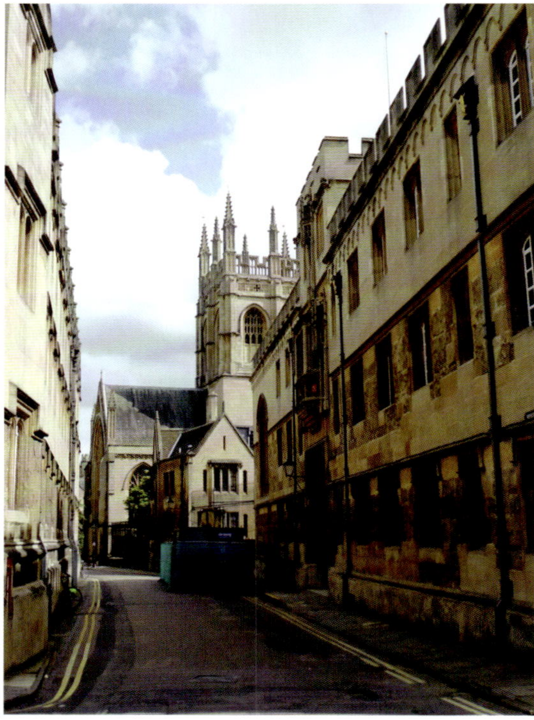

Corpus Christi College

This college, which is situated in picturesque Merton Street, was founded by Richard Fox (*c.* 1447–1528), Bishop of Winchester, on 1 March 1517, with provision for a president, twenty fellows, and twenty scholars. The main gateway, which can be seen in this Victorian view, gives access to the Front Quad, which was built in the sixteenth century. The tall Gothic building that can be seen in the background is Merton College chapel. The colour photograph was taken in 2012 and, like the upper view, it is looking eastwards along Merton Street. The large building that can be seen to the left is Oriel College.

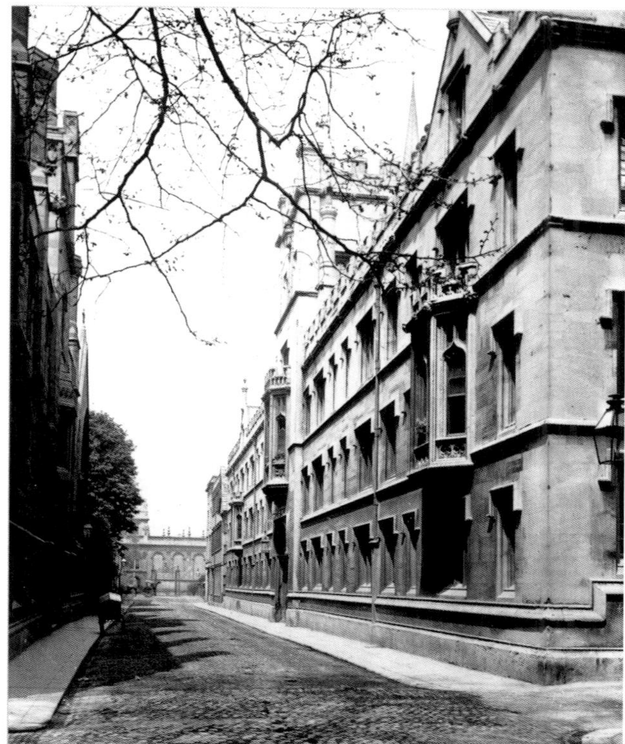

Exeter College
Associated from its inception
with the West Country, Exeter
College was founded in 1314
by Walter de Stapleton, Bishop
of Exeter, and refounded by
Sir William Petre (1505/6–72)
in 1566. Many of its buildings
are of seventeenth- or
eighteenth-century origin,
but the impressive chapel,
which was inspired by La
Sainte Chapelle in Paris, was
designed by Sir Gilbert Scott
(1811–78) and completed in
1860. The upper view shows
the exterior of the college from
Turl Street, while the lower view
shows the chapel; both of these
photographs were taken by
Henry Taunt around 1880.

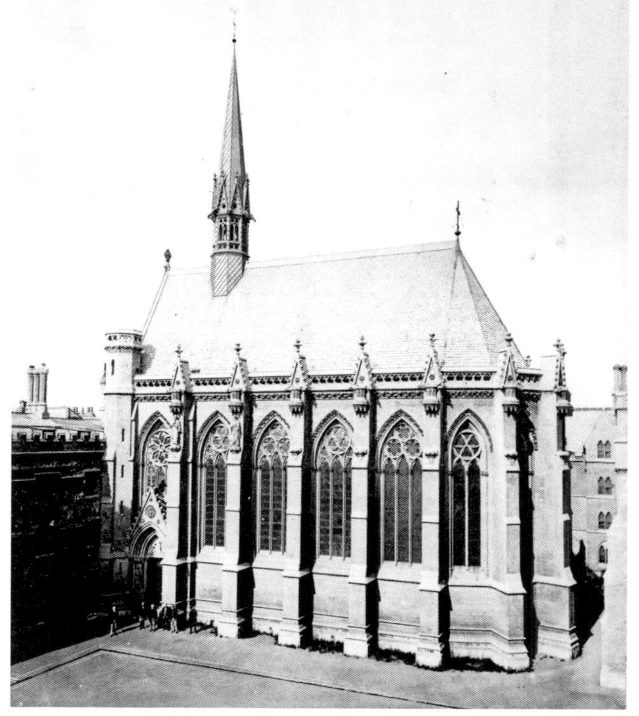

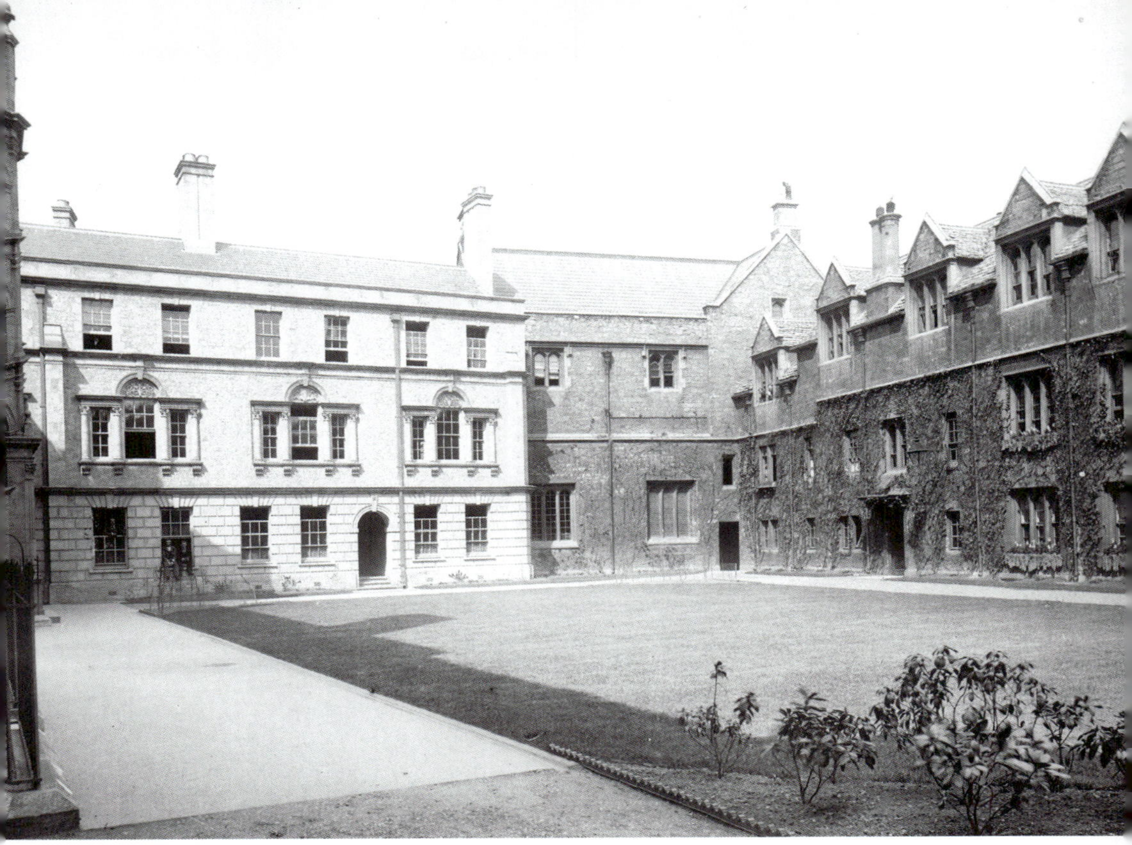

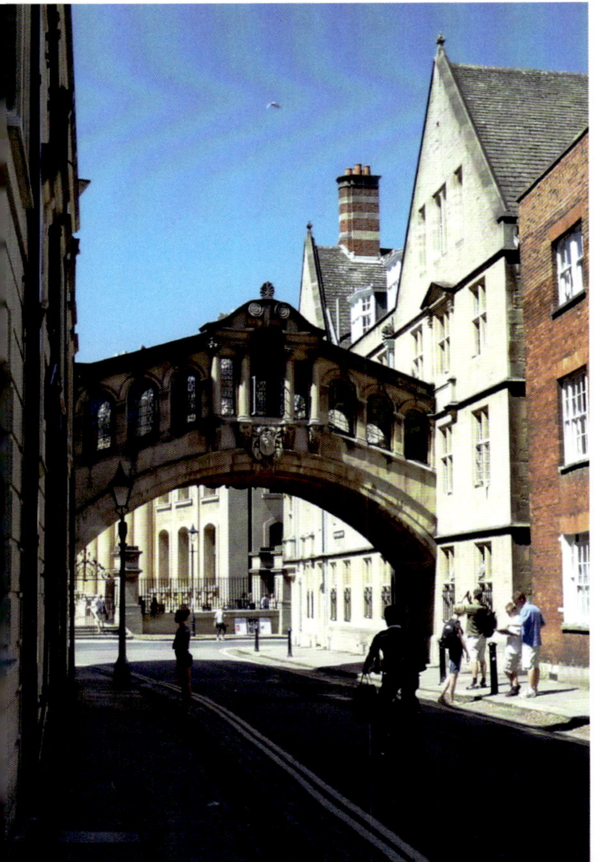

Hertford College and Hart Hall

Hertford was founded as a college in 1740 when Dr Richard Newton, the Principal of 'Hart Hall', obtained a charter of incorporation. Unfortunately, there were insufficient funds to sustain the new foundation and the institution went into decline, its buildings being taken over by Magdalen Hall. After many vicissitudes, Hertford College was revived by Act of Parliament in 1874, the necessary endowment having been provided through the generosity of Thomas Baring (1831–91), a member of the famous banking family. The refounded college was laid out by Sir Thomas Jackson (1836–1924) in his favourite English Renaissance style. The main quadrangle, shown in the upper view, was built during the late nineteenth century, while the extension on the north side of New College Lane was added during the early twentieth century. The two parts of the college are linked by Jackson's famous 'Bridge of Sighs'.

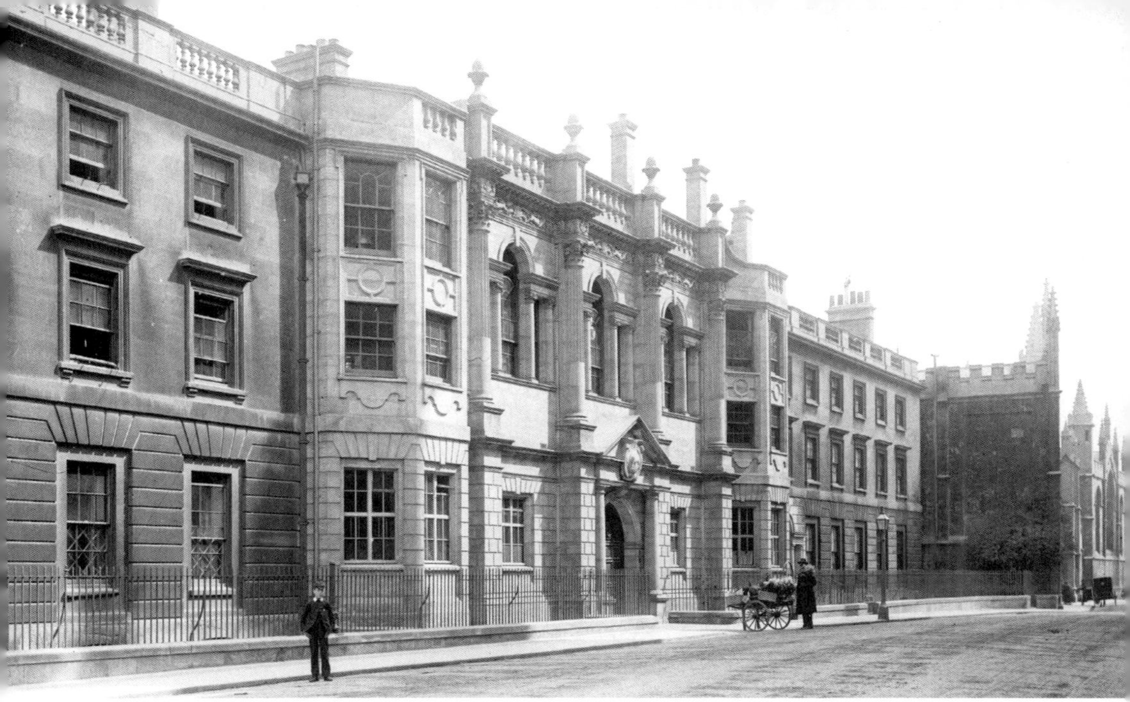

Hertford College and Hart Hall
Most of the Hertford College buildings are of Victorian or Edwardian origin, but the main quadrangle incorporates portions of the much older Hart Hall. The upper photograph shows the Catte Street façade during the 1880s, while the lower view provides a further glimpse of the main quadrangle. Although Hertford College is a relatively new foundation, it can claim several famous alumni including Lord Clarendon, Charles James Fox (1749–1806), the philosopher Thomas Hobbes (1588–1679), and the Bible translator William Tyndale (*c.* 1494–1536), all of whom had studied at Hart Hall or Magdalen Hall.

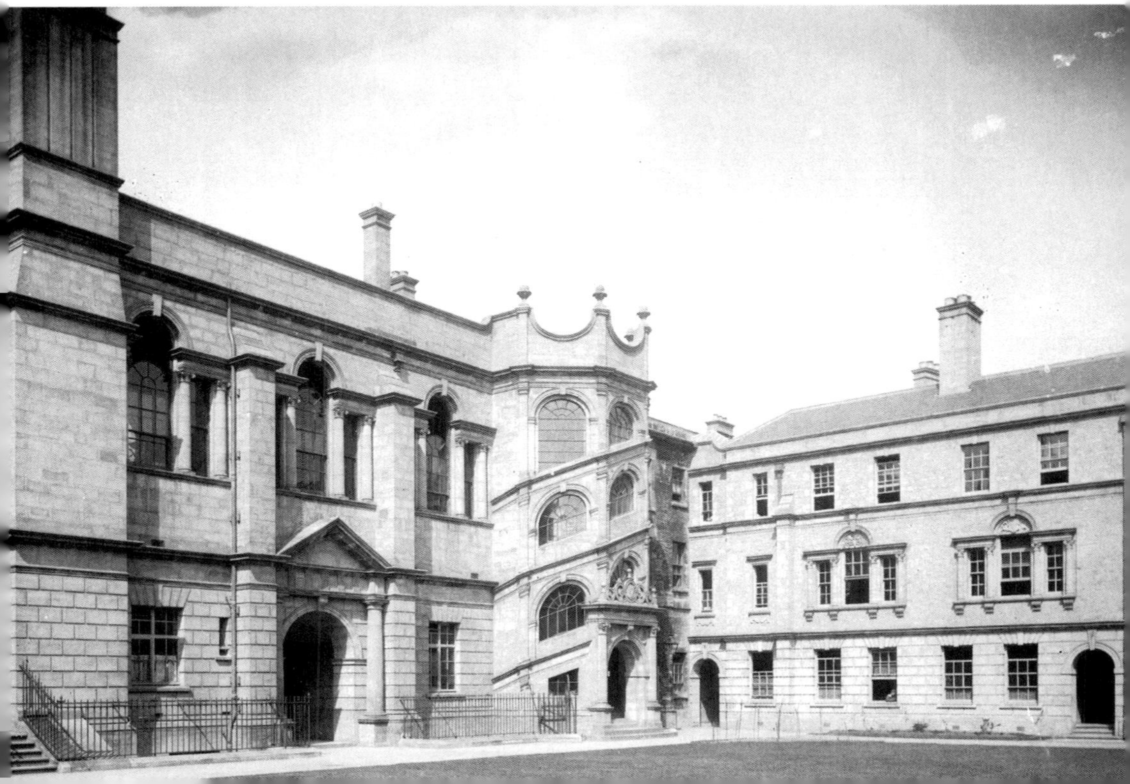

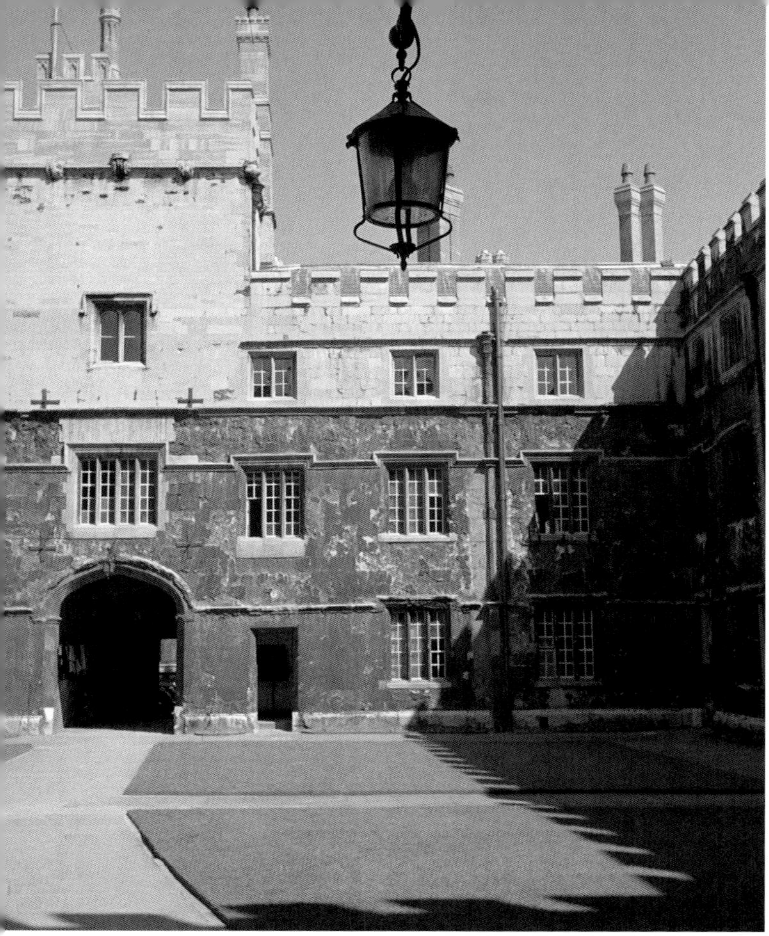

Jesus College
Sited on the west side of Turl Street, Jesus College was founded by Elizabeth I in 1571 as the result of a petition from Hugh Price (*c.* 1495–1574), the treasurer of St David's Cathedral. This college has always been intimately connected with Wales, and many of its students have been Welshmen. There are two quadrangles, together with an additional range of buildings flanking Ship Street, which was added in the early twentieth century. The upper picture shows the part of the First Quad, while the lower view depicts the Inner Quad. Jesus College is associated with many eminent people – T. E. Lawrence (1888–1935) and former Prime Minster Harold Wilson (1916–95) being two of its most famous alumni.

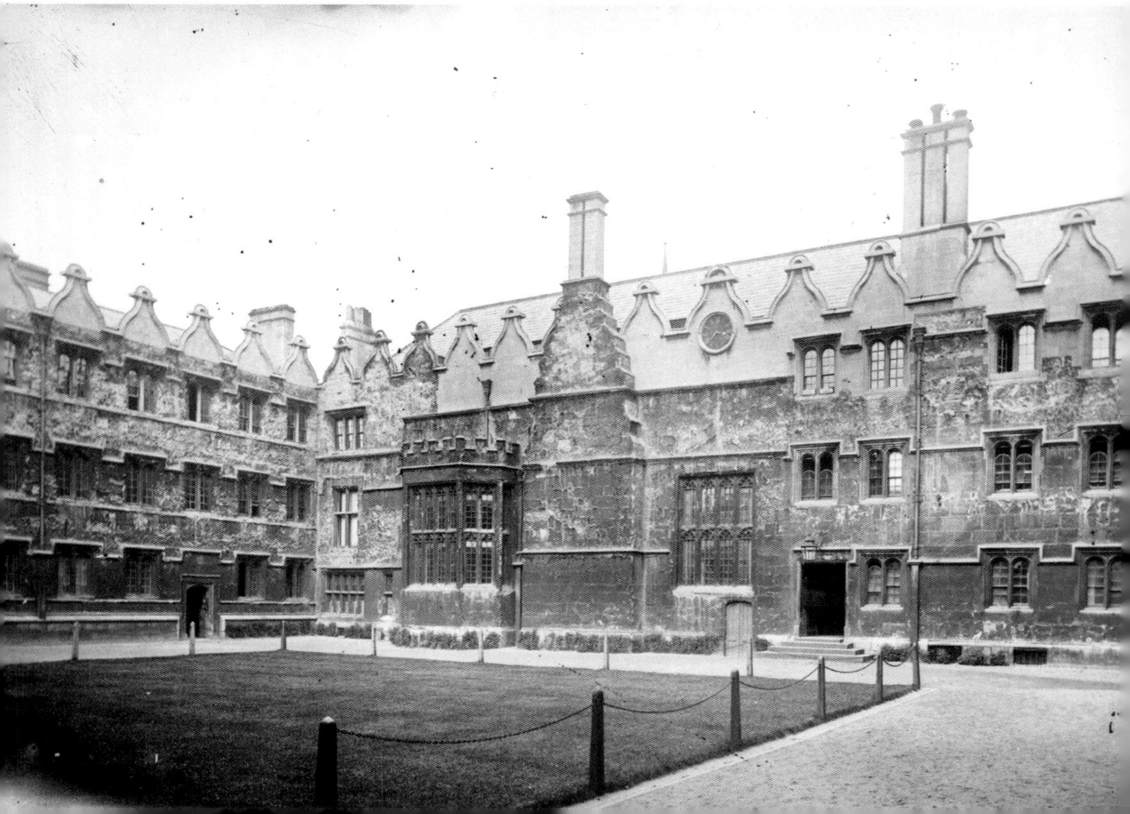

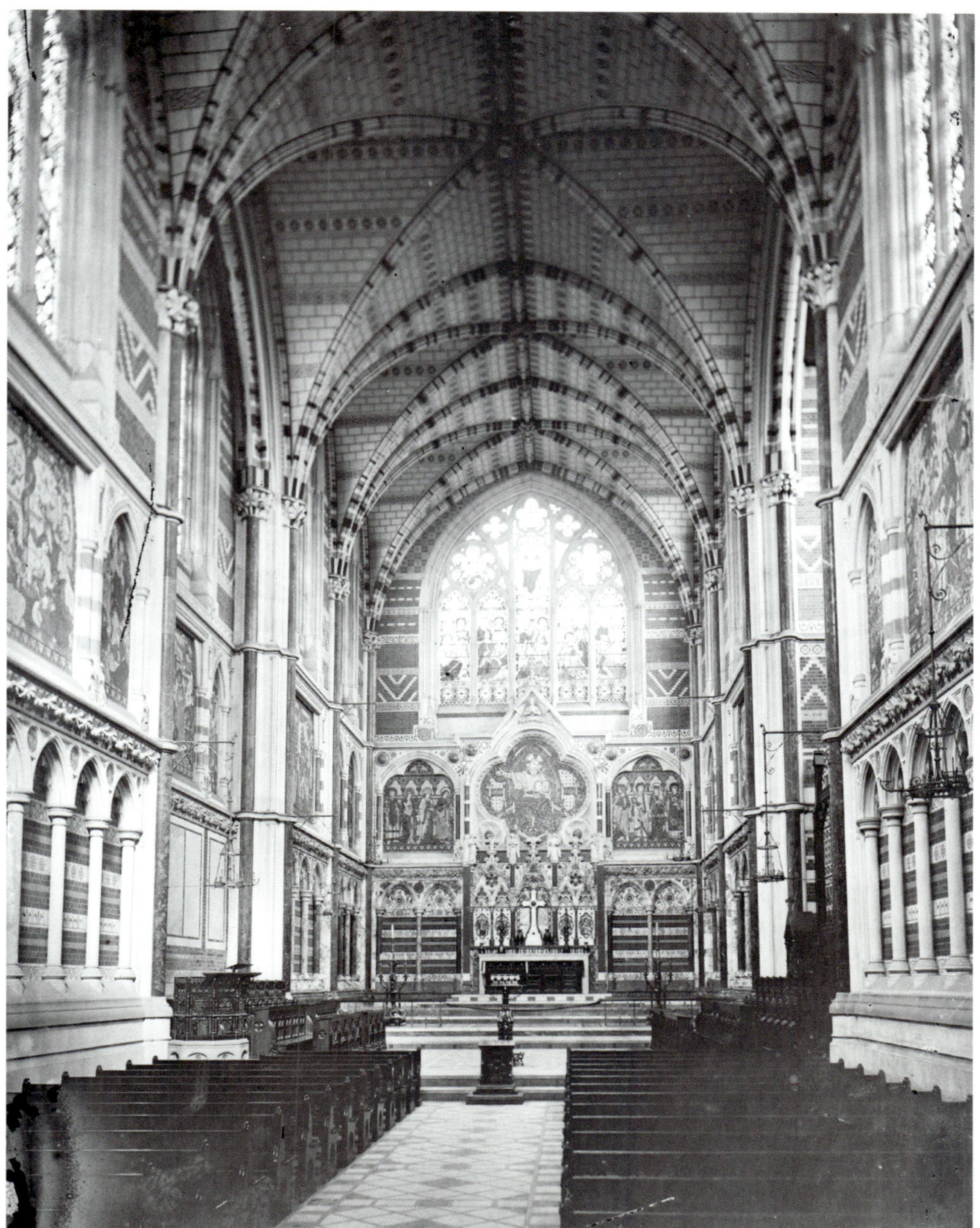

Keble College

Keble College, in Parks Road, is now regarded as an archetypal Victorian building. Designed by William Butterfield, and notable for its eye-catching polychromatic brickwork, the college was formally opened by Lord Salisbury on 21 June 1870. There are two quadrangles, known as Pusey Quad and Liddon Quad, while a range of twentieth-century buildings have been added along Blackhall Road. The chapel, in Liddon Quad, is shown around 1912.

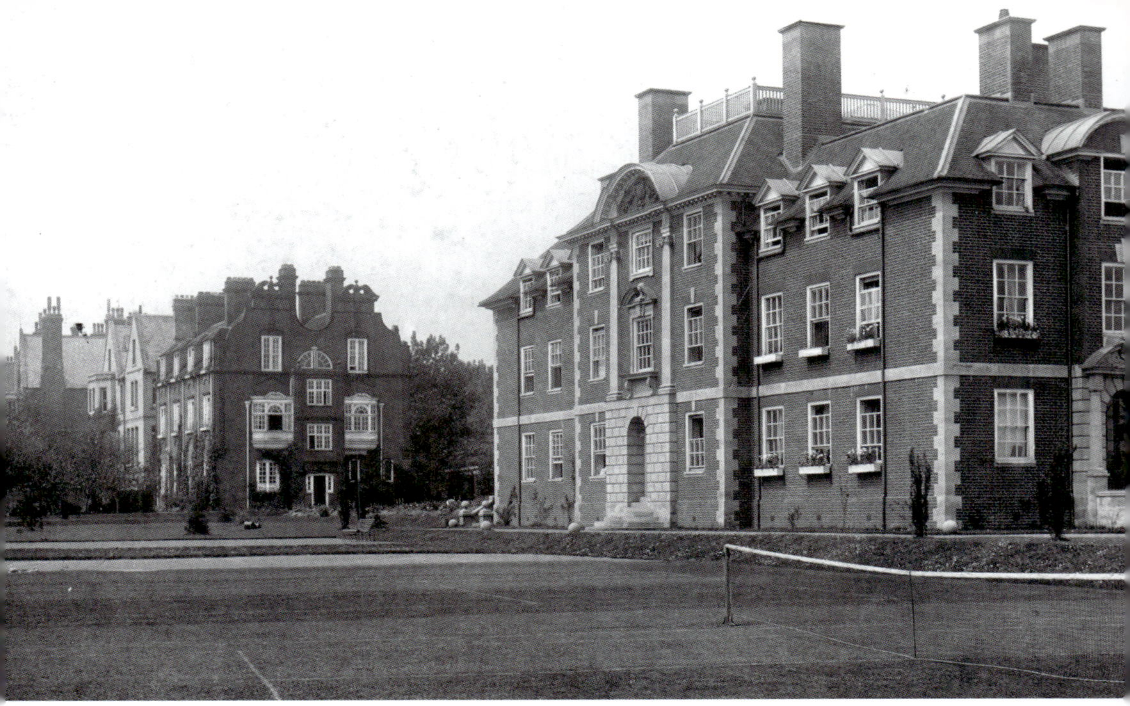

Lady Margaret Hall

Women were first admitted to Oxford in the 1870s, although they were not allowed to become members of the university until 1920. Lady Margaret Hall and Somerville, the first ladies' colleges, were founded as hostels for Anglican and Nonconformist students respectively, and they both became full colleges in 1960; men were first admitted in 1979. Lady Margaret Hall boasts some surprisingly grand buildings in the Queen Anne style.

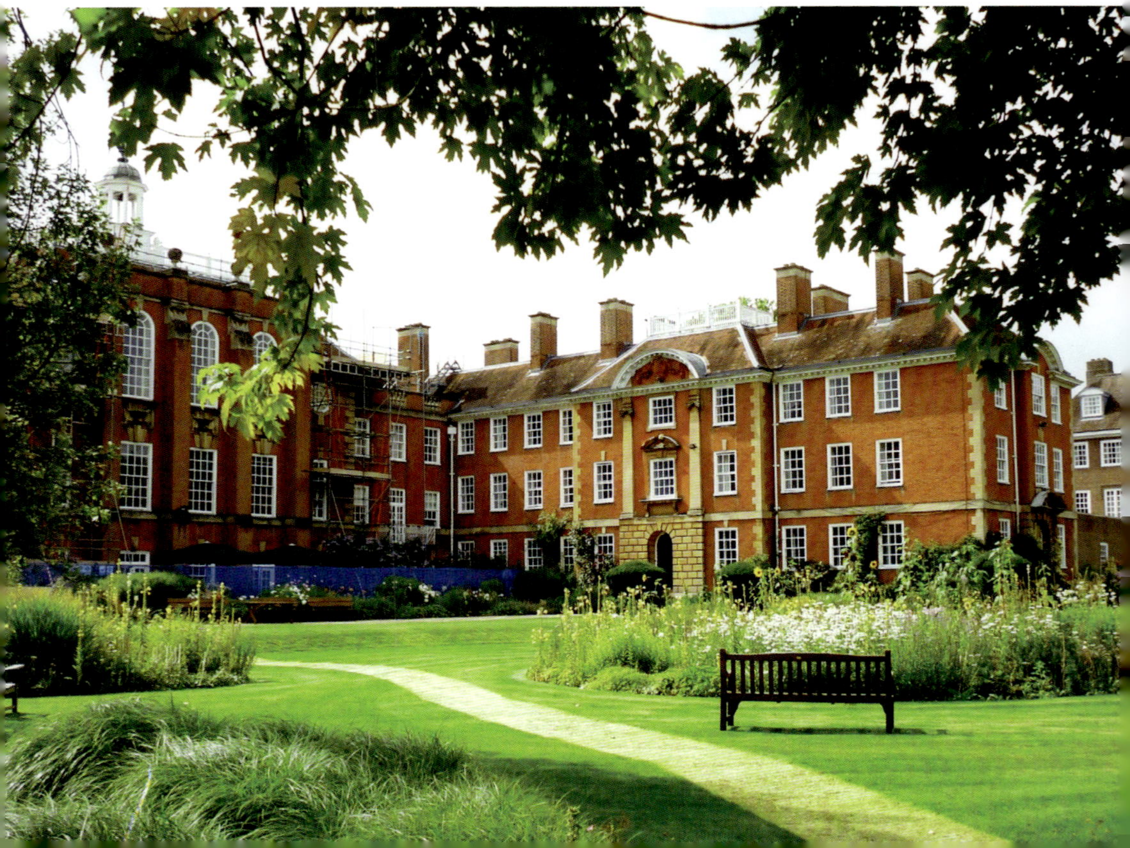

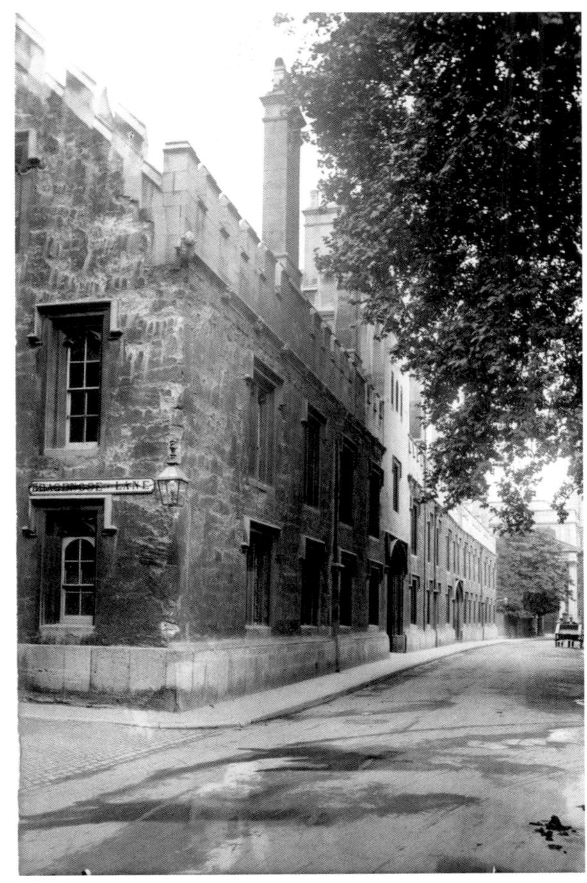

Lincoln College

Lincoln College was founded by Richard Flemming (*c.* 1385–1431), Bishop of Lincoln, who, in 1427, received royal licence to unite the parishes of All Saints, St Michael-at-the-Northgate, and St Mildred to form a 'little college of theologians' to combat the supposed 'heretical' teachings of John Wycliffe and the Lollards, who were questioning Catholic orthodoxy. St Mildred's Church was demolished to make way for the new college, which has two quadrangles and a lengthy façade on the east side of Turl Street. The photographs, both of which were taken by Henry Taunt, show the Turl Street frontage in 1875 and the Front Quad in 1885. John Wesley (1703–91), a graduate of Christ Church, was elected a Fellow of Lincoln College in 1726; he received his MA in the following year, and was ordained as a priest on 22 September 1728. His rooms in Chapel Quad are marked by a commemorative plaque.

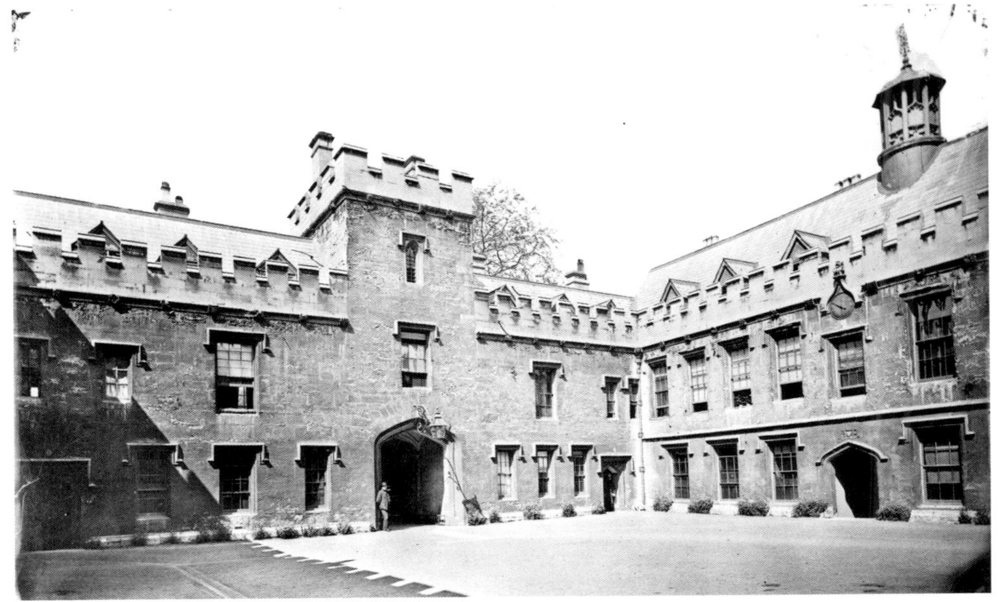

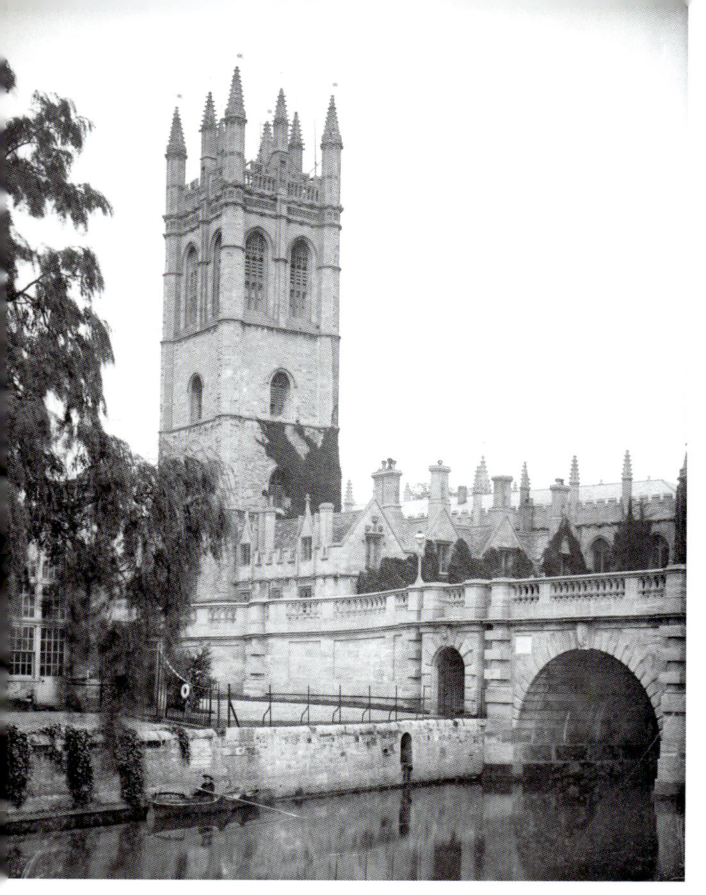

Magdalen College

Magdalen College was founded by William Patten of Waynflete in Lincolnshire (*c*. 1400–86), Bishop of Winchester, in 1458 – the dedication being a reflection of the Bishop's devotion to St Mary Magdalen. Construction commenced in 1467 and the main buildings, including the cloister and the famous Magdalen Tower, were completed by around 1509, the principal architect being William Orchard (*ob*. 1504), who was Oxford's leading master mason. The left view, dating from the 1880s, shows the tower and part of the adjacent Magdalen Bridge, while the lower photograph shows the south-western corner of the cloister, with the Founder's Tower to the right and Magdalen Tower visible in the background; the latter structure has a height of 144 feet.

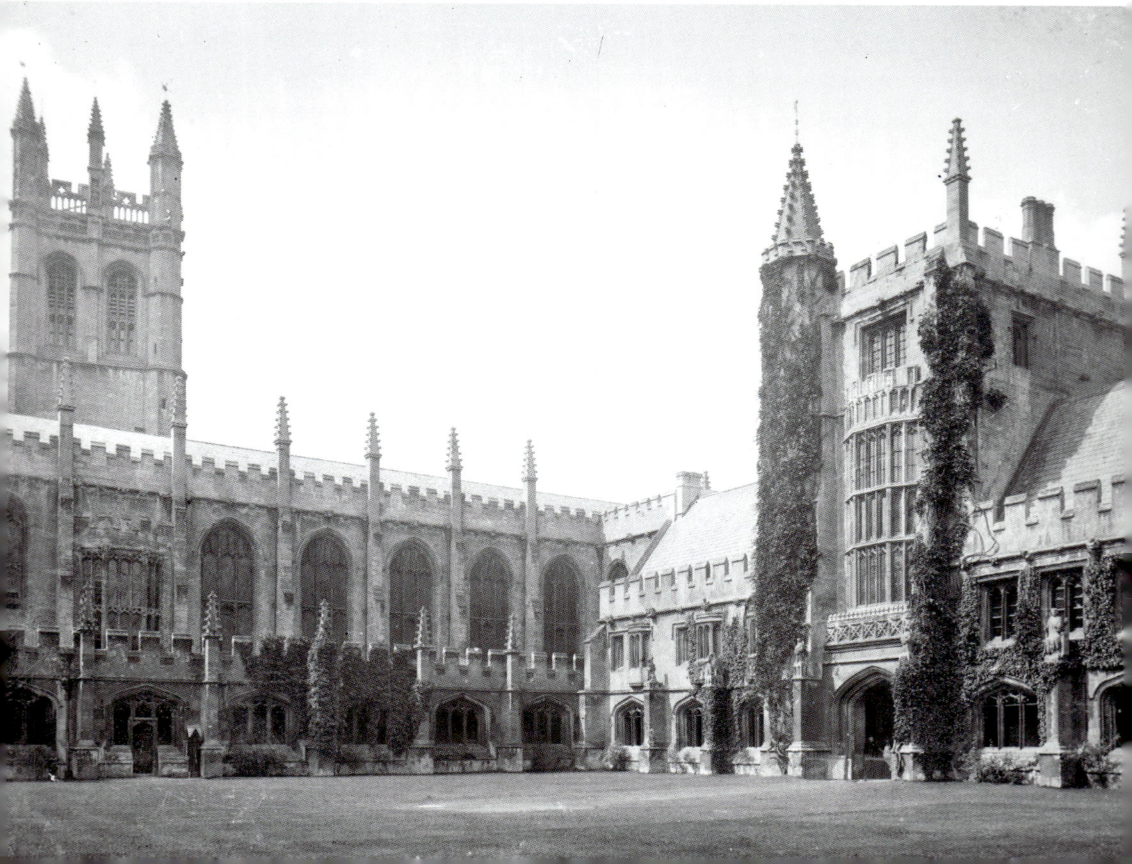

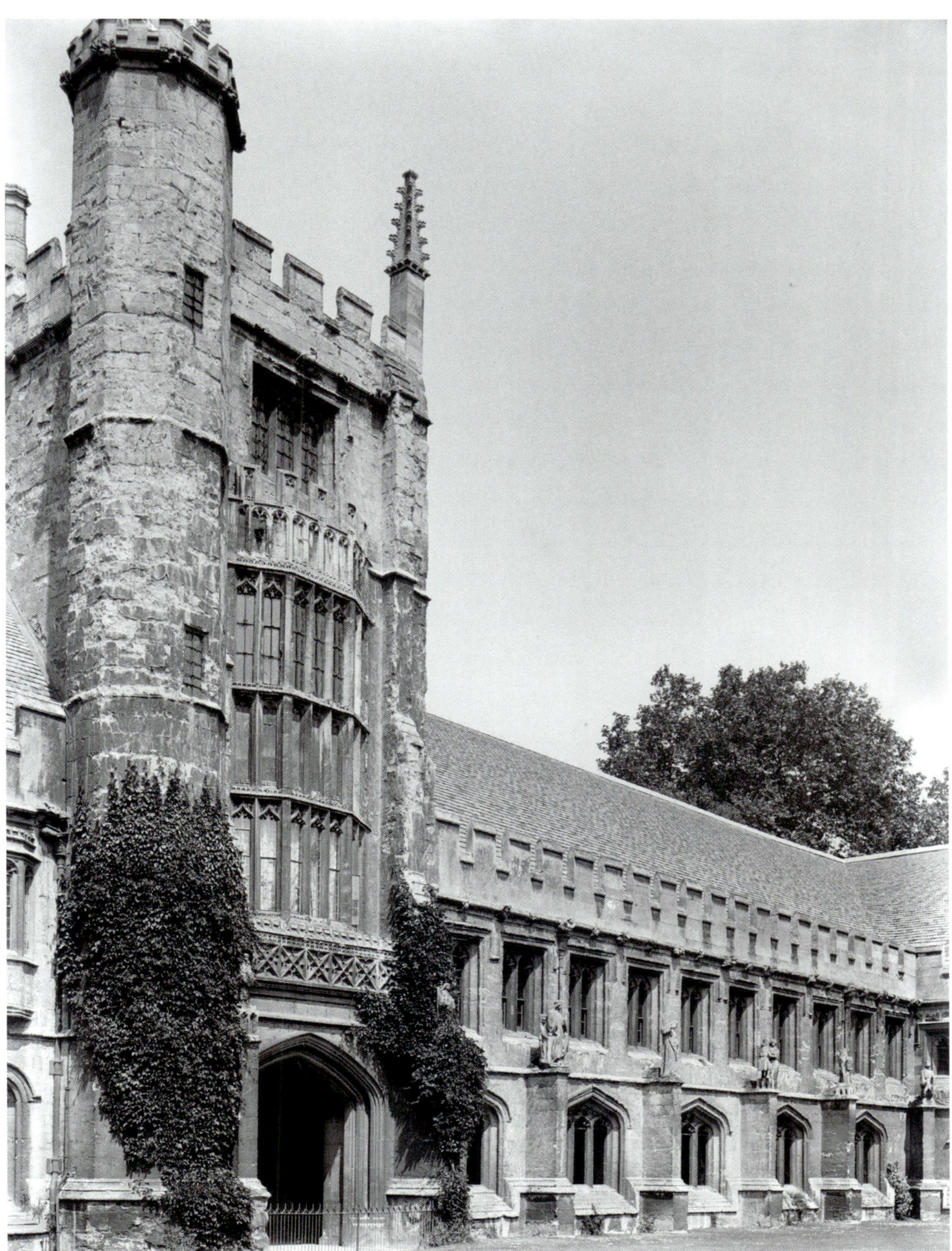

Magdalen College

The Founder's Tower, which is on the west side of the cloister, had been the gate tower of the original college buildings, but it now forms a link between the cloister and the adjacent St John's Quad.

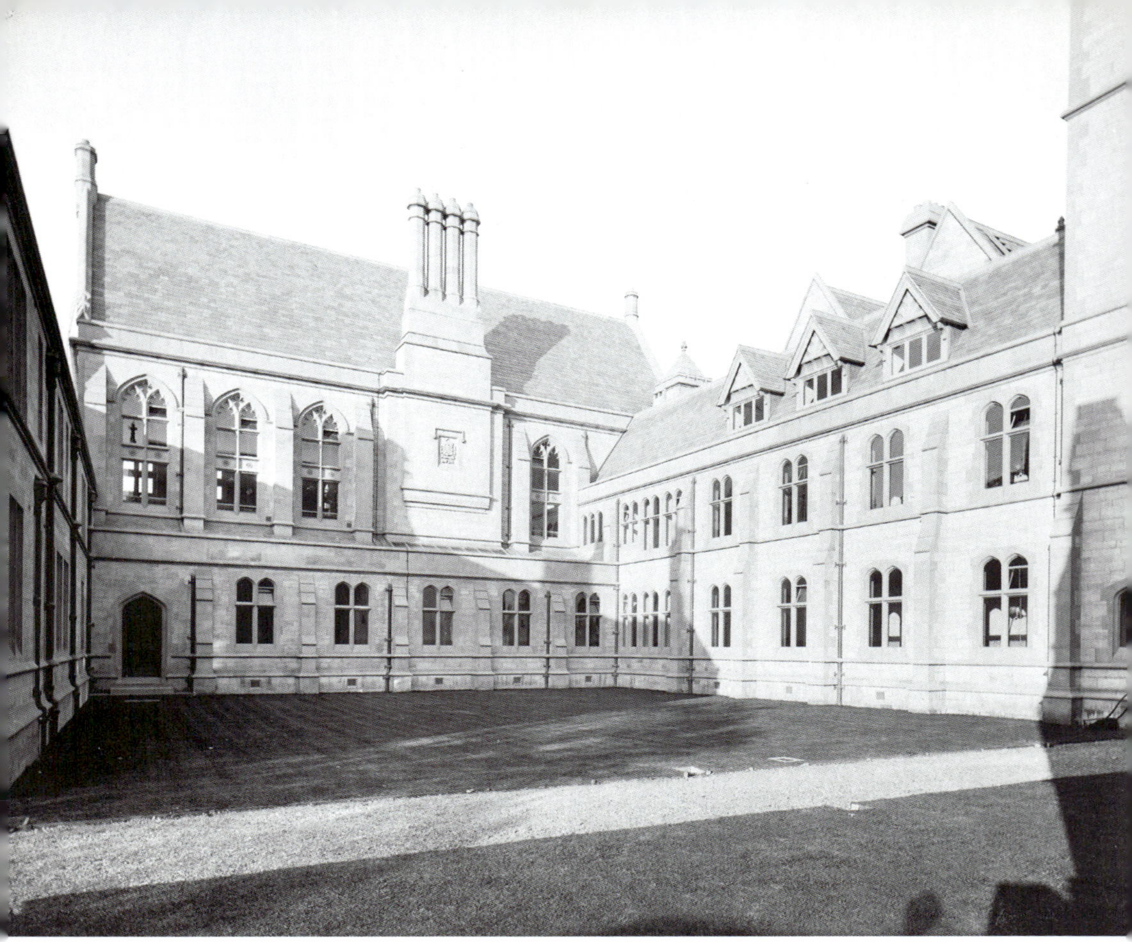

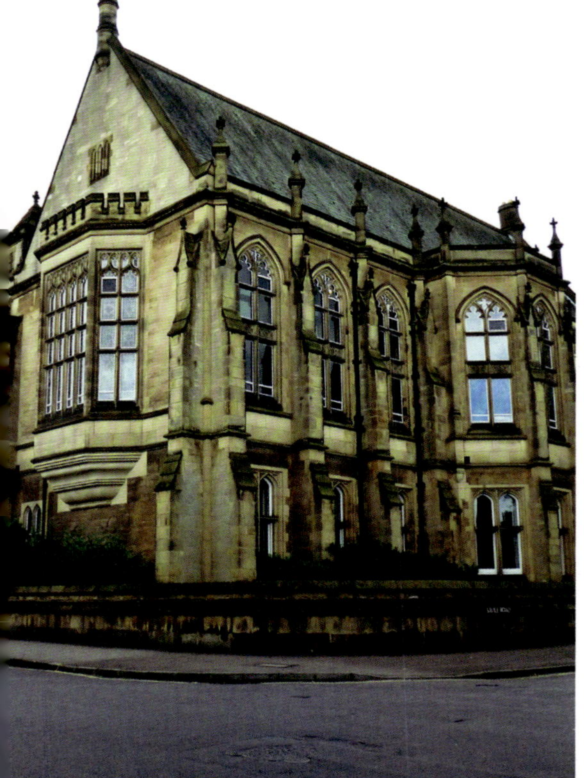

Harris Manchester College

Oxford and Cambridge had traditionally been exclusively Anglican institutions, Nonconformists being barred. This prohibition led to the establishment of various 'dissenting academies' including Manchester College, which was founded in Manchester in 1786 and moved to Oxford in 1889. Manchester became a university hall in 1990, and in 1996 it was granted a royal charter, thereby becoming a constituent college of the University of Oxford. Although justifiably proud of its Nonconformist and specifically Unitarian origins, the college is now open to mature students of all denominations. The college buildings in Mansfield Road were designed by the Manchester architect Thomas Worthington (1826–1909), and they are of traditional appearance, as shown in the accompanying photographs.

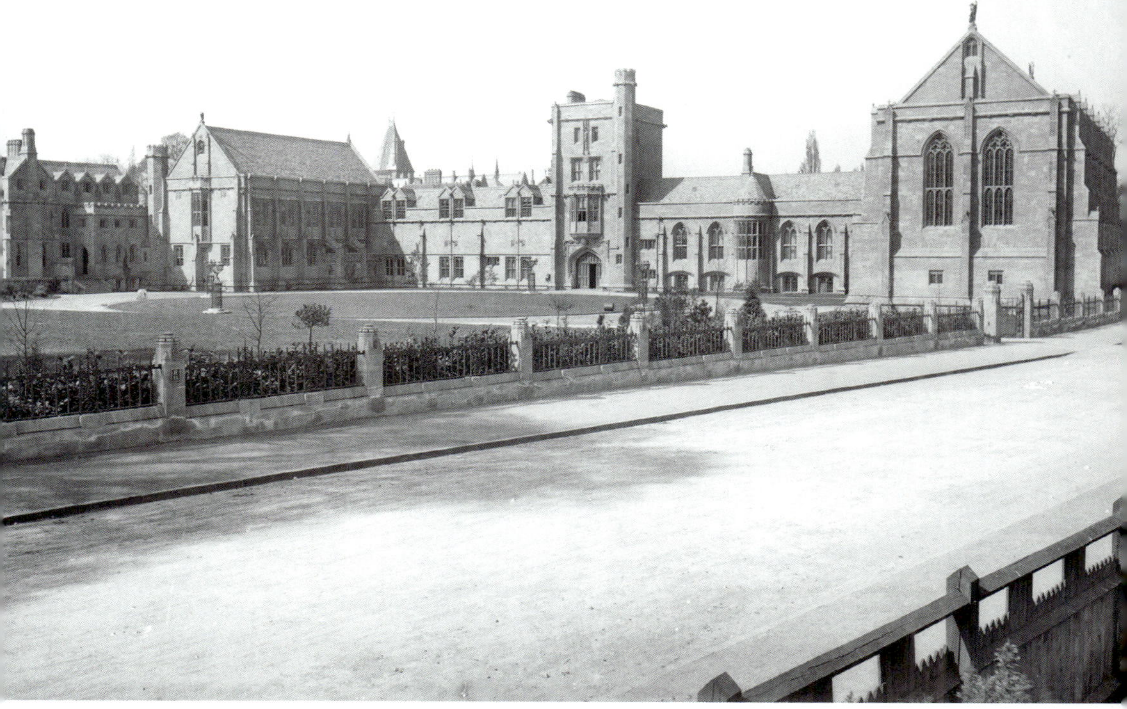

Mansfield College

Several of Oxford's younger colleges are situated north of the centre, one of these being Mansfield College, which is sited in Mansfield Road, to the north of Harris Manchester College. Mansfield College originated in Birmingham as a Nonconformist training college, but it moved to Oxford in 1886. The buildings, designed by Basil Champneys (1842–1935), are in traditional medieval style.

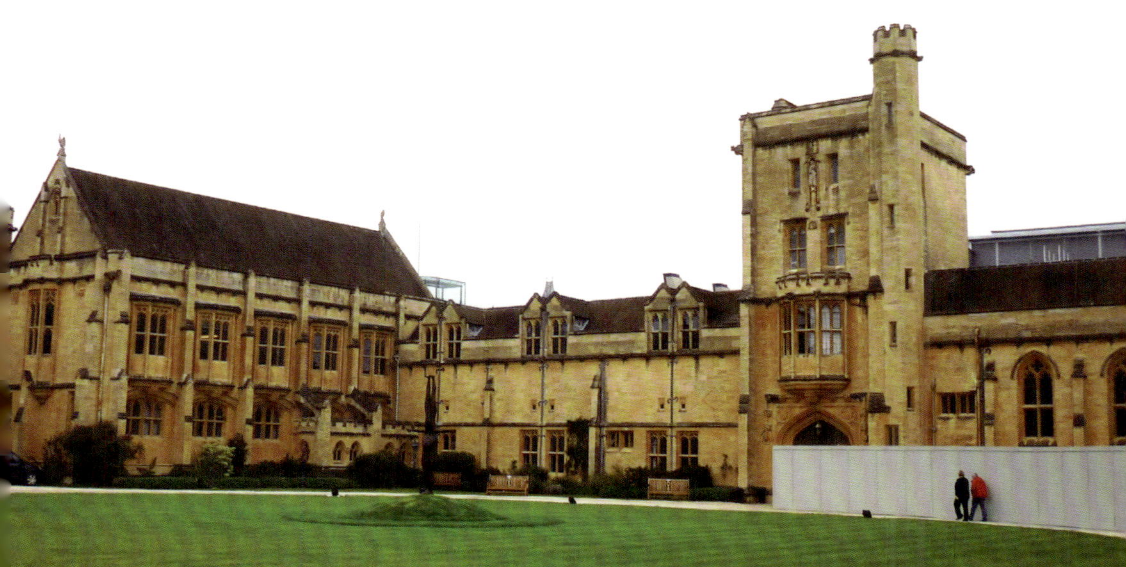

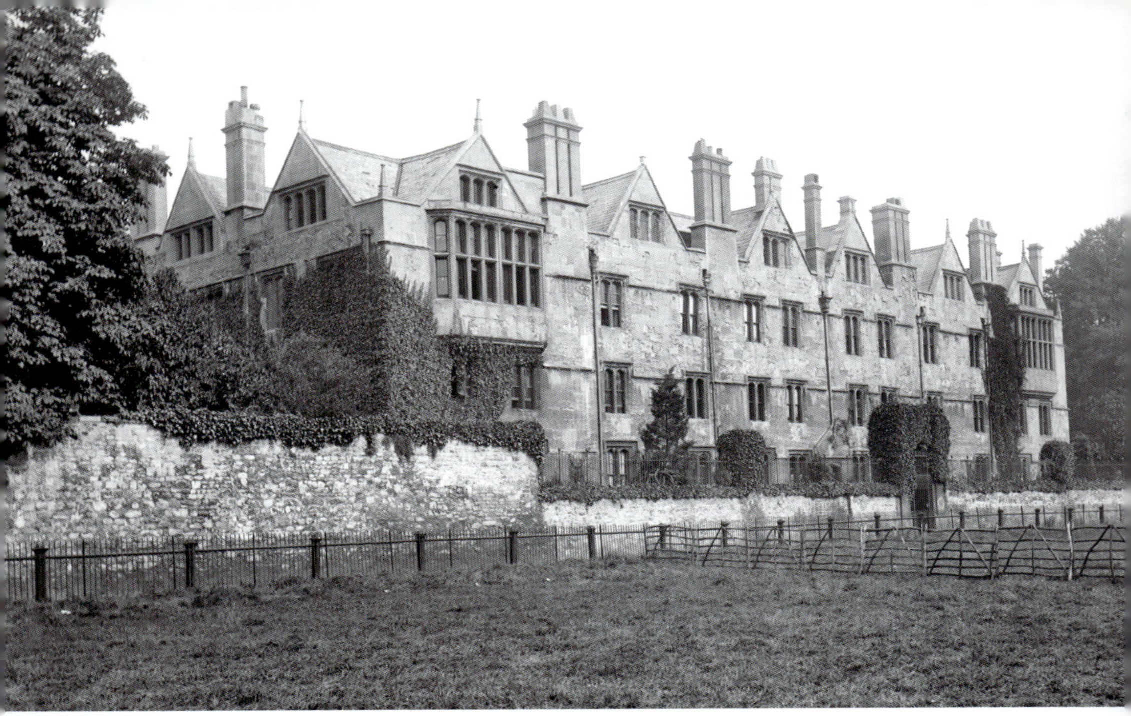

Merton College

Merton College is situated in Merton Street, which runs parallel to High Street. Christ Church Meadows and Merton Field are immediately to the south, and these classic Oxford scenes show the south façade of Merton College from the Meadows -- the upper photograph having been taken in 1907, while the colour view was taken from a similar vantage point in 2012. The college is arguably the oldest in Oxford, having been founded in 1264 by Walter de Merton (*c.* 1205–77), Lord Chancellor and Bishop of Rochester.

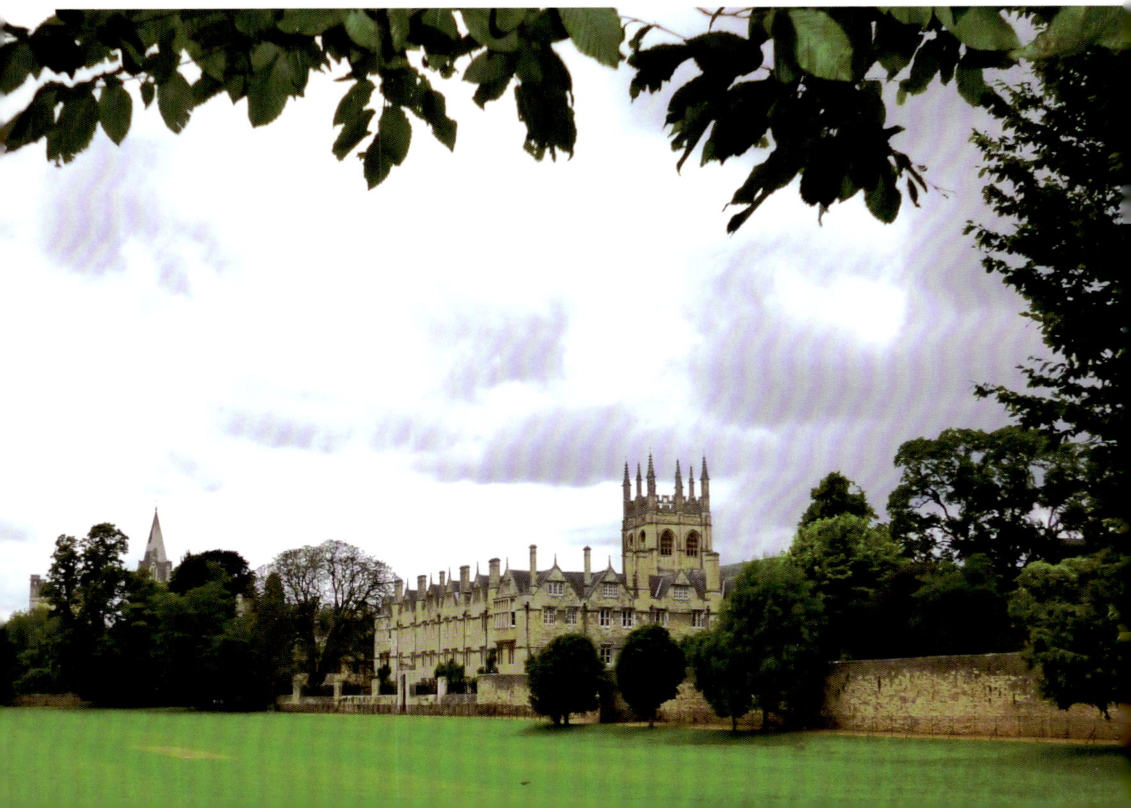

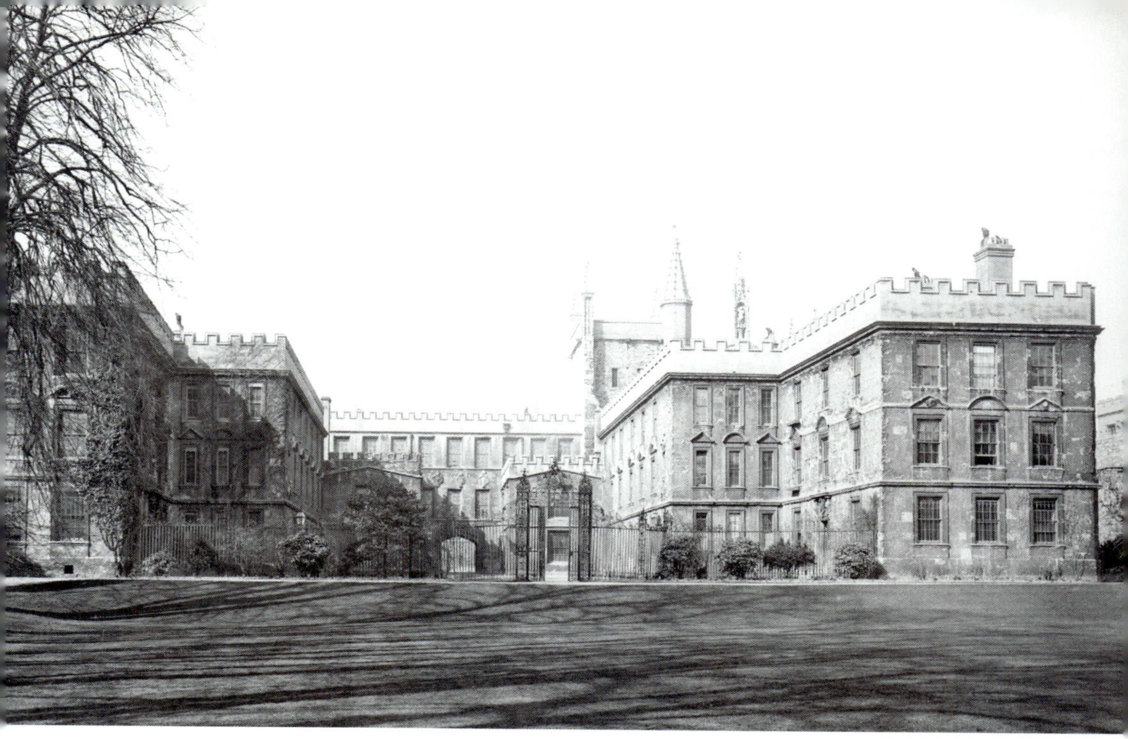

New College

Despite its name, New College is in fact a very old institution, which was founded by William of Wykeham (*c.* 1324–1404), Bishop of Winchester, in 1379. The 'Great Quad' was completed by 1386, while the cloister and bell tower were added in 1400. The upper photograph shows the Garden Quad, while the lower view shows the interior of the college chapel – the very large reredos having no less than five tiers of figures.

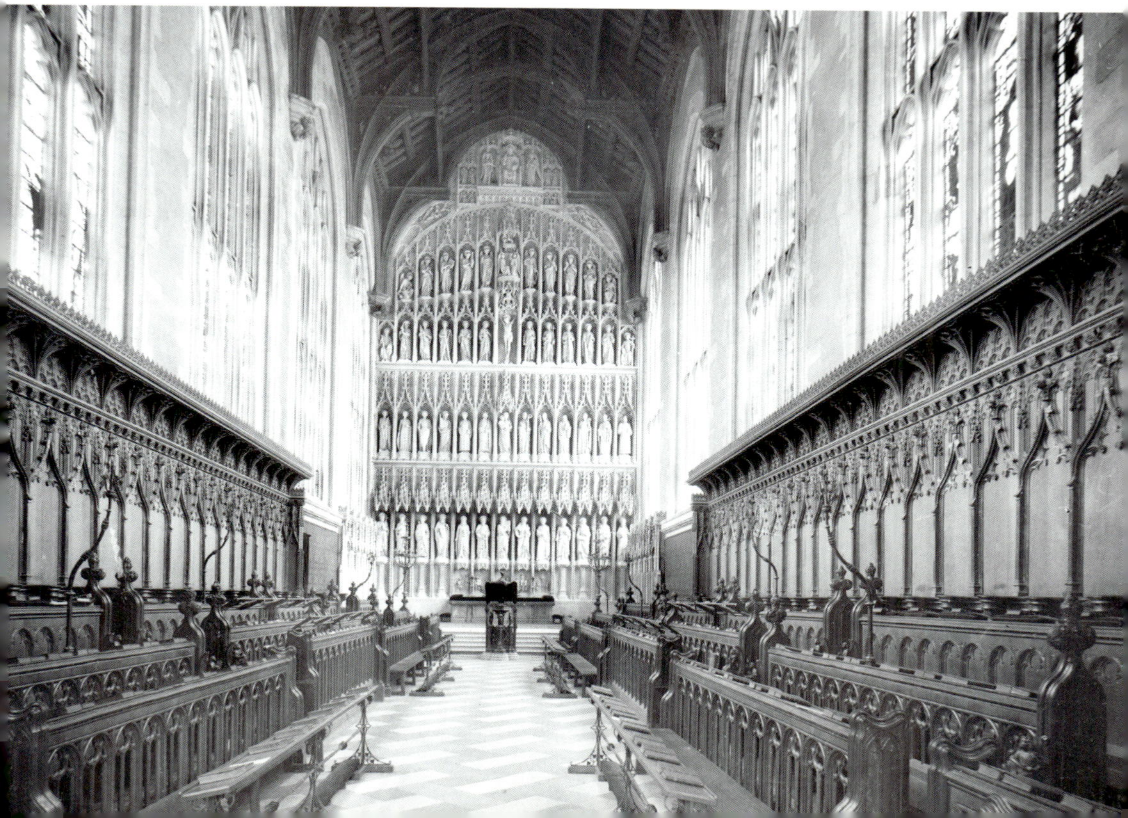

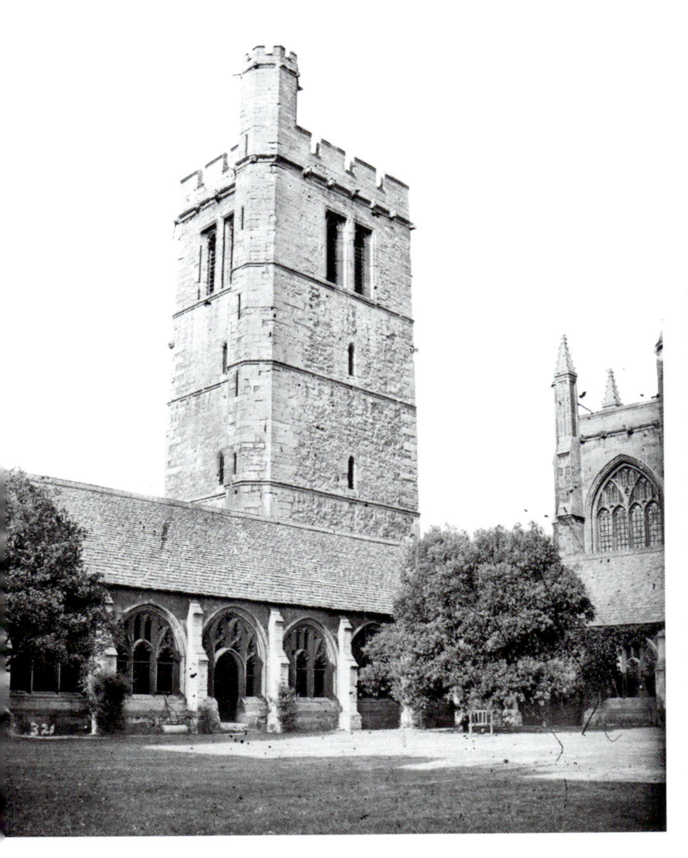

New College

In architectural terms, New College can be seen as the prototype for all later Oxford colleges, insofar as it was built to a regular plan comprising a quadrangle, with gate tower, hall, chapel and library – this more or less standardised layout being similar to that of contemporary monastic foundations. Like other early colleges, New College features a range of monastic-style cloisters, which are shown in these Victorian views of around 1875. New College has now expanded well beyond the confines of its original site, and the college now includes nineteenth- and twentieth-century buildings, in addition to its medieval core.

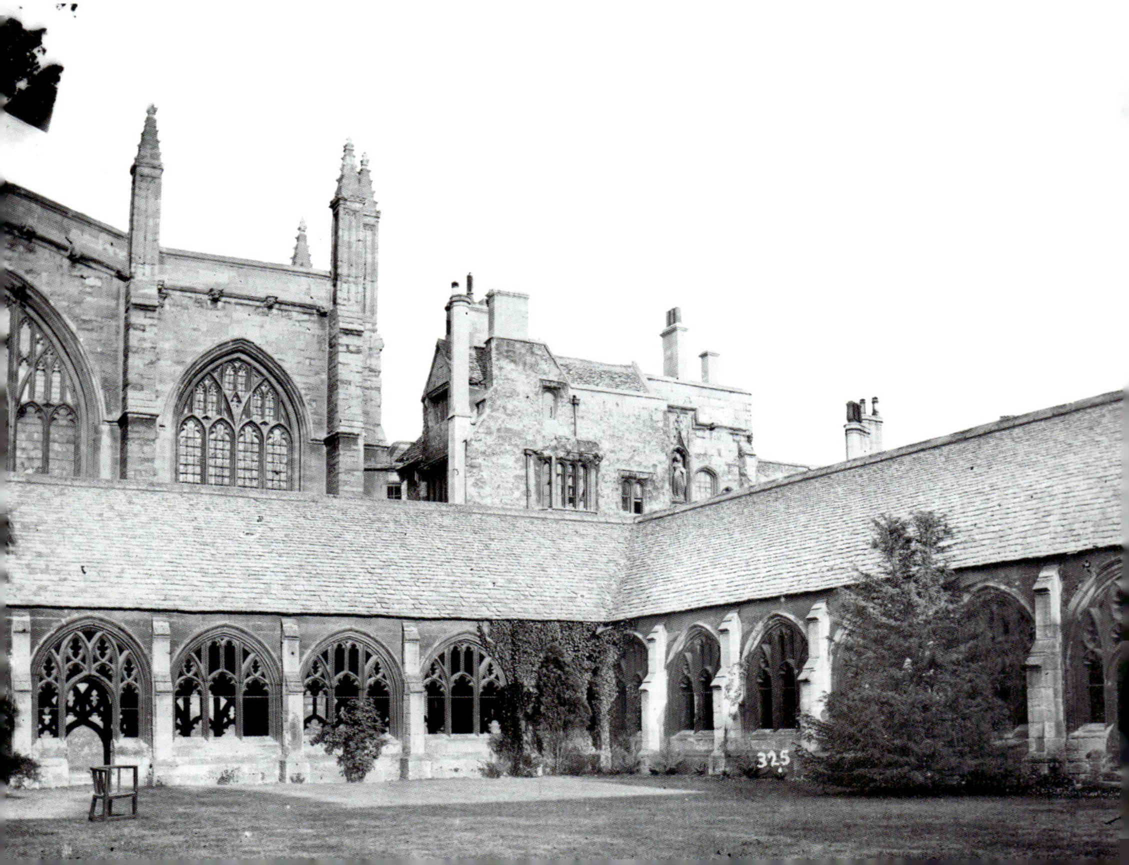

New College – The City Walls

A substantial section of the city wall can be seen in New College gardens, and five open-backed bastions remain in situ. These medieval defences were obsolete by the time of the Civil War, necessitating the provision of a complex system of earthwork defences, which formed an outer 'rim' or perimeter that extended well beyond the confines of the medieval city. The upper photograph shows one of the still-extant bastions, while the lower view shows a surviving length of the medieval wall.

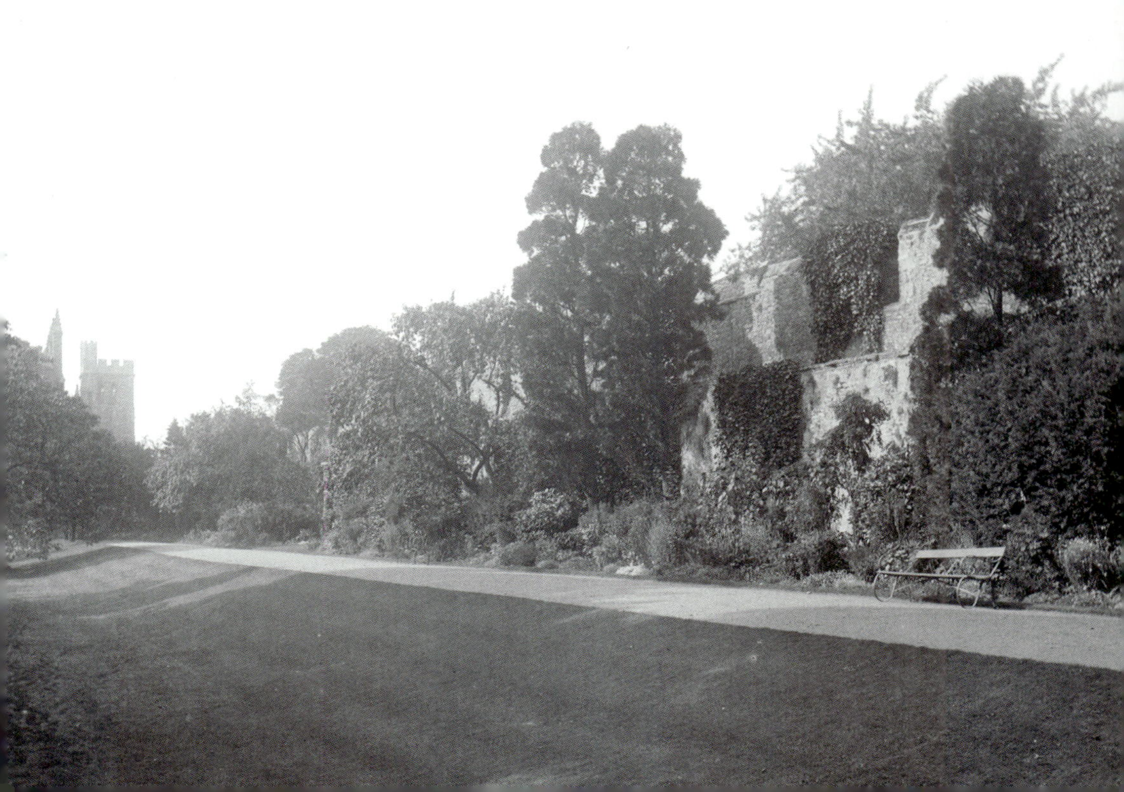

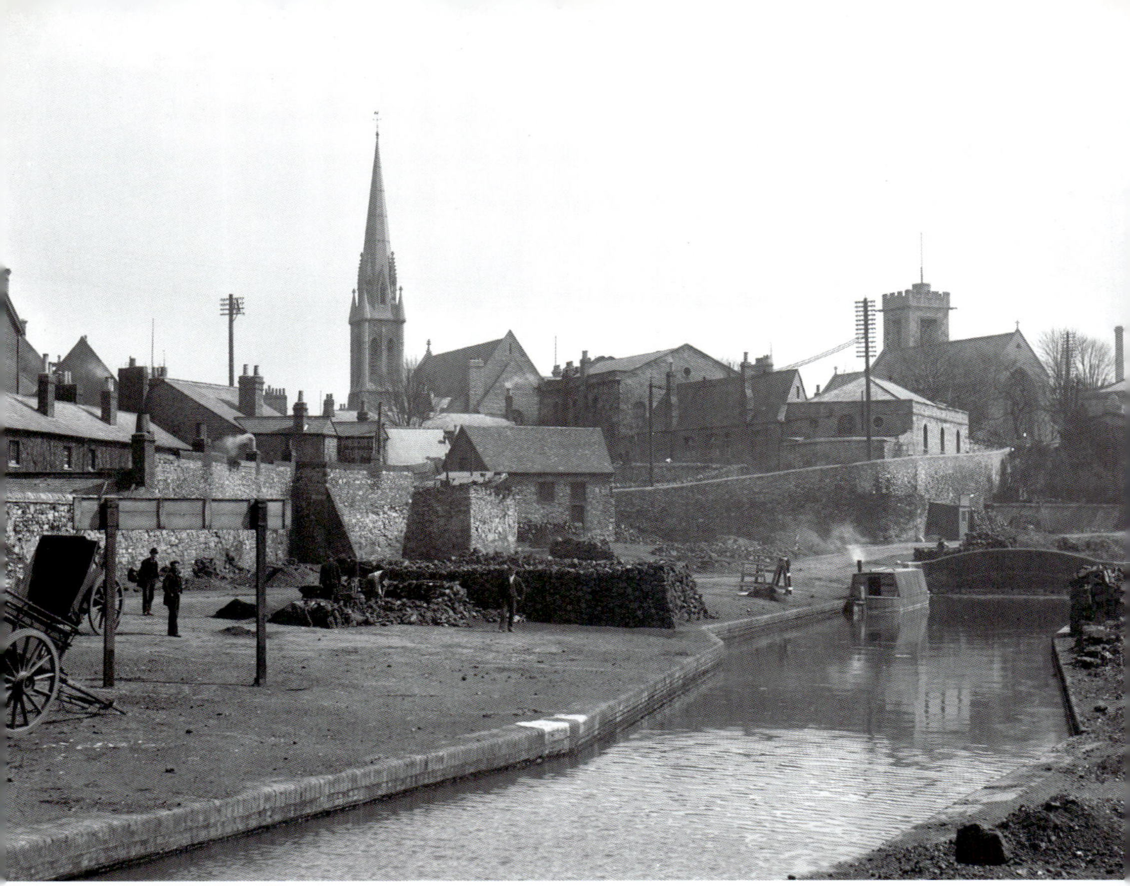

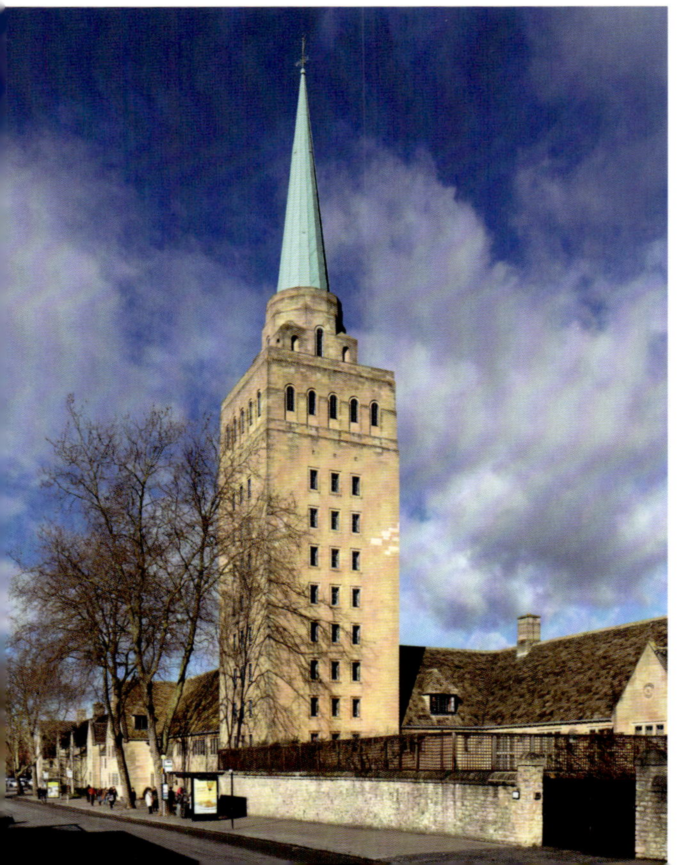

Nuffield College

The Oxford Canal was incorporated by Act of Parliament in 1769, and opened between Hawkesbury Junction and Banbury around 1778. The canal was extended southwards to Oxford in 1789–90, and although rapidly eclipsed by the railway, the waterway carried commercial traffic until the 1950s. In 1937 the canal's terminal basin, shown in the upper view, was purchased by the philanthropist Lord Nuffield in order to provide a site for Nuffield College. The college was constructed in 1949–60, and it received its charter from the Queen in 1958 – full collegiate status being assumed in 1963. This modern college boasts extensive Cotswold-style buildings and an impressive tower that rises 150 feet to the top of the spire.

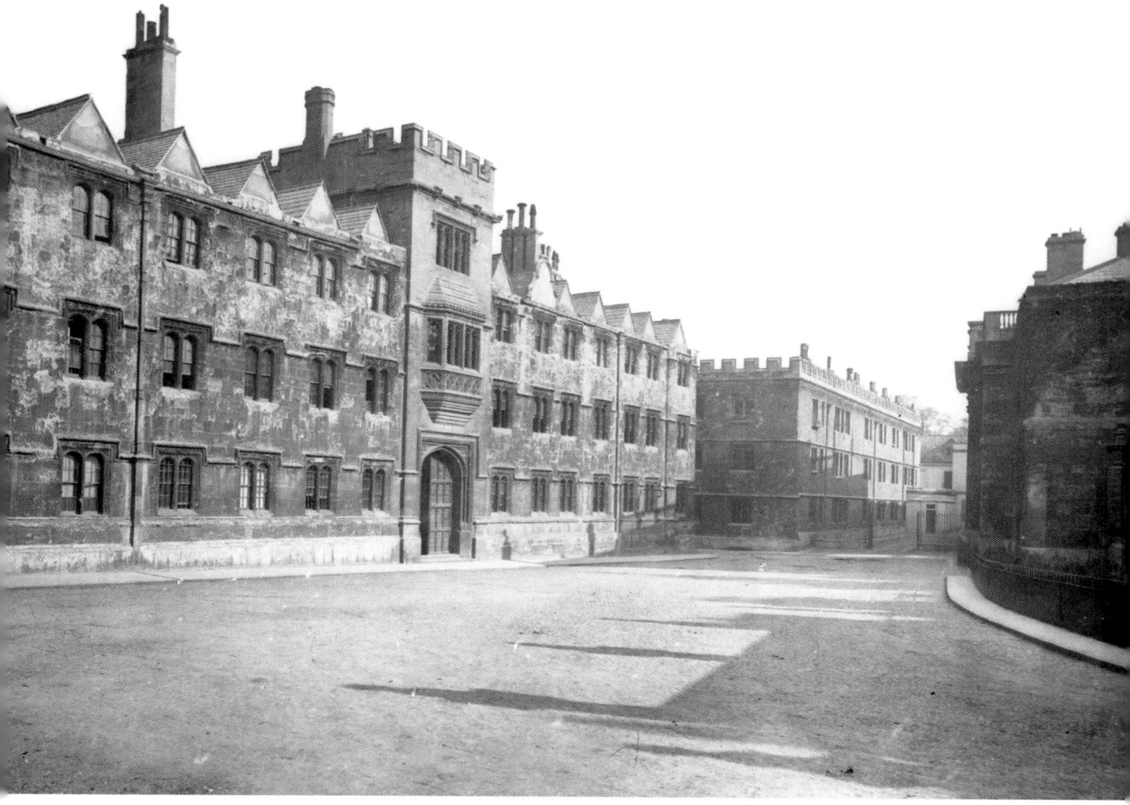

Oriel College

Oriel College was founded in 1324 by Adam de Brome, the rector of St Mary's Church, under the patronage of the ill-fated Edward II. The college buildings incorporate three quadrangles, the hall, buttery and ante-chapel being on the east side of Front Quad. The name 'Oriel' is derived from a house known as La Oriele that had stood on the site of the present-day college buildings. These two Victorian photographs show the college from Oriel Square, the embattled gate tower with its canted oriel window being prominent in both views.

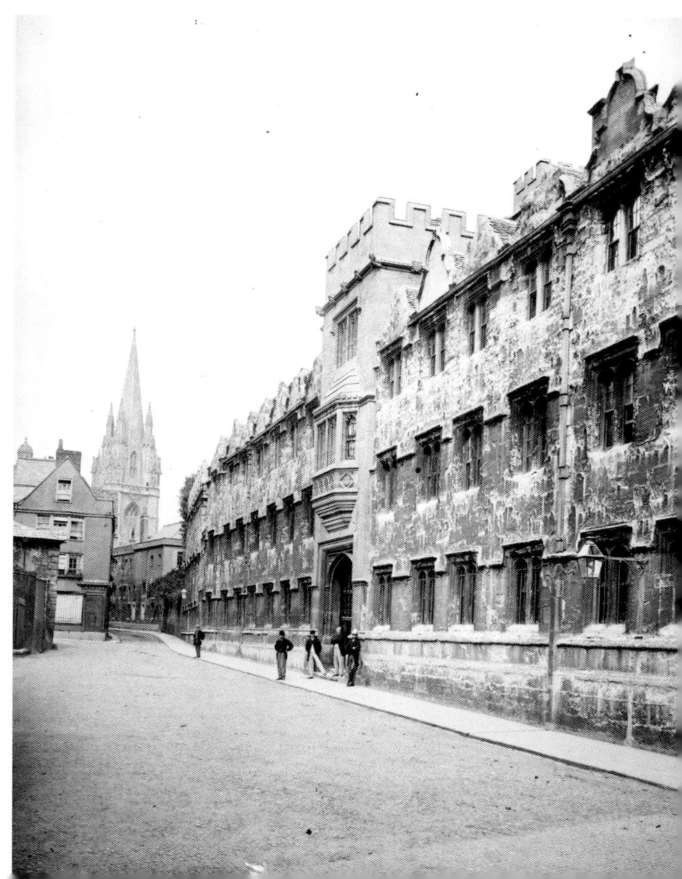

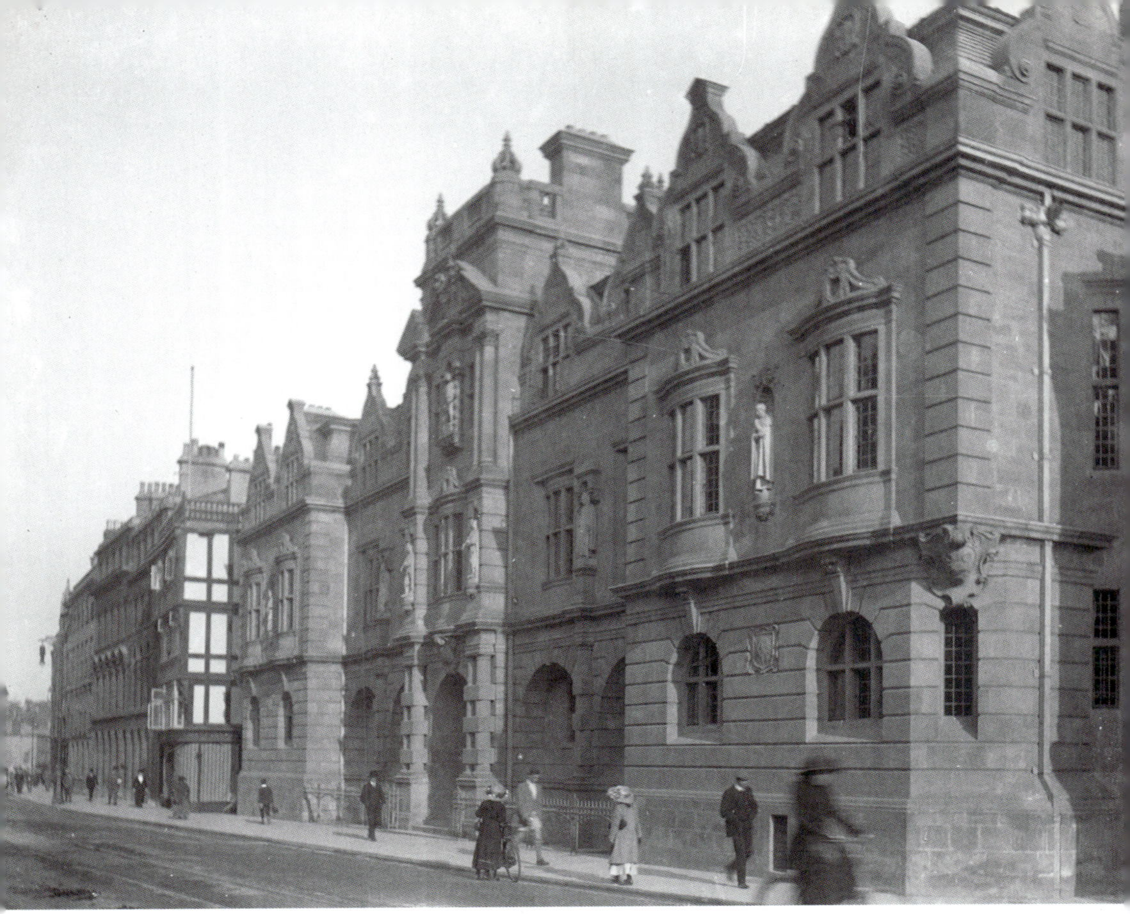

Oriel College – The Rhodes Building

At the end of the nineteenth century a group of old buildings on the south side of High Street were ruthlessly swept away to make way for an extension of Oriel College known as the Rhodes Building, which was built in 1908–11 and named in honour of the mining entrepreneur and African imperialist Cecil Rhodes (1853–1902), who left £100,000 to pay for its construction. The upper view shows the Rhodes Building shortly after its completion, while the lower view shows the south-west corner of the Back Quad.

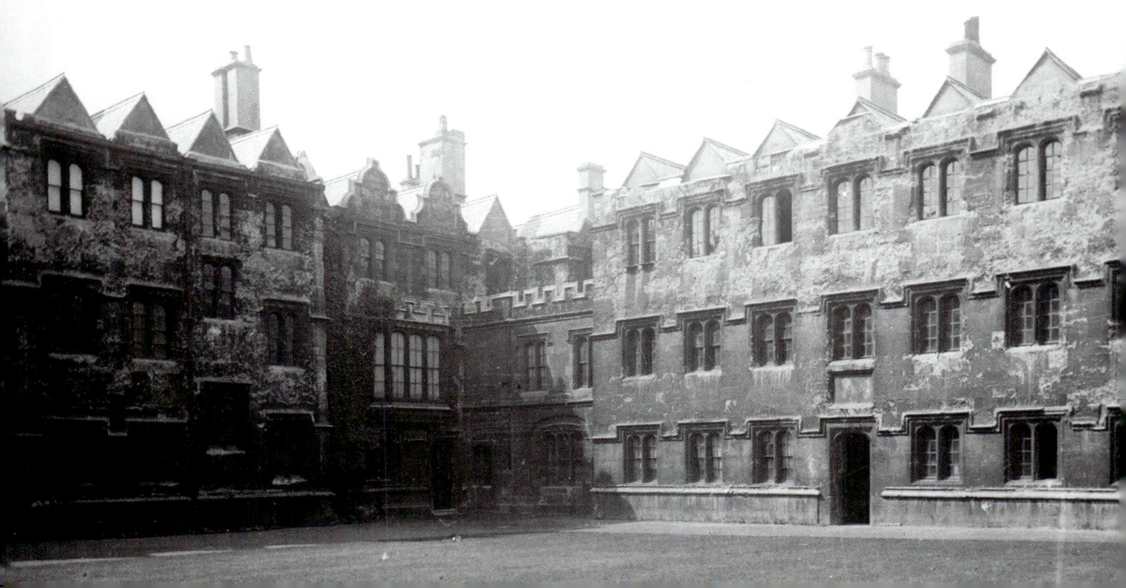

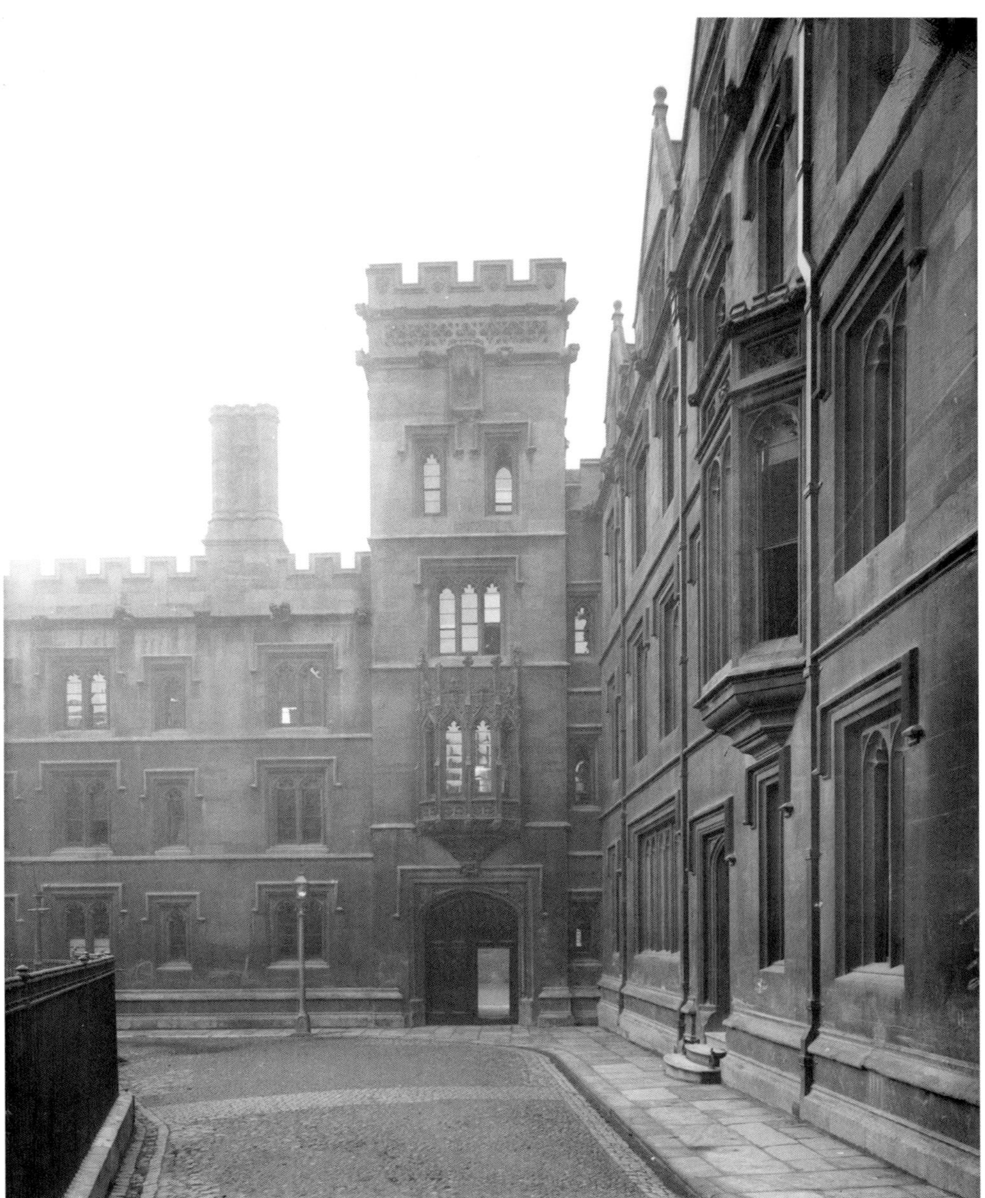

Pembroke College

Thomas Tesdale (1547–1610), a former mayor of Abingdon, bequeathed £5,000 to establish places at Balliol College for six scholars and seven fellows from Abingdon School, but after many frustrating delays the Tesdale Bequest was used to found Pembroke College on the site of the medieval Broadgates Hall. Additional funding was provided by Richard Wightwick, and the new college, which derived its name from the 3rd Earl of Pembroke (who was then Chancellor of Oxford University), was opened in 1624. The college is situated in Pembroke Square, the entrance and gate tower being shown in the upper view. Passing through the gate tower, one enters the 'Old Quad', which was built in the seventeenth century and remodelled in 1829–30.

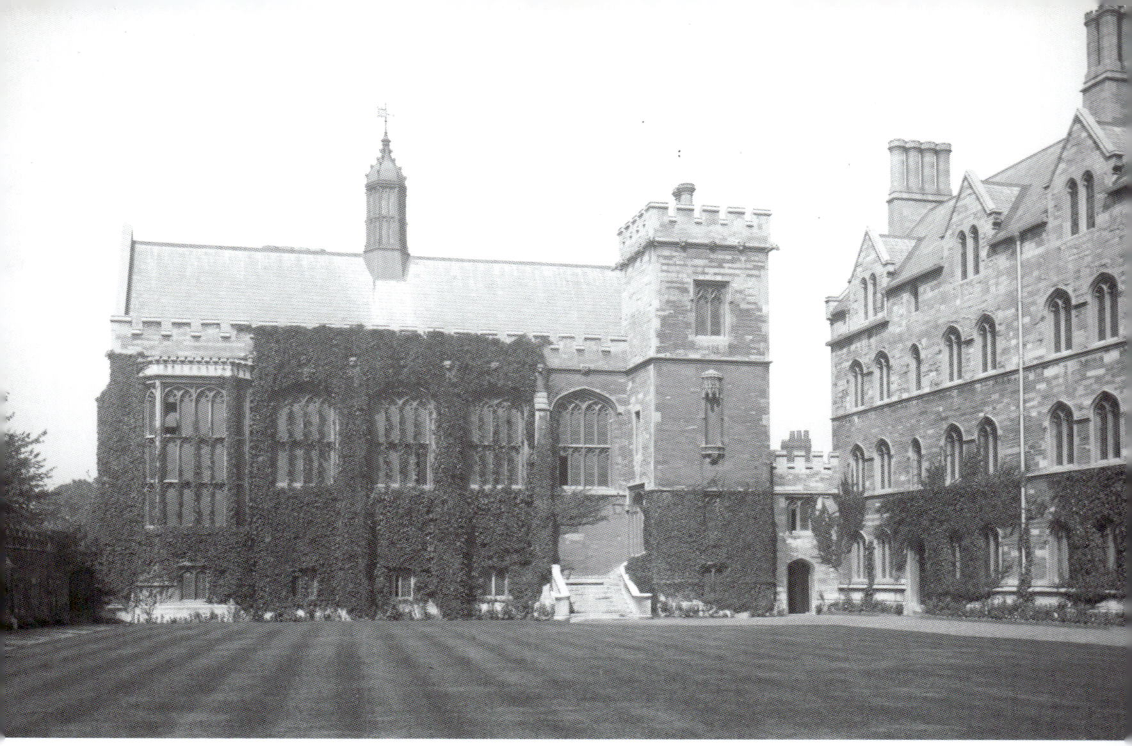

Pembroke College

The much larger 'Chapel Quad' contains an eighteenth-century chapel and a nineteenth-century hall with tall windows and a staircase tower. The architect was John Hayward of Exeter (1807–91). Pembroke's most famous resident was the lexicographer Samuel Johnson (1709–84), who entered the college as a commoner in 1728 and lodged in a room above the gateway during his unhappy sojourn at the college – eventually leaving without taking his degree. However, in 1755 the university awarded him an MA in recognition of the work that he had undertaken in connection with his *Dictionary of the English Language*.

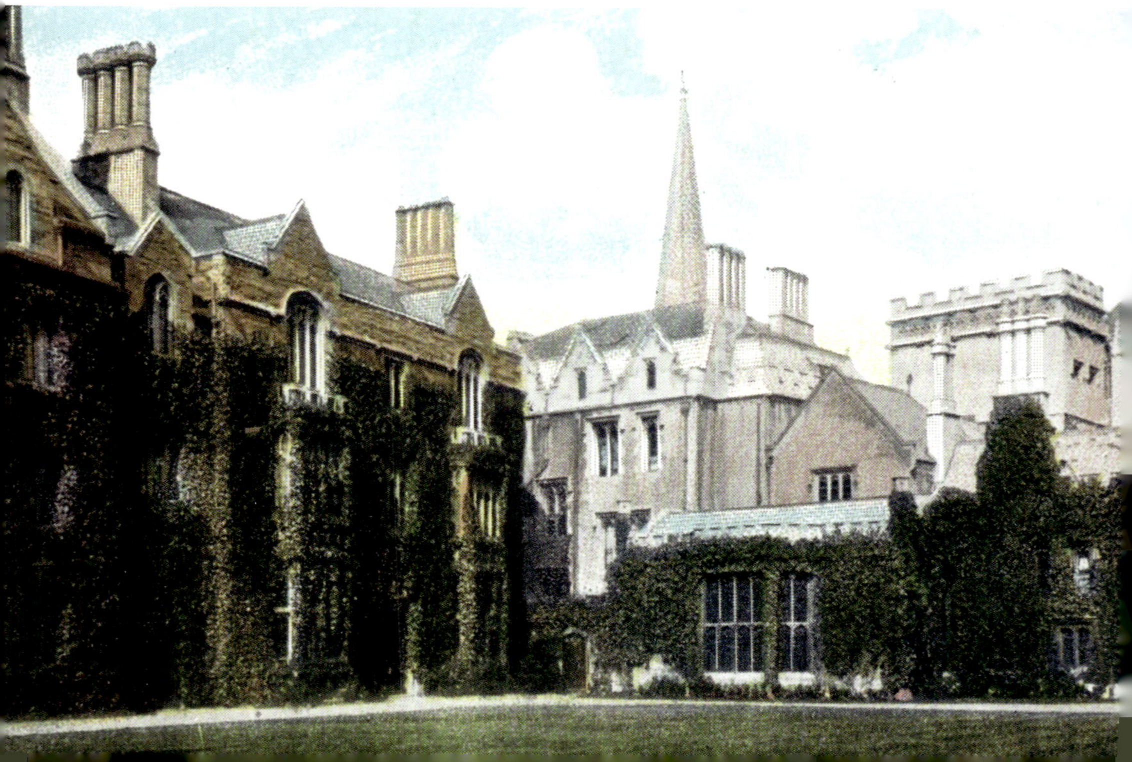

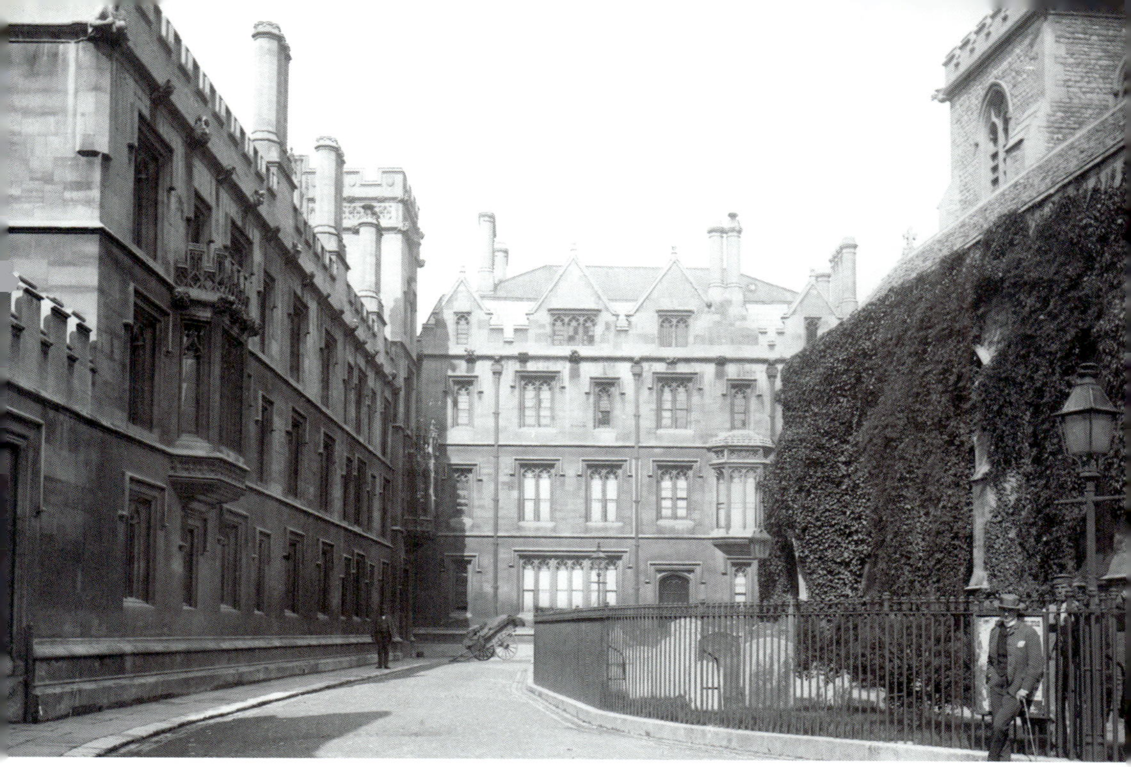

The upper view provides a further glimpse of Pembroke Square – the college gate tower being visible in the distance, while St Aldates Church can be seen to the right of the picture. The lower picture shows the interior of the Victorian dining hall, which features a hammer-beam roof and is one of the grandest halls in Oxford. It has been suggested that this magnificent hall was inspired by the hall at Eltham Palace in London.

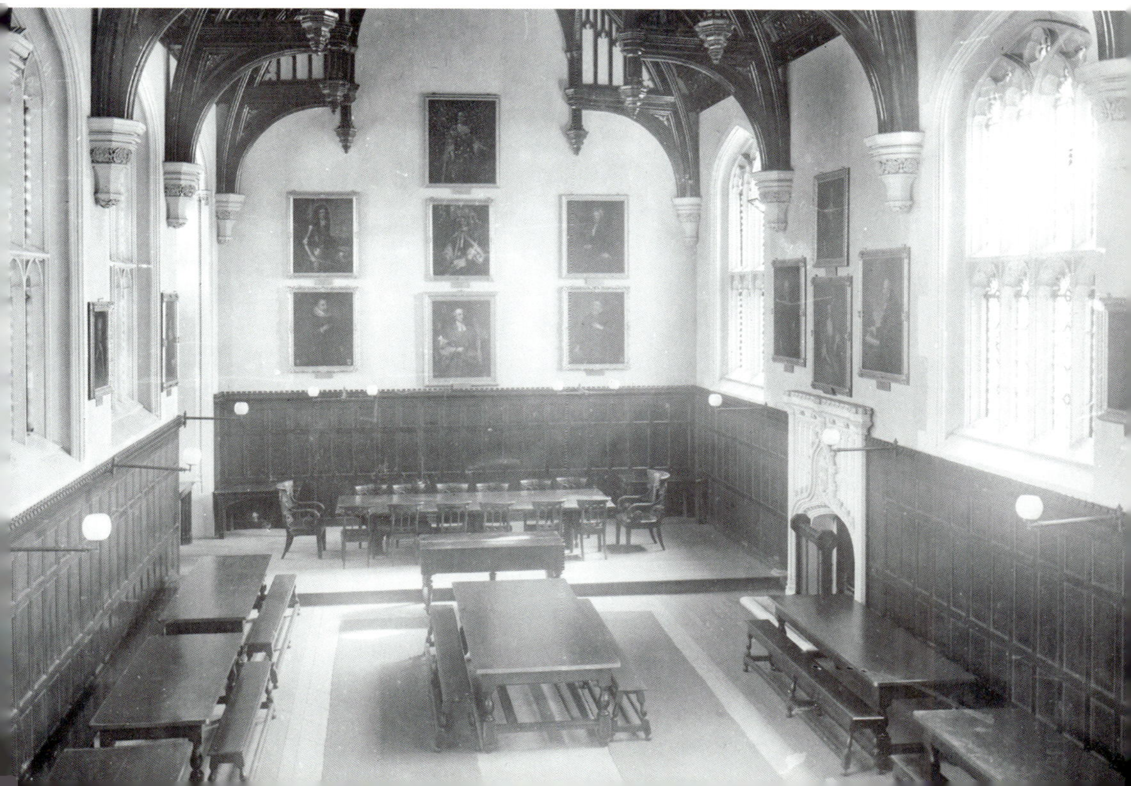

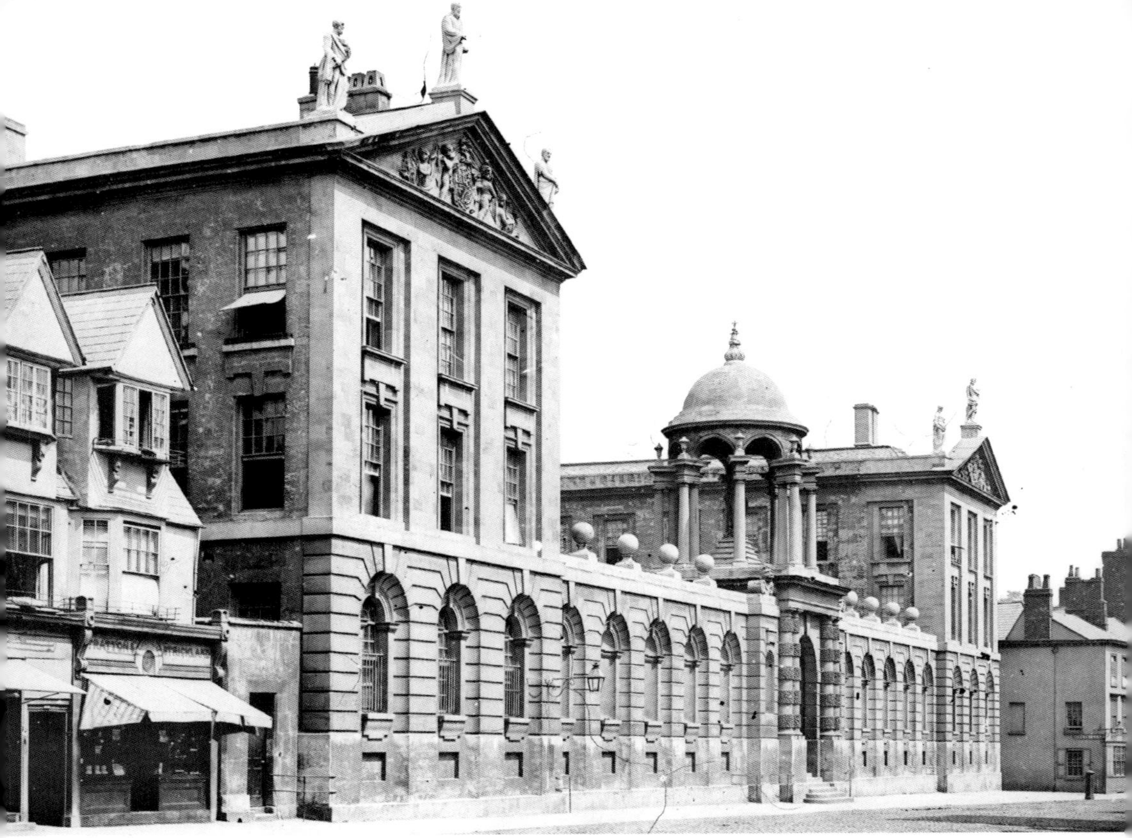

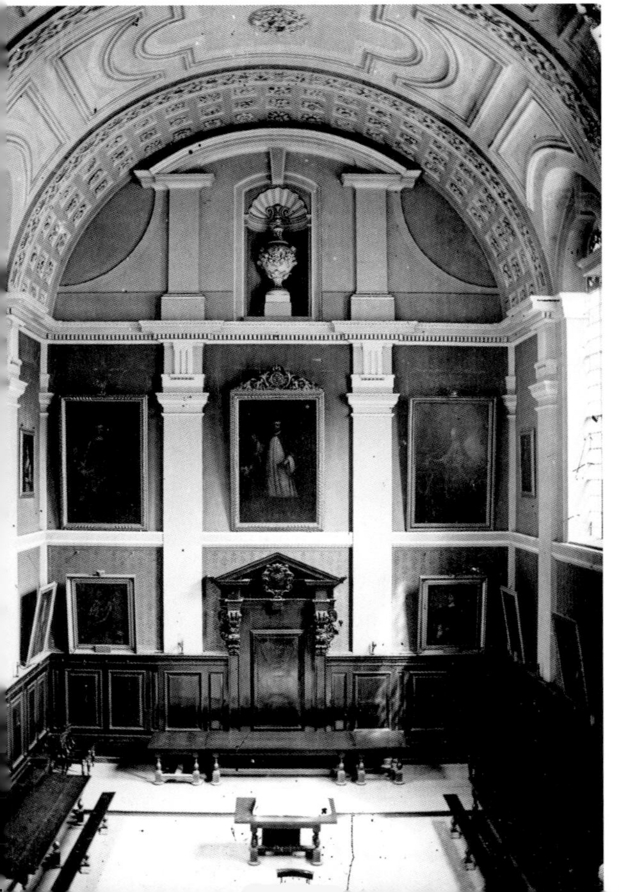

Queen's College
Queen's College was founded in 1340 by Robert of Eglesfield, chaplain to Queen Philippa. Notwithstanding its medieval origins, the classical architecture of Queen's College dates mainly from the seventeenth and early eighteenth centuries. The façade of Front Quad, depicted on a Henry Taunt photograph taken in 1870 (above), incorporates a baroque gatehouse, which is flanked by the much taller gable ends of the east and west ranges to form a pleasing and symmetrical composition. The two wings are linked by a rusticated screen, and the gatehouse is surmounted by a domed rotunda, containing a statue of Queen Caroline (the wife of George II). The lower view shows the interior of the lavishly decorated hall, looking west and showing the huge pilasters and decorated ceiling.

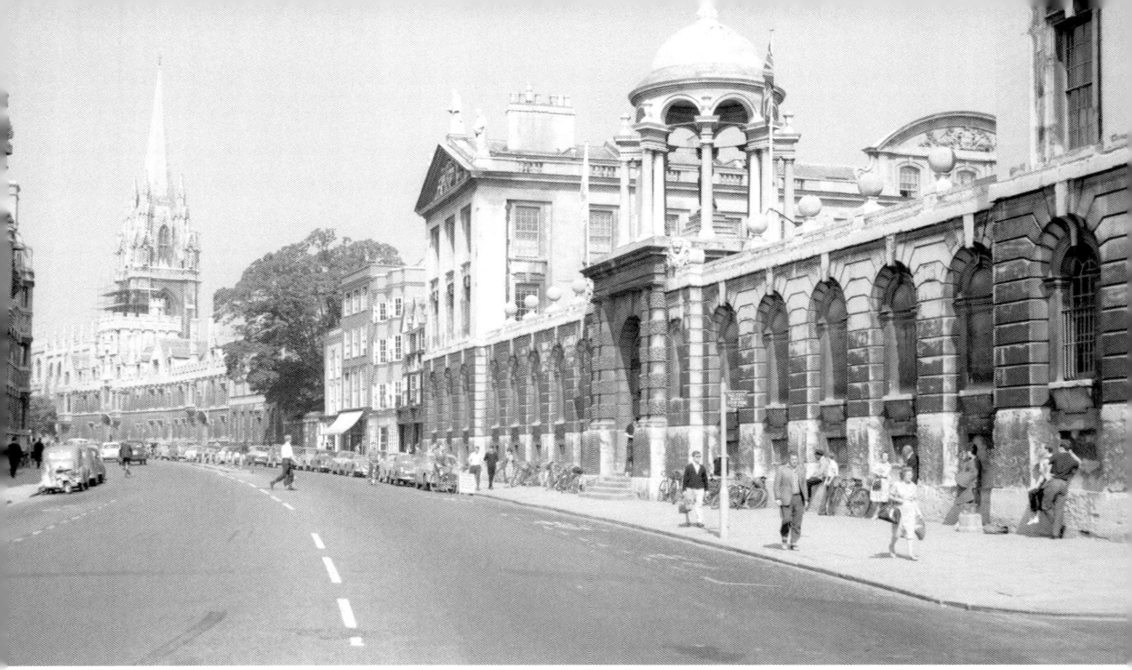

Queen's College

Above: A further view of the High Street frontage, looking west towards Carfax, with All Souls College and the spire of St Mary the Virgin Church visible in the background.

Below: The library, which forms the west side of the North Quadrangle, was built in 1692–95. The rusticated ground floor was originally an open arcade, but it was walled in in 1841. The north range, which can be seen to the right, was remodelled at the start of the eighteenth century.

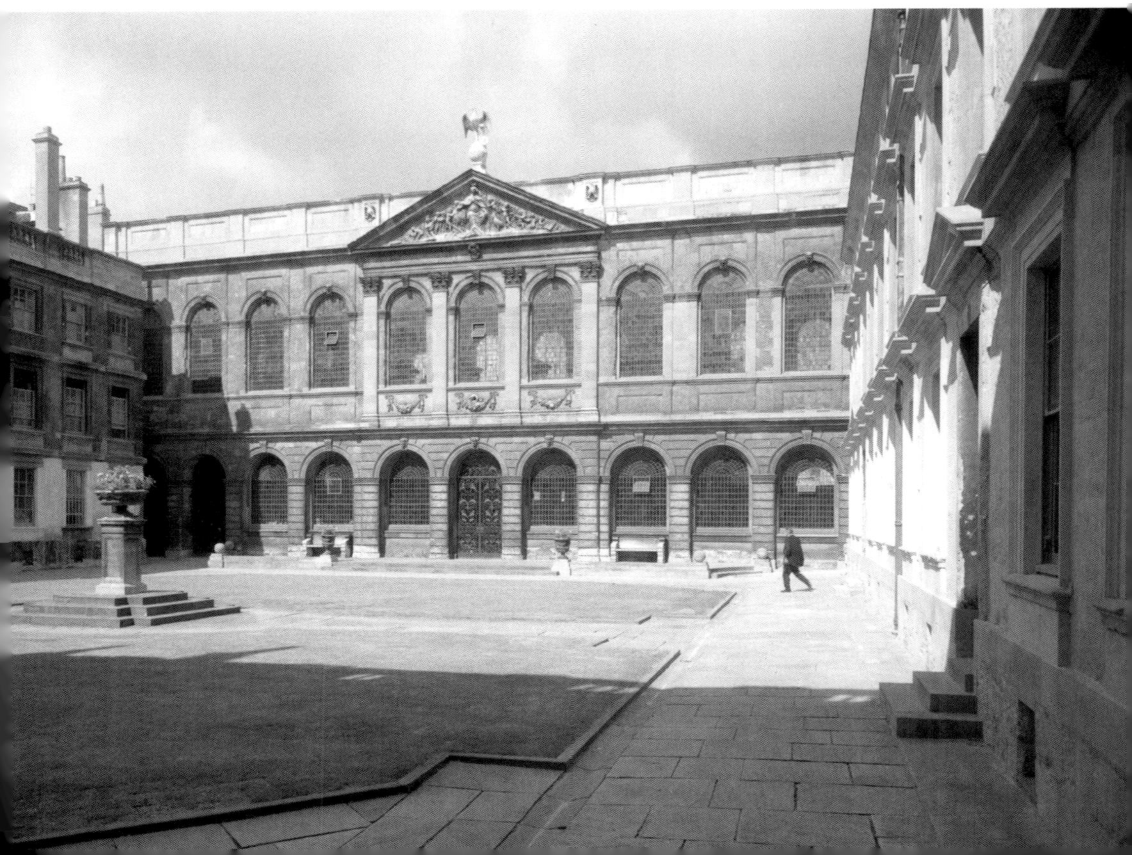

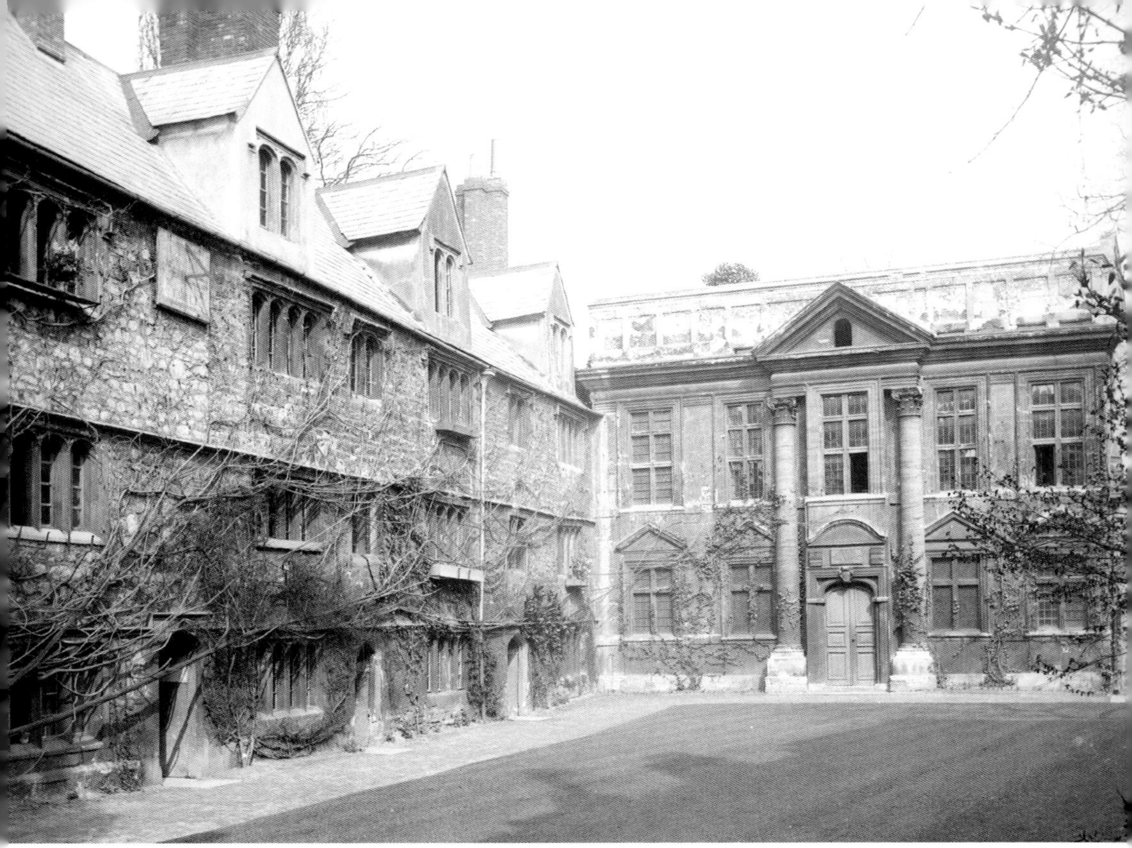

St Edmund Hall
St Edmund Hall originated in the mid-thirteenth century as a hall of residence for undergraduates, but in 1957 it was granted a charter of incorporation by Elizabeth II and thereby became a conventional college. In contrast to neighbouring Queen's College, the buildings are small in scale, and have an intimate, domestic quality.

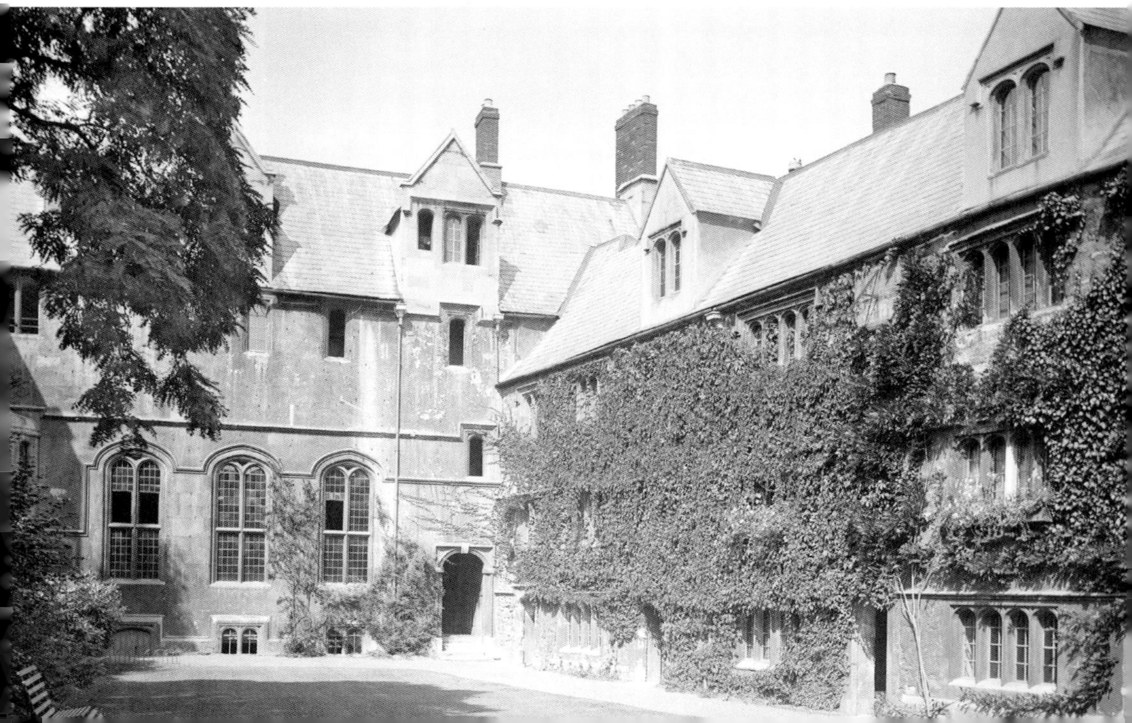

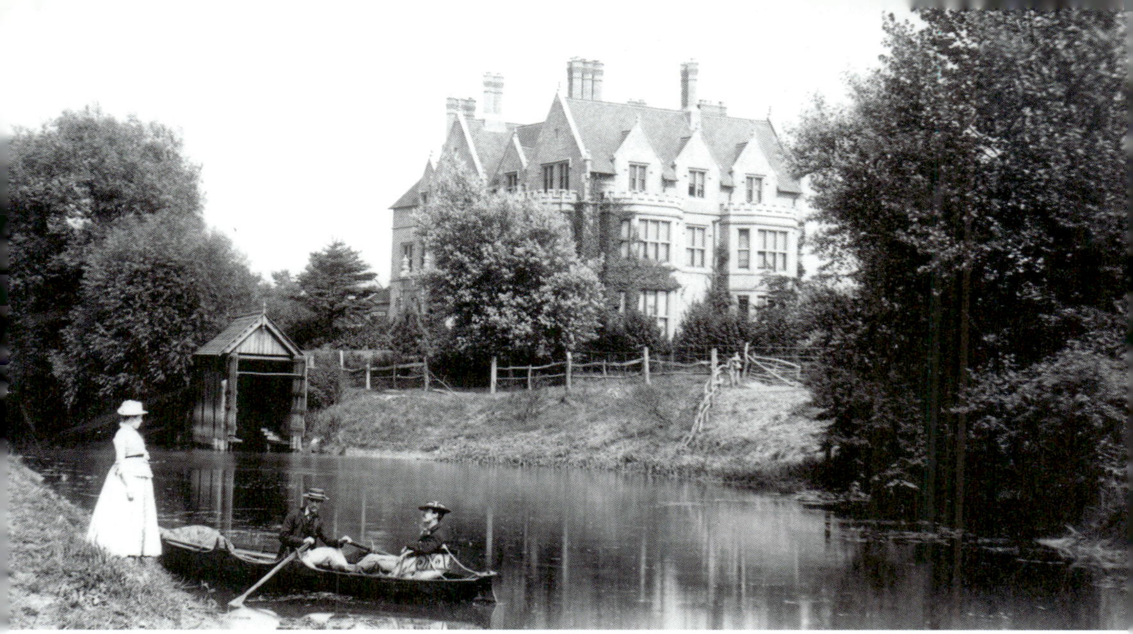

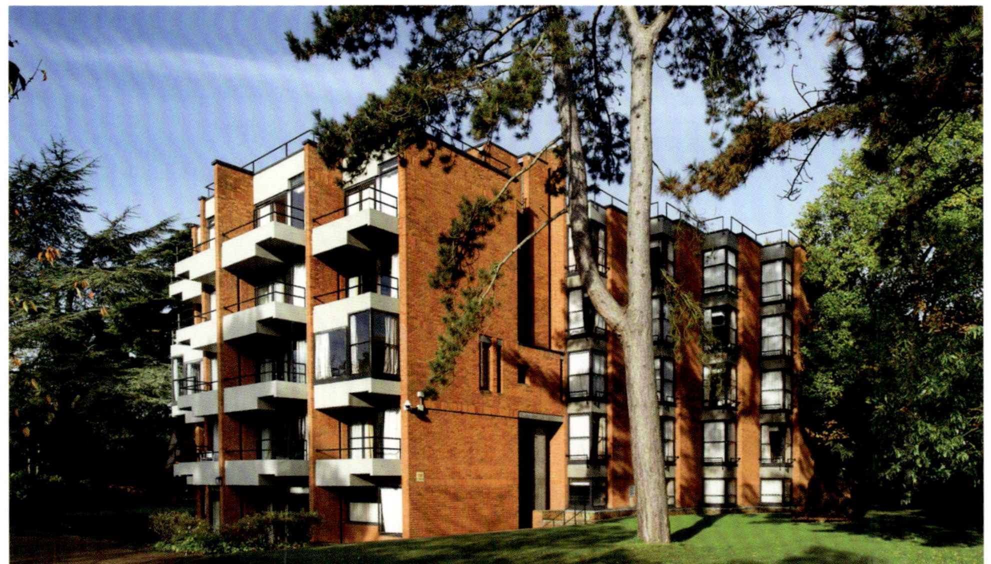

St Hilda's College

St Hilda's College was founded in 1893 by Dorothea Beale (1831–1906), the principal of Cheltenham Ladies' College. Men have been admitted since 2008, but St Hilda's was, until that time, an exclusively female establishment. The college, which is sited in attractive surroundings beside the River Cherwell, boasts a diverse range of buildings, some of which predate the college, while others were added during the nineteenth and twentieth centuries.

St Hugh's College

Founded in 1886 by Elizabeth Wordsworth (1840–1932), the first principal of Lady Margaret Hall, St Hugh's College, in St Margaret's Road, was intended to cater for clergymen's daughters and others who could not afford the fees at the other ladies colleges; male students were first admitted in 1986. The college boasts some attractive Queen Anne-style buildings while the Wolfson building was added in 1964–66.

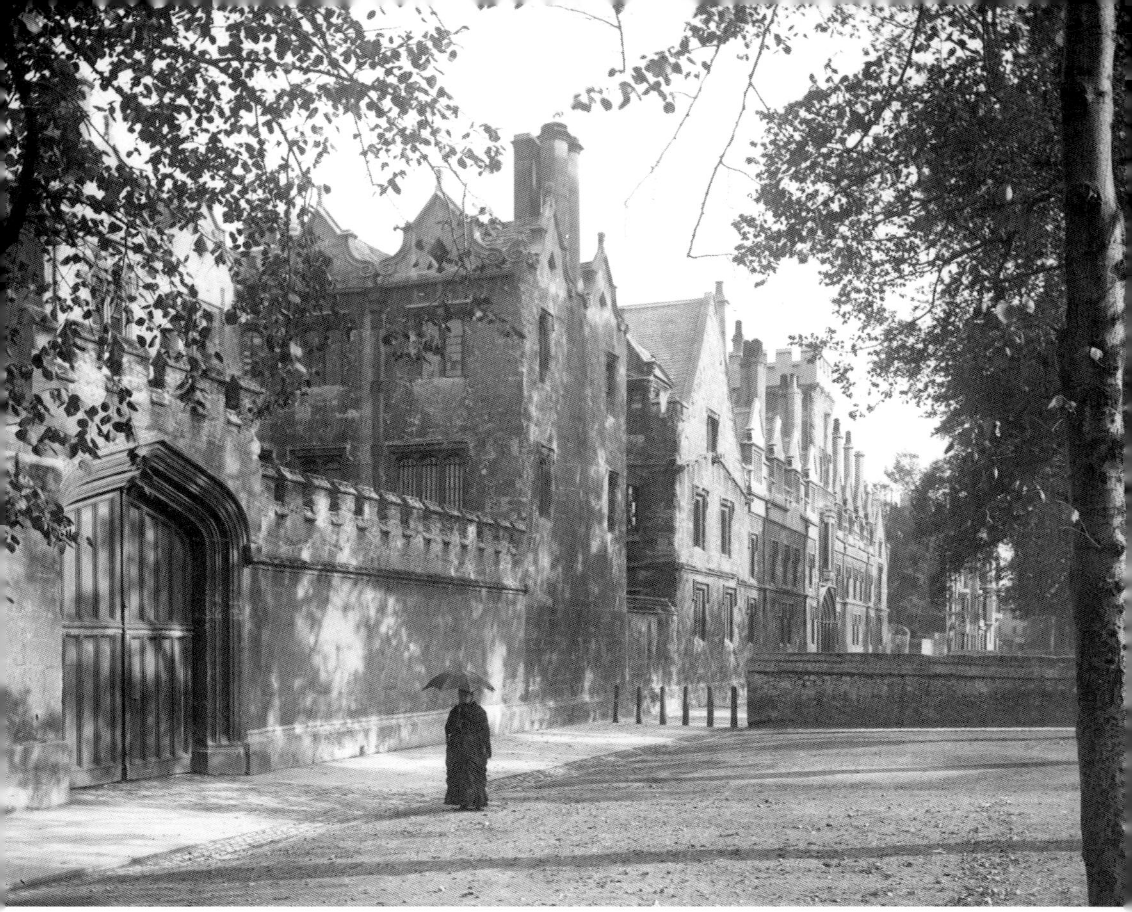

St John's College
St John's College, on the east side of
St Giles', traces its history back to 1437
when Archbishop Chichele founded
'St Bernard's College' as a college for
Cistercian monks. The college was
dissolved during the Reformation, but
in 1555 it was refounded by Sir Thomas
White (*c.* 1550–1624), a prosperous
London merchant. St John's claims to
have seven quadrangles, the façade of
Front Quad (shown above during the
1880s) being the former St Bernard's
College, while the lower photograph
provides a detailed view of the gate
tower in 1917. A statue of St Bernard
can be seen standing in a niche on the
upper storey. The college's recent alumni
include former Prime Minister Tony Blair.

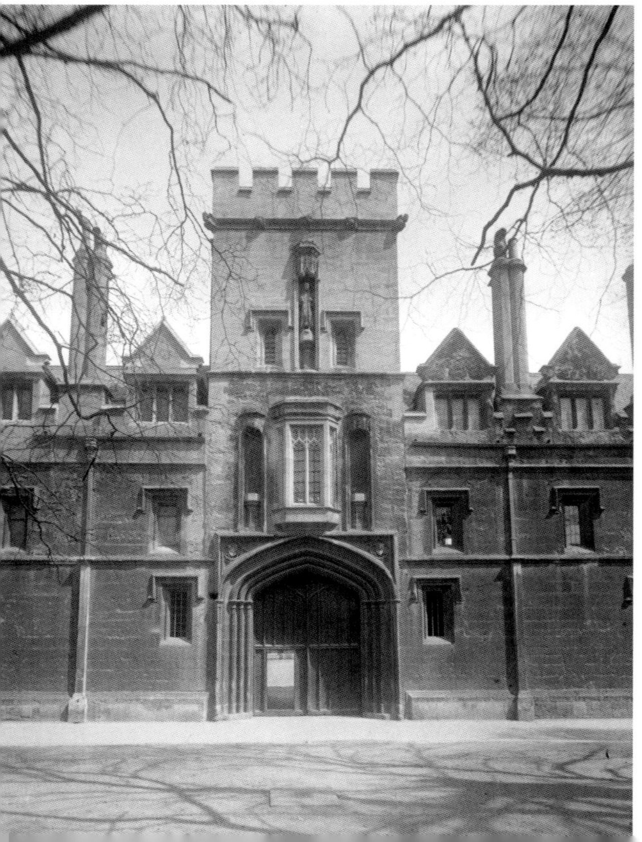

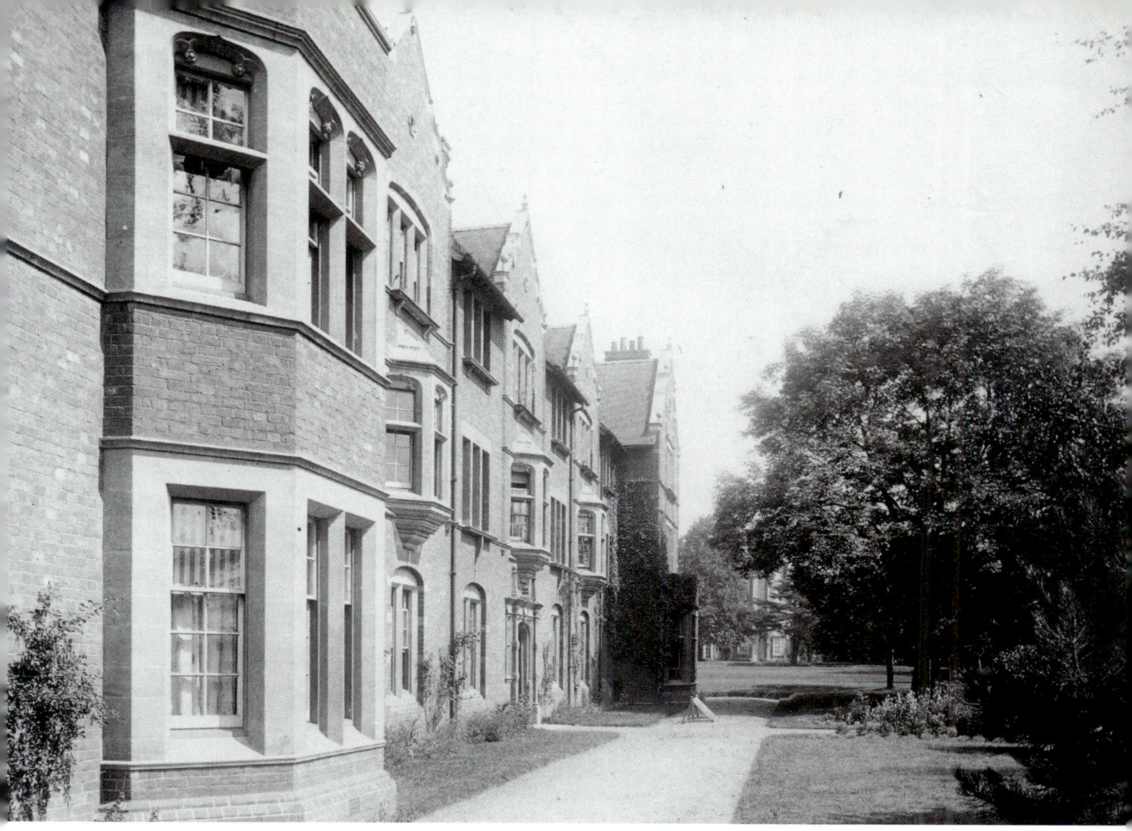

As mentioned earlier, Lady Margaret Hall and Somerville, the first ladies' colleges, were founded in 1879 as hostels for Anglican and Nonconformist students respectively, but they both became full colleges in 1960. Men were first admitted as undergraduates in 1994. The black-and-white view is looking along the garden front of the West Building, while the recent photograph shows the college entrance in 2013. Somerville's most famous alumnae include former Prime Minister Margaret Thatcher , together with Indira Ghandi, Iris Murdoch and Dorothy L. Sayers.

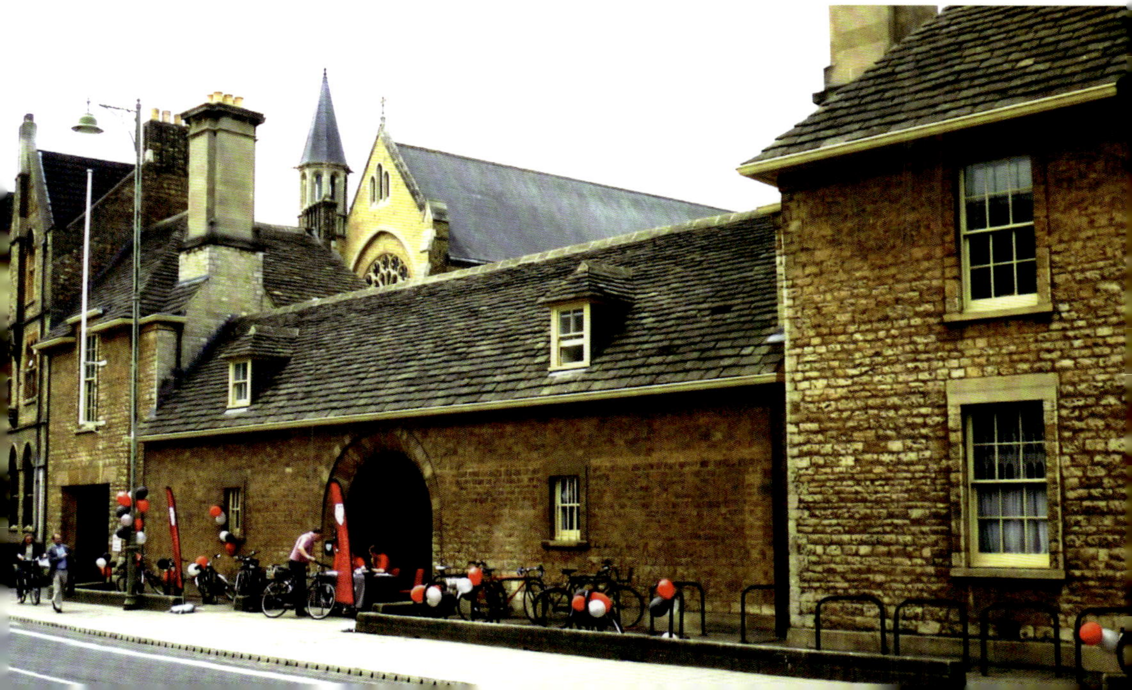

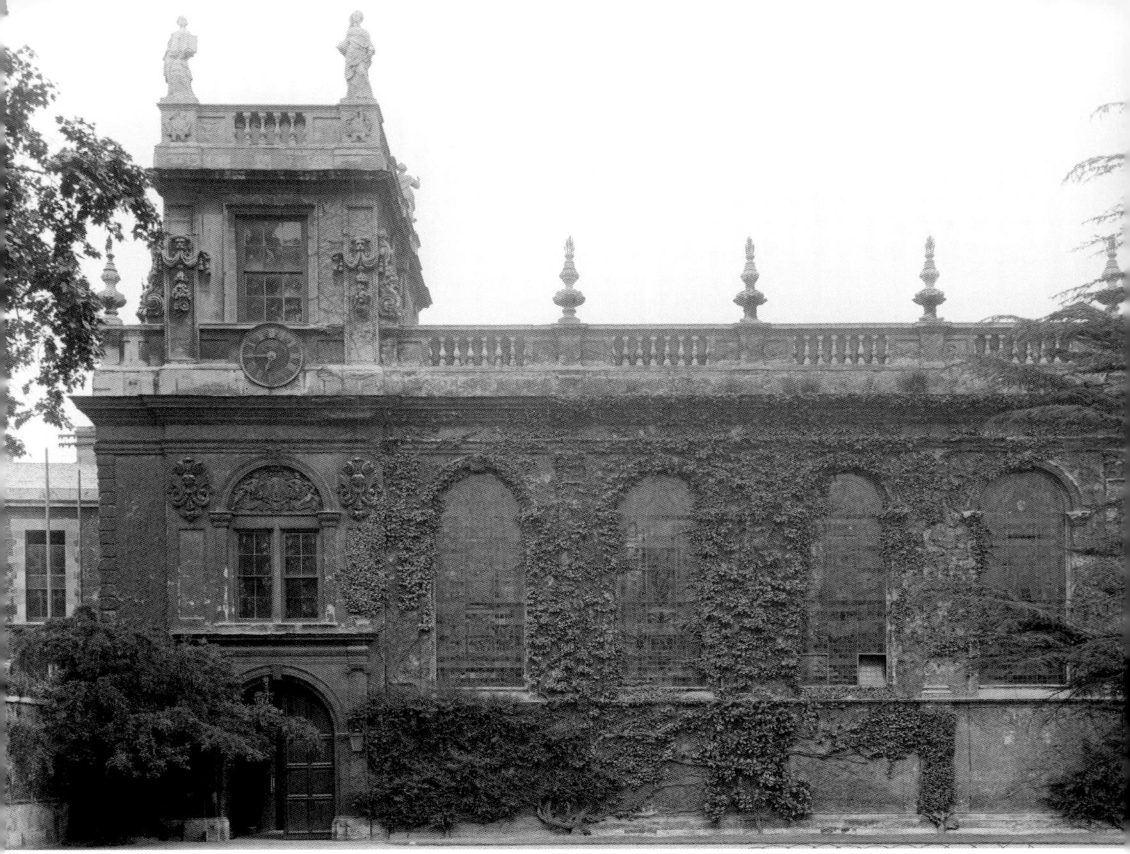

Trinity College
Built on the site of the much earlier Durham College, which was suppressed at the Reformation, Trinity College was founded in 1555 by Sir Thomas Pope (*c.* 1507–59), the son of an Oxfordshire yeoman who had risen to prominence as a Tudor civil servant and Privy Councillor. Trinity has four quadrangles, its seventeenth-century chapel (above) being in the north-western corner of Front Quad. The Garden Quadrangle (below) has just three ranges, the north wing having been designed by Christopher Wren.

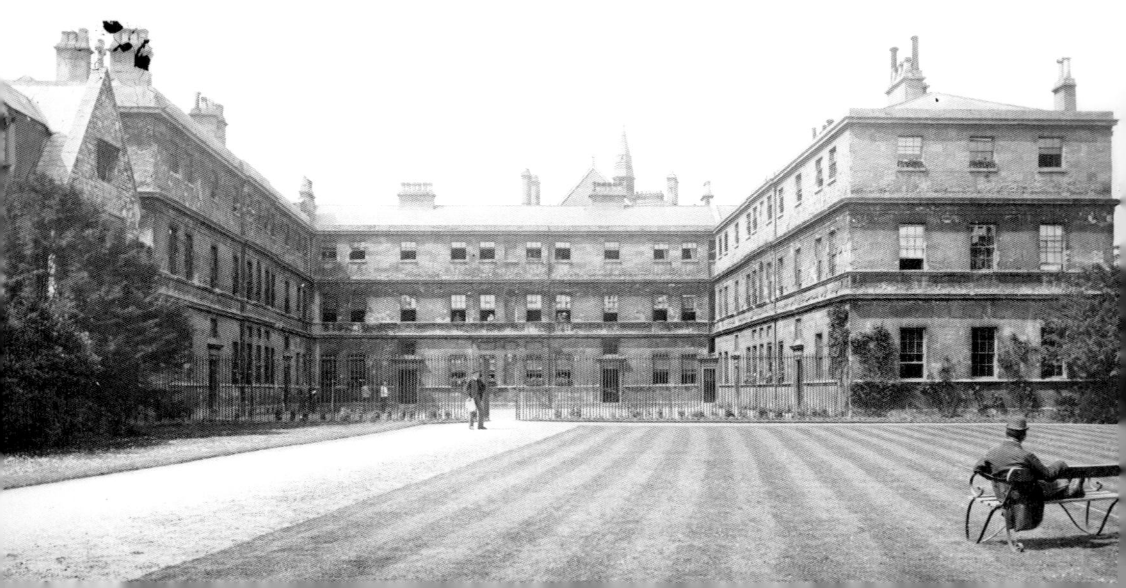

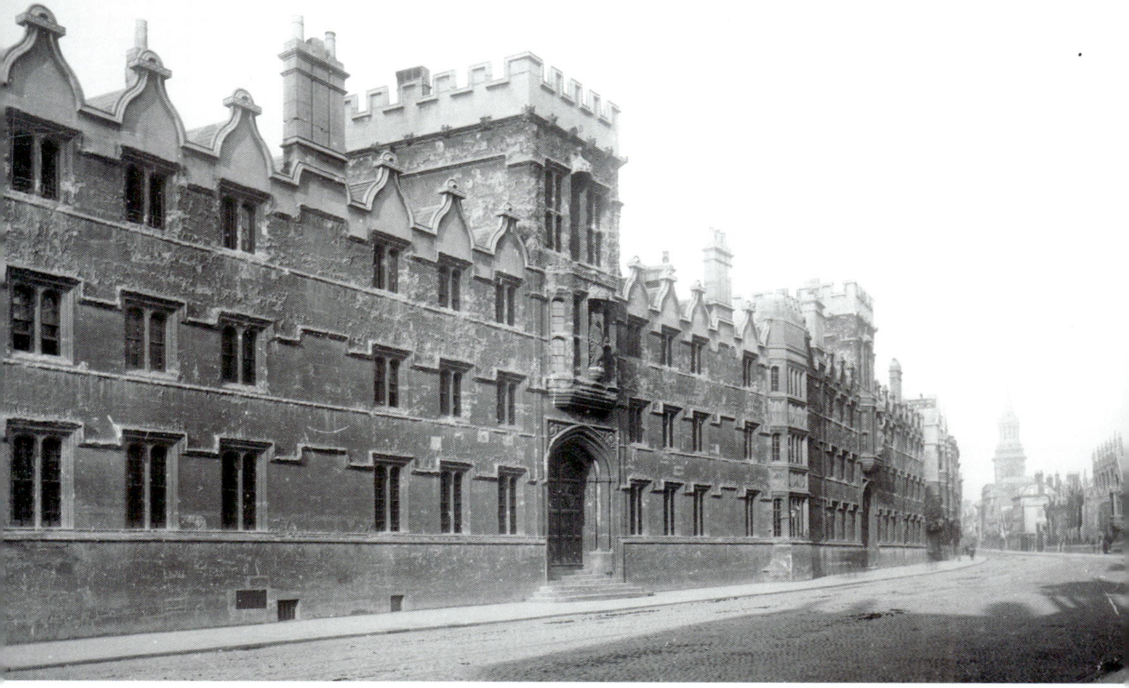

University College

Situated on the south side of High Street, University College claims to be the oldest college in Oxford, having been founded by William of Durham in 1249. The upper picture shows part of the long and impressive street façade, which incorporates two periods of construction – the western end having been built in the seventeenth century, while the eastern extension was added during the eighteenth century. The colour view shows the seventeenth-century building in 2012.

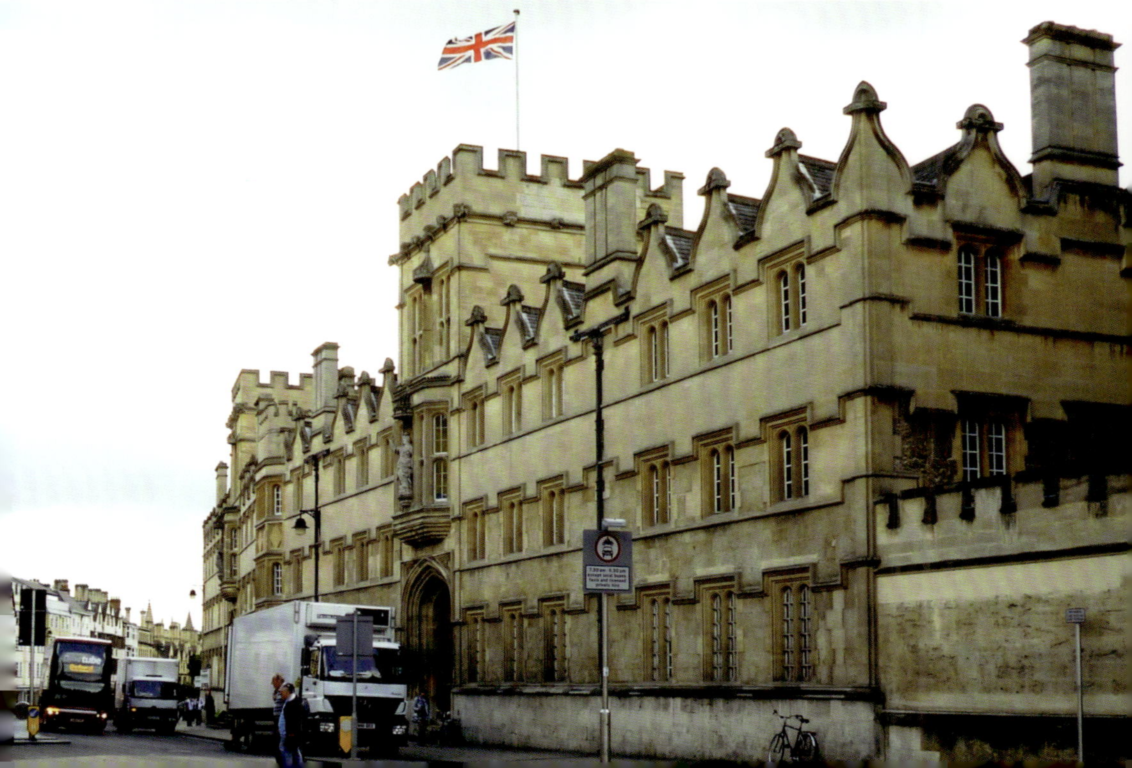

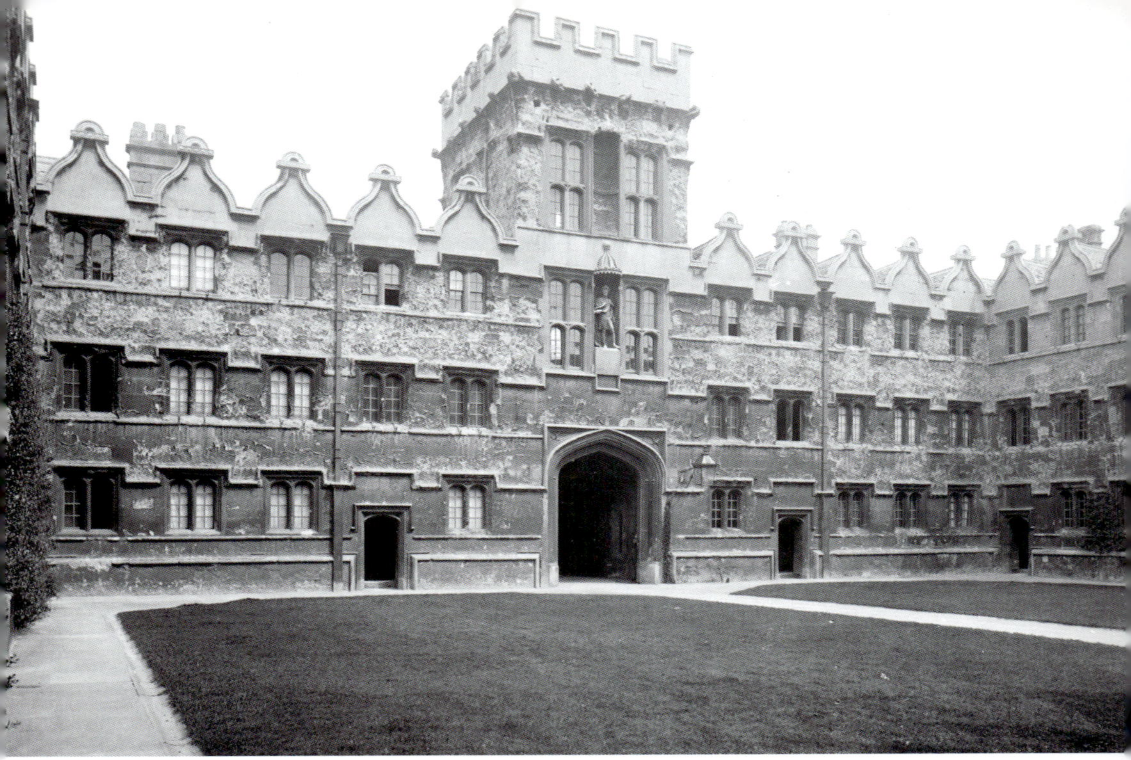

The college has two gate towers, the east gateway having a statue of Mary II, while the west gate, which gives access to the Front Quadrangle, is graced by a statue of Queen Anne. The upper view shows the western gate tower from the Front Quadrangle, the niche above the entrance being graced by a statue of James II (the father of Queen Anne). The lower illustration provides a further view of the Front Quad – the distinctive gables and windows being similar to those on the north frontage.

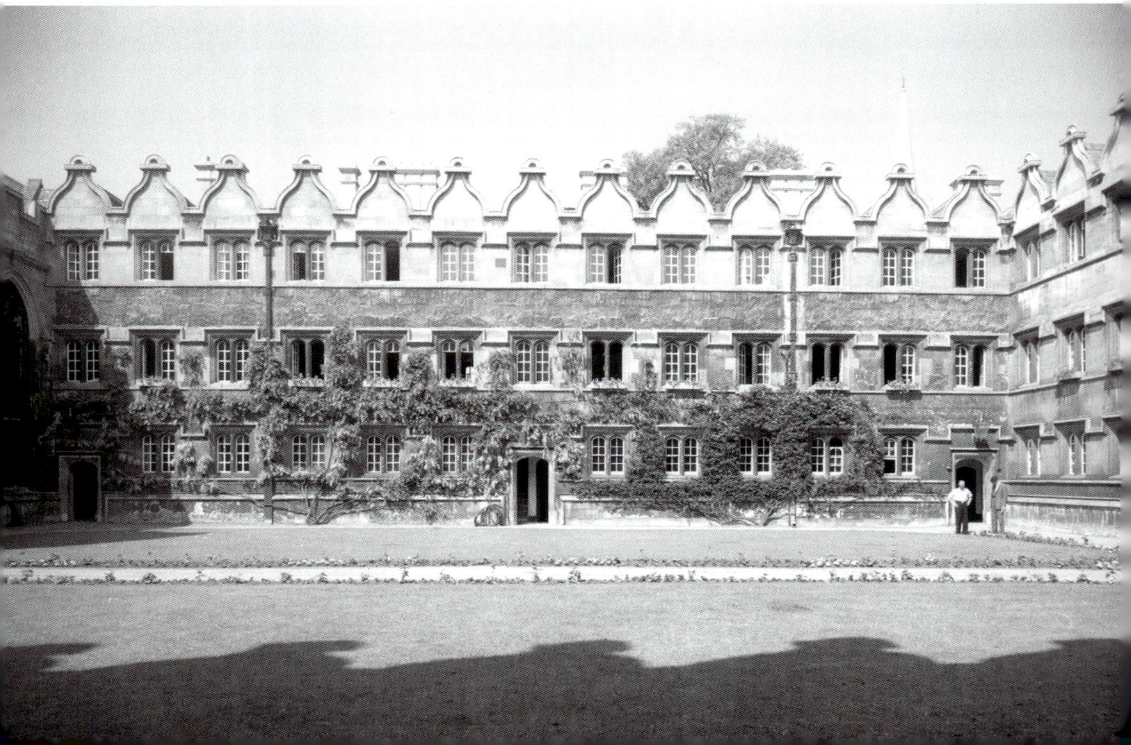

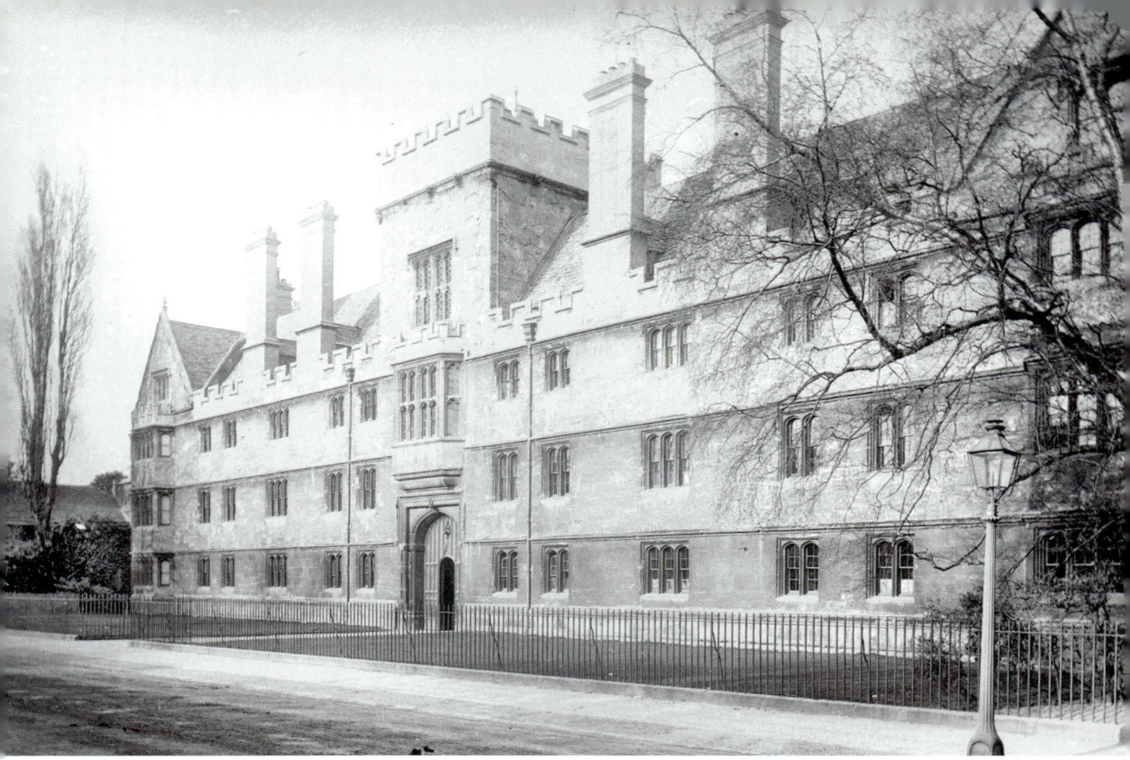

Wadham College was founded by Nicholas Wadham (1532–1609) and his wife Dorothy (1534/5–1618) who, as his executrix, obtained a royal letter patent in 1610 and undertook all of the work that was required to bring the scheme to completion by 1613, when the new college was opened. These two photographs show the gate tower and the west side of the Front Quadrangle, which flanks Parks Road – the colour photograph having been taken in 2012, while the black-and-white view, by Henry Taunt, dates from 1870.

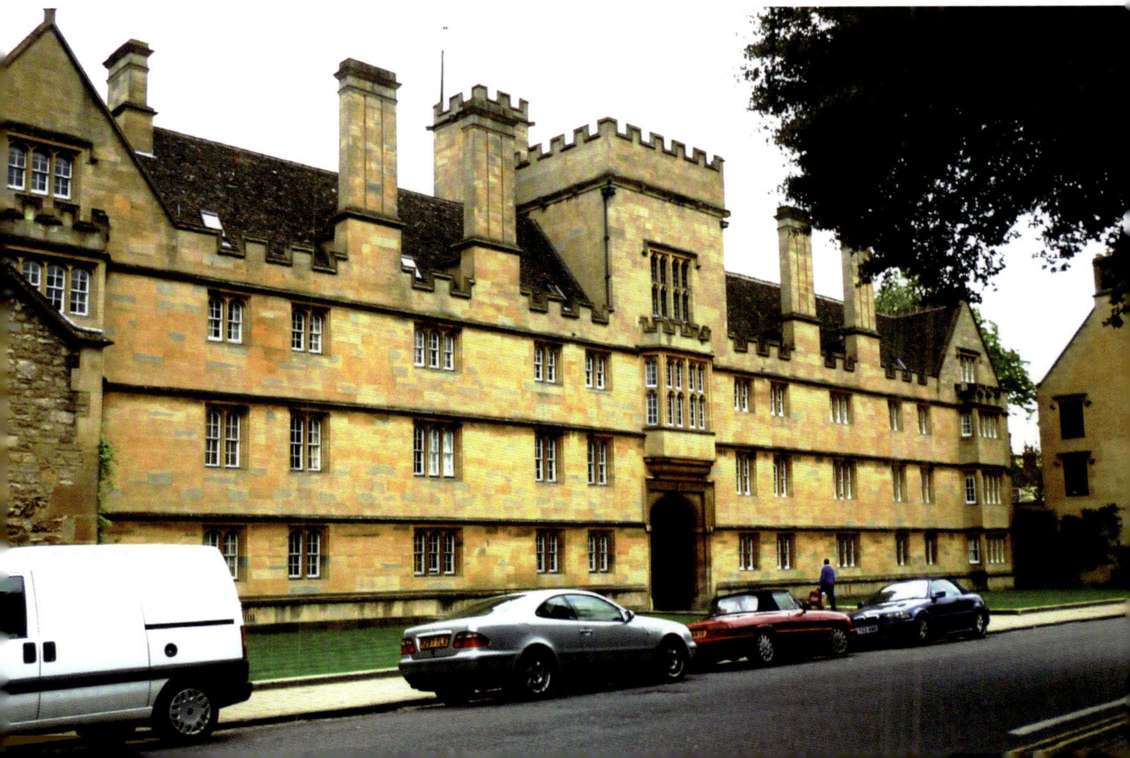

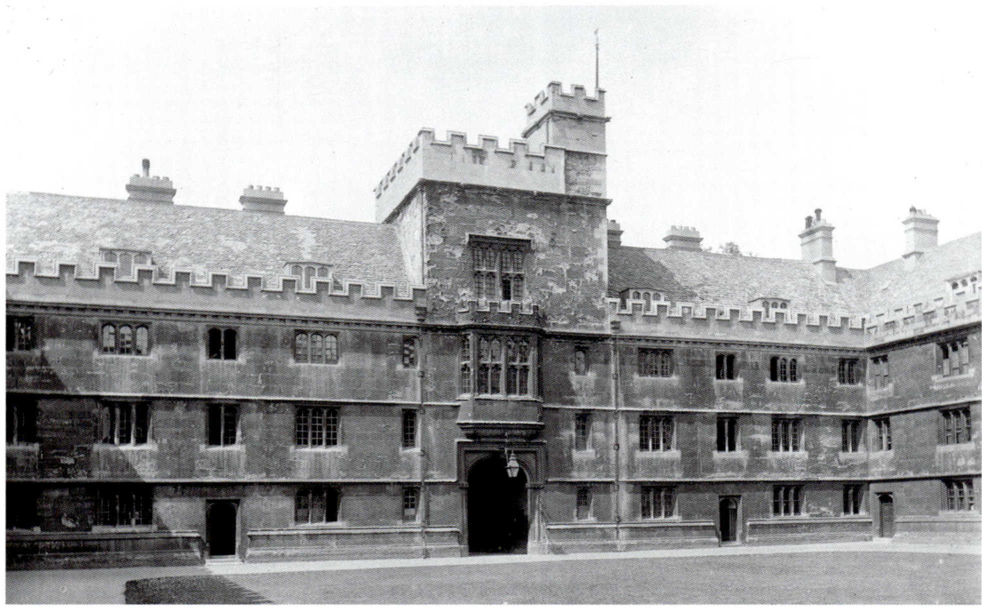

Wadham College

The upper view shows the west side of the Front Quadrangle in 1904, while the lower view provides a detailed look at the statues of Nicholas and Dorothy Wadham, which stand in niches between coupled Ionic columns on the east side of the quadrangle. Although she was widowed at the age of seventy-five, Dorothy lived long enough to see the college flourish before her death in 1618. The Wadhams are buried in the north transept of Ilminster Church, in their native Somerset.

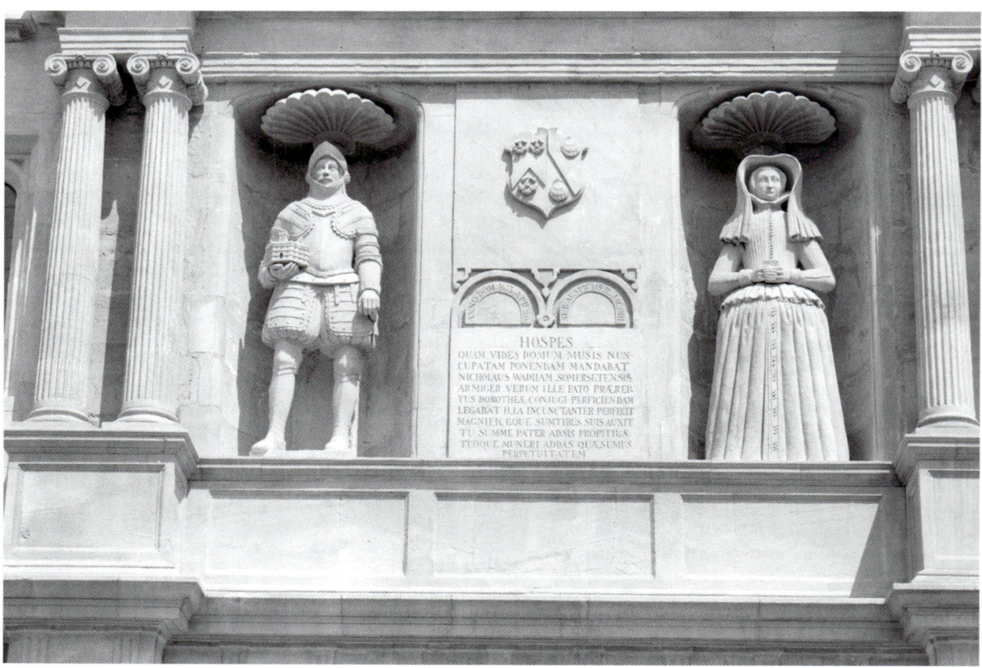

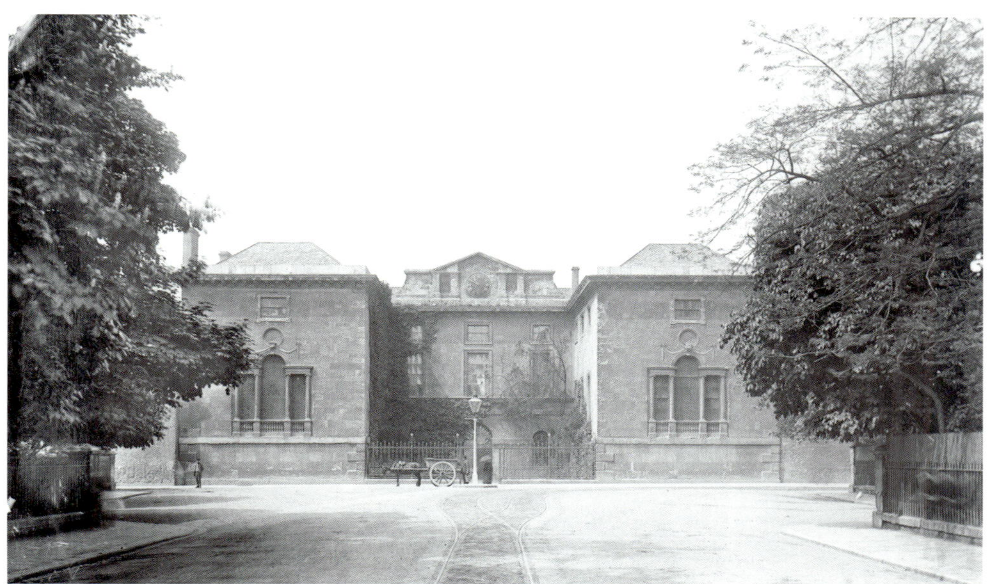

Worcester College

Situated in Worcester Street, Worcester College received its charter in 1714 after Sir Thomas Cookes (1648–1701), a Worcestershire baronet, had bequeathed £10,000 to the university, with the aim of founding a college for students from his native county. Work commenced in 1720, but the construction of the college was a curiously protracted process, and building operations were still underway during the 1790s. The Worcester Street façade has a slightly forbidding appearance – the projecting wings being not unlike the bastions of a fortress (above) – but the north wing of the Front Quad is an impressive, three-storey structure sited on a raised terrace (below).

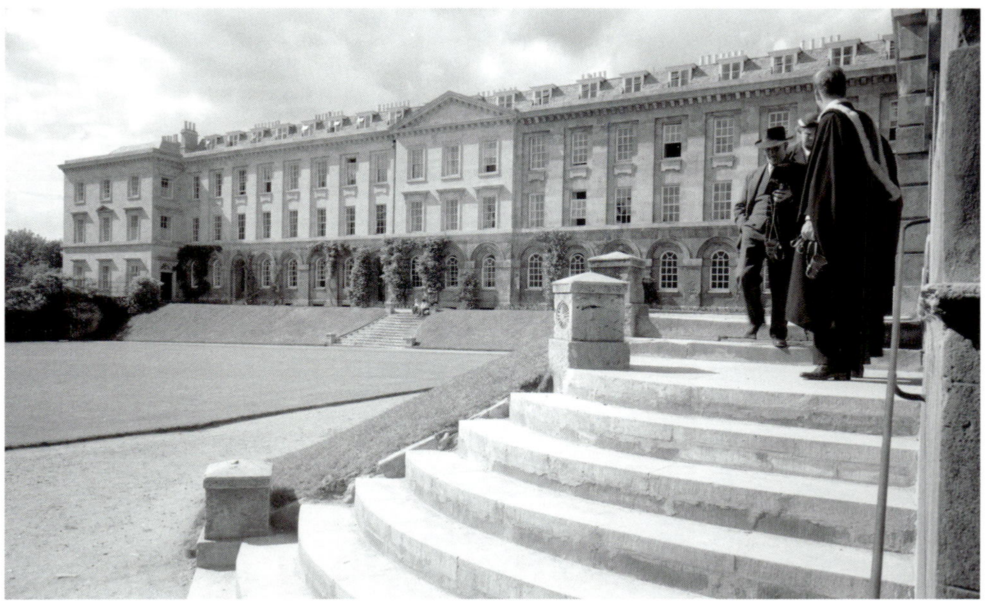

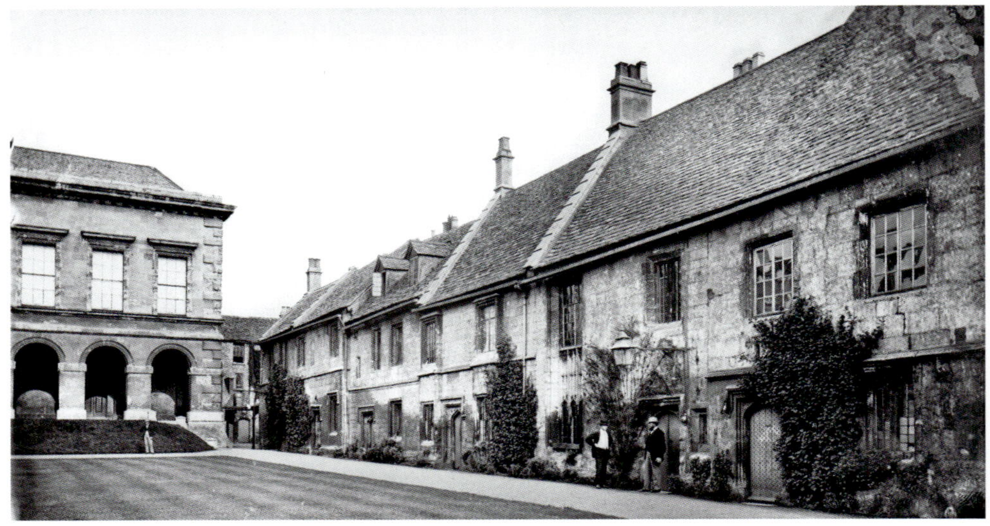

Worcester College

The college was built on the site of Gloucester Hall, which had been established in 1283 as a school for Benedictine monks, and some of the medieval buildings have survived – the south side of the quadrangle, shown in the upper view, being of fifteenth-century origin. These picturesque old houses were associated with particular monasteries – the arms of Pershore, Glastonbury and Malmesbury abbeys among those emblazoned above the doorways of each house. The lower view shows the south side of the medieval range in 1880.

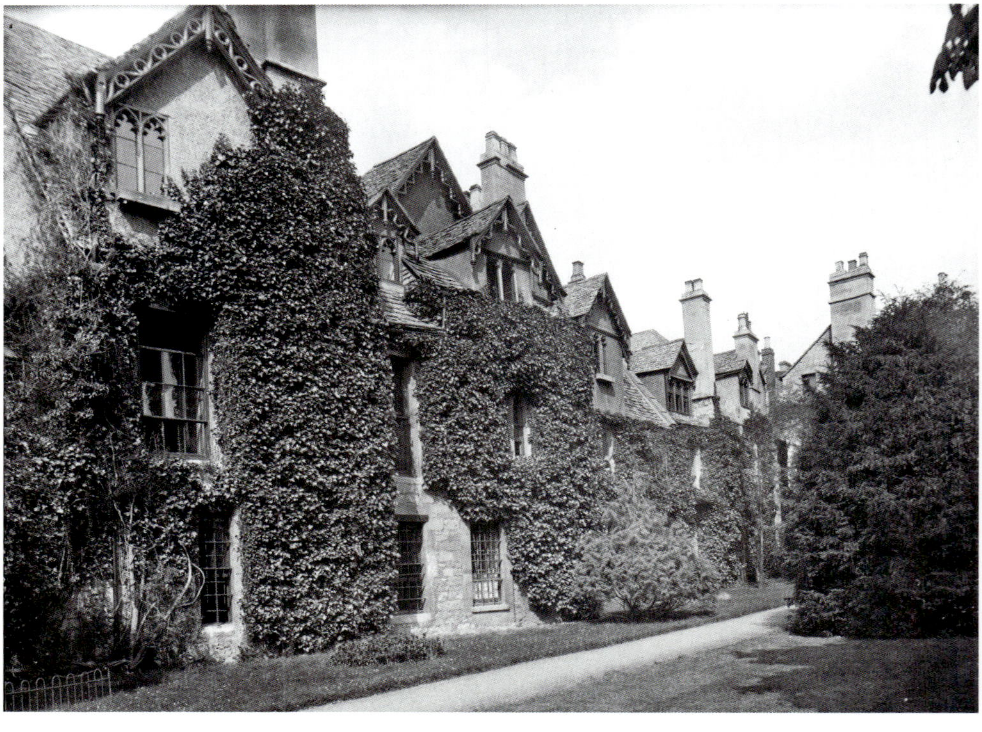

University Buildings

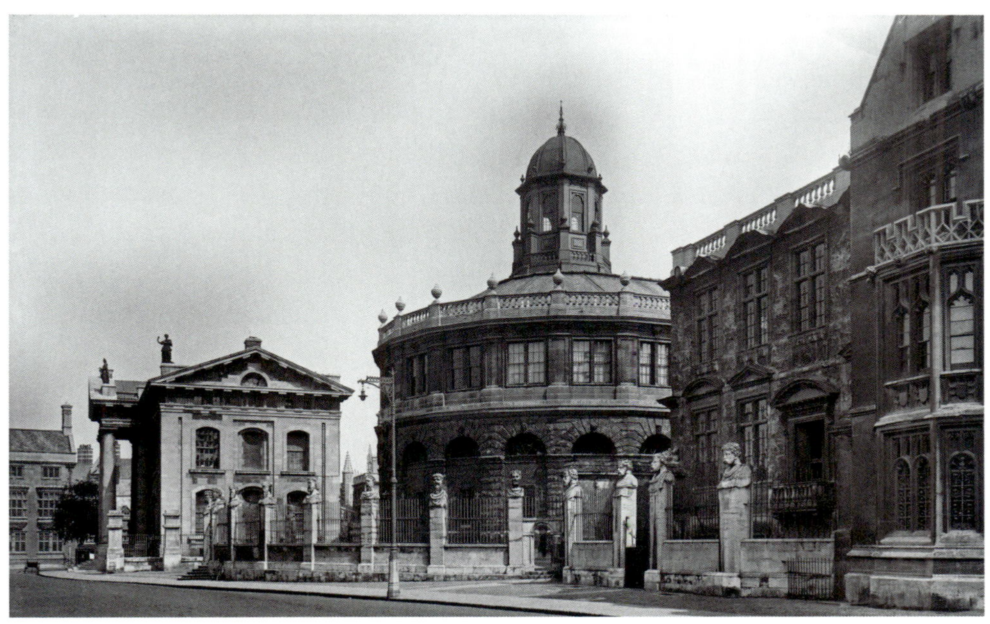

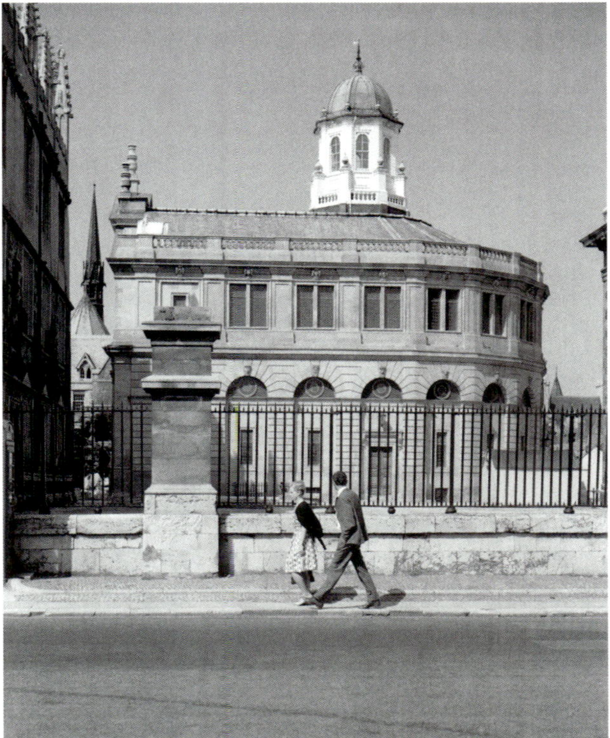

The Sheldonian Theatre

Inspired by the Temple of Marcellus in Rome, the Sheldonian Theatre was funded by Archbishop Gilbert Sheldon (1598–1677) and designed by Christopher Wren in order to provide a 'theatre' in which university ceremonies could be held. The building was formally handed over to the university at a ceremony held in 1669. The upper picture shows the Sheldonian from Broad Street around 1900, the neighbouring Clarendon Building being visible to the left. The lower photograph shows the east side of the building from Catte Street.

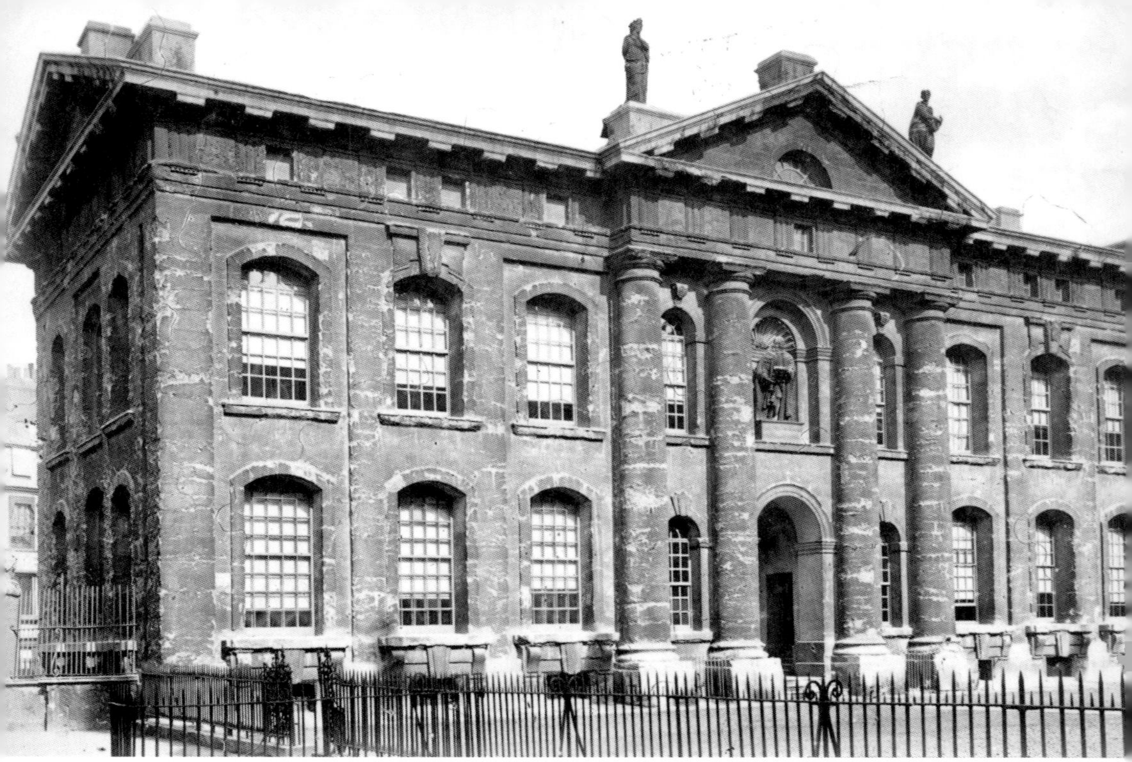

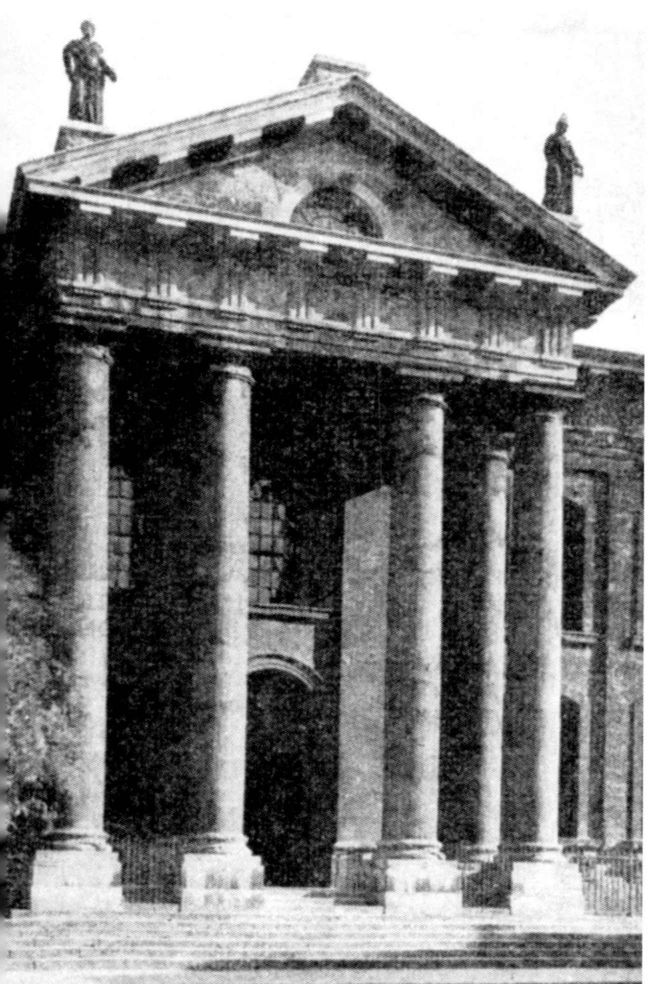

The Clarendon Building
Designed by Nicholas Hawksmoor, this impressive structure was paid for by the profits of Clarendon's *History of the Great Rebellion*, which had been written by Edward Hyde, 1st Earl of Clarendon (1609–74), and published posthumously in 1702–04 – the royalties having been given to the university. The Clarendon Building was completed in 1715 and it was, until 1830, the home of the Oxford University Press. The building, which is now used as offices by the Bodleian Library, features porticoes on its north and south façades, the monumental north portico having detached Tuscan columns, whereas the corresponding portico at the rear has attached columns. The female figures that adorn the top of the building represent the nine Muses; the present statues are fibre-glass replicas.

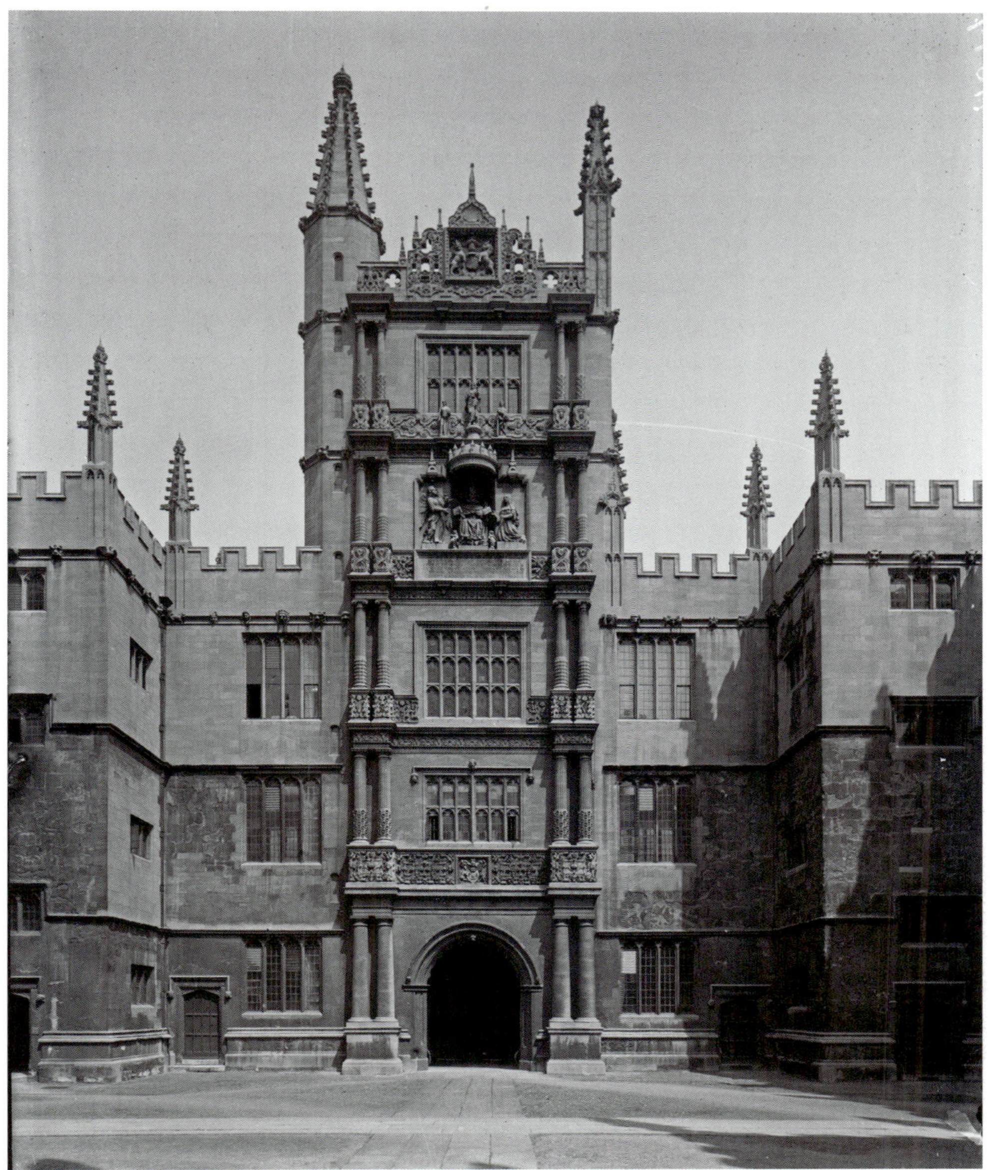

The Bodleian Library: The Schools Quadrangle and Tower of Five Orders
The university library was originally housed in St Mary's Church, but in the fifteenth century Duke Humphrey of Gloucester (1391–1447) donated his magnificent library to the university, and the books and manuscripts were then moved to a new home that had been constructed for them above the Divinity School – the new room being known as 'Duke Humphrey's Library'. Sadly, the collection was dispersed during the reign of Edward VI, although the library was restored by Sir Thomas Bodley (1545–1613) and reopened, with 2,000 books, in 1602. The 'Old Bodleian' occupies a group of historic buildings including the 'Schools Quadrangle', with its celebrated 'Tower of Five Orders', the Divinity School, Convocation House and the Proscholium. The photograph provides a detailed view of the Tower of Five Orders.

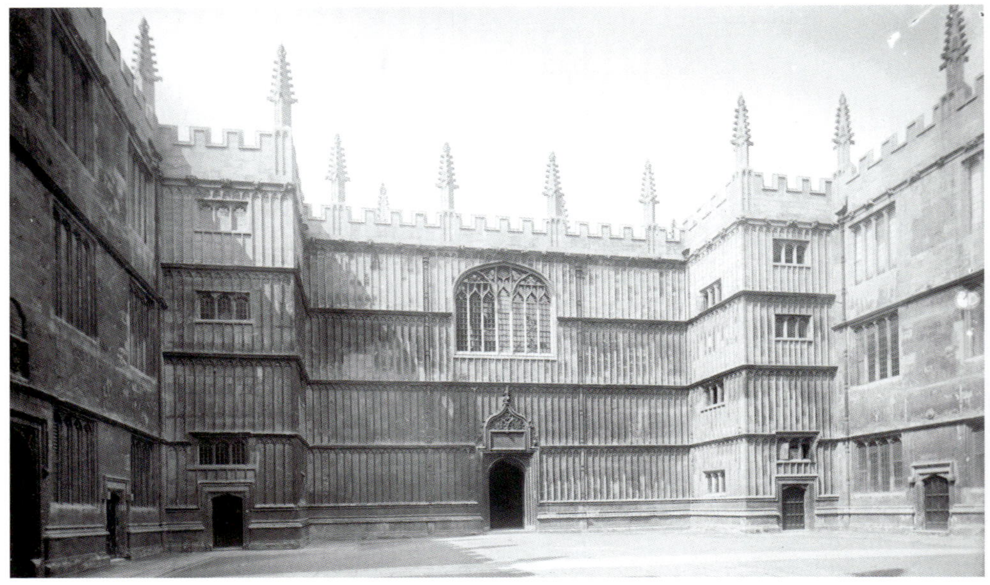

The Bodleian Library – The Proscholium and the 'Arts End'

Above: The entrance to the Bodleian is opposite the Tower of Five Orders, on the west side of the Schools Quadrangle – the bronze statue in front of the doorway being a representation of the Earl of Pembroke. The single doorway gives access to a vaulted entrance hall known as the Proscholium.

Below: This Victorian photograph, taken in 1885, shows the part of the library known as the 'Arts End', which is situated on the upper floor above the Proscholium.

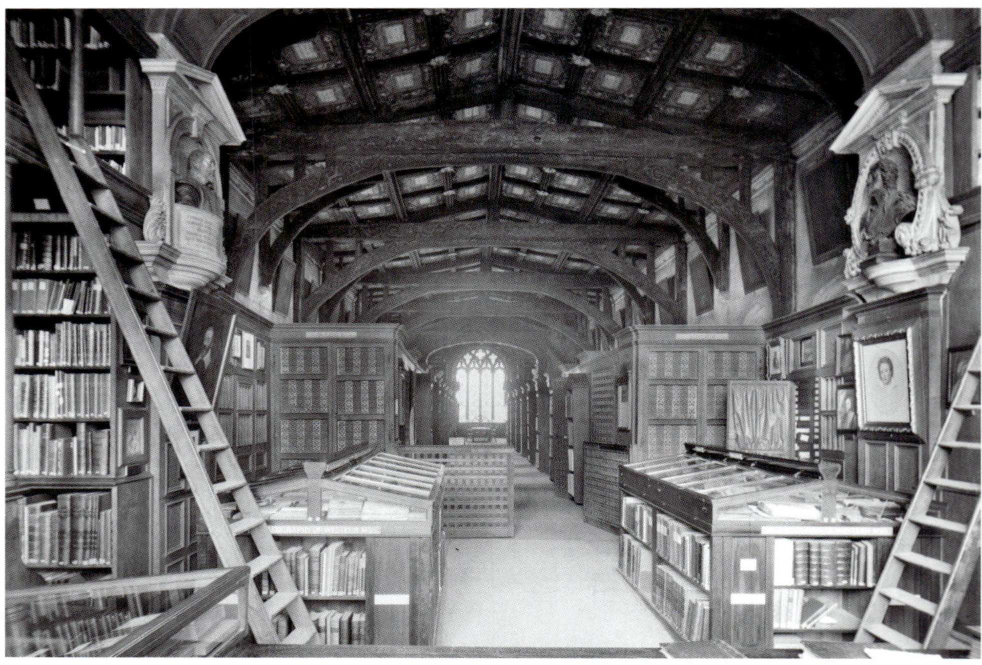

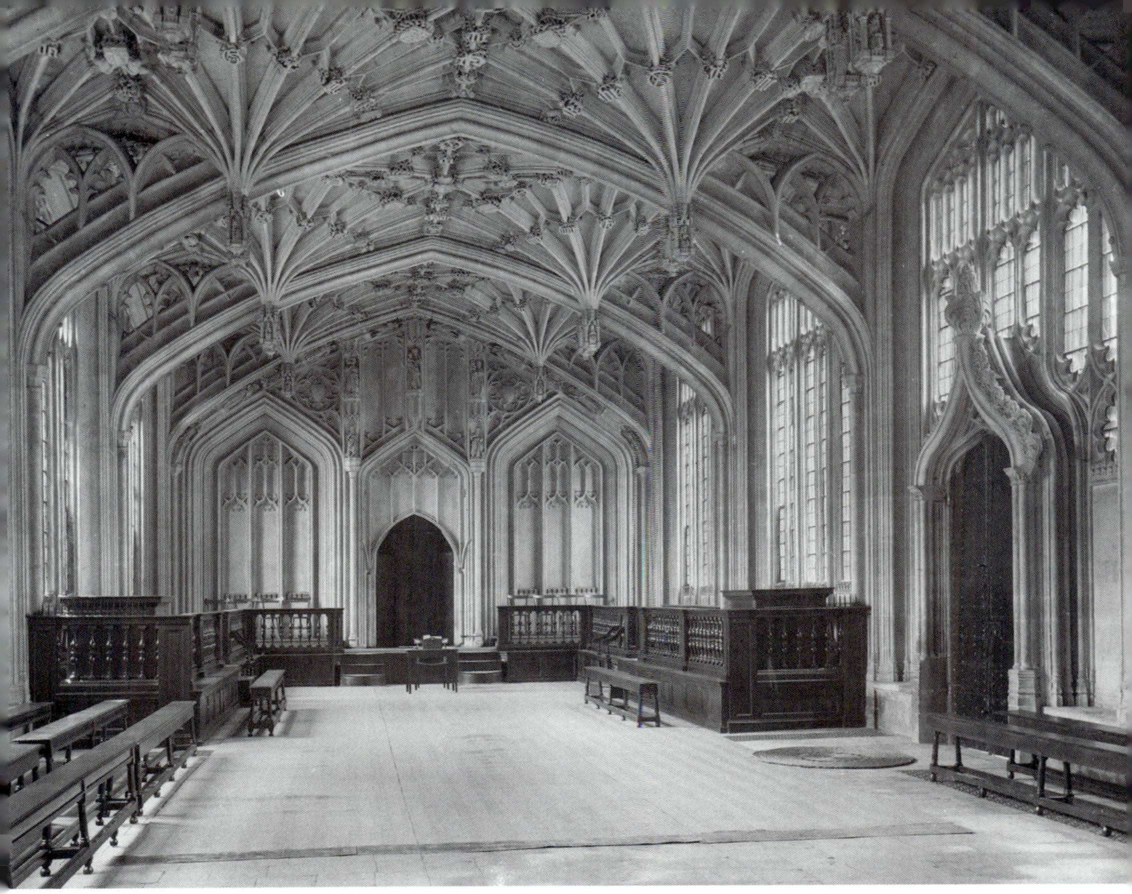

The Bodleian Library – The Divinity School

Above: A 1919 view of the Divinity School, which is situated below Duke Humphrey's Library, and entered via the Proscholium. The Divinity School was built in at least two stages over a period of years, much of the work having been accomplished in the 1420s, although the magnificent vaulted ceiling was added around sixty years later, after the decision had been taken to increase the height of the building to two storeys, so that the library could be accommodated on the upper floor.

Right: Details of the remarkable vaulting, which has often been described as a 'fan vault', although it would be more accurate to describe it as a 'lierne vault'. The architect is thought to have been William Orchard, whose initials 'WO' appear on several of the vault bosses.

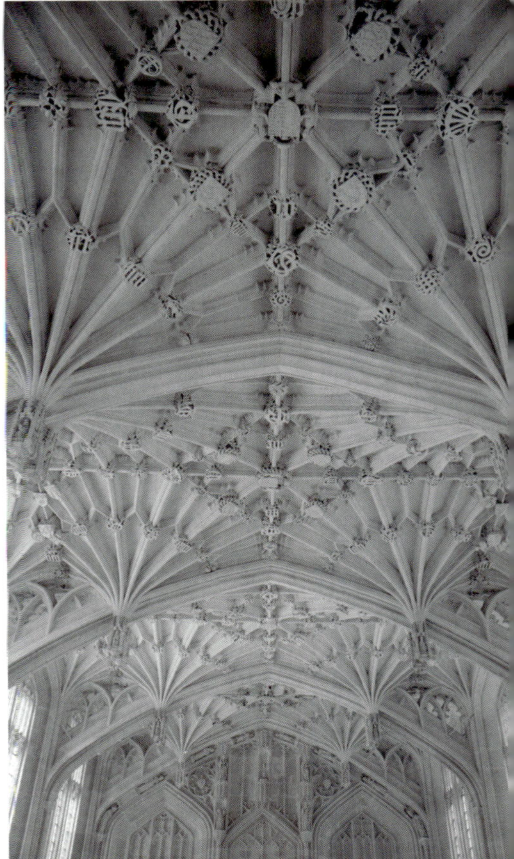

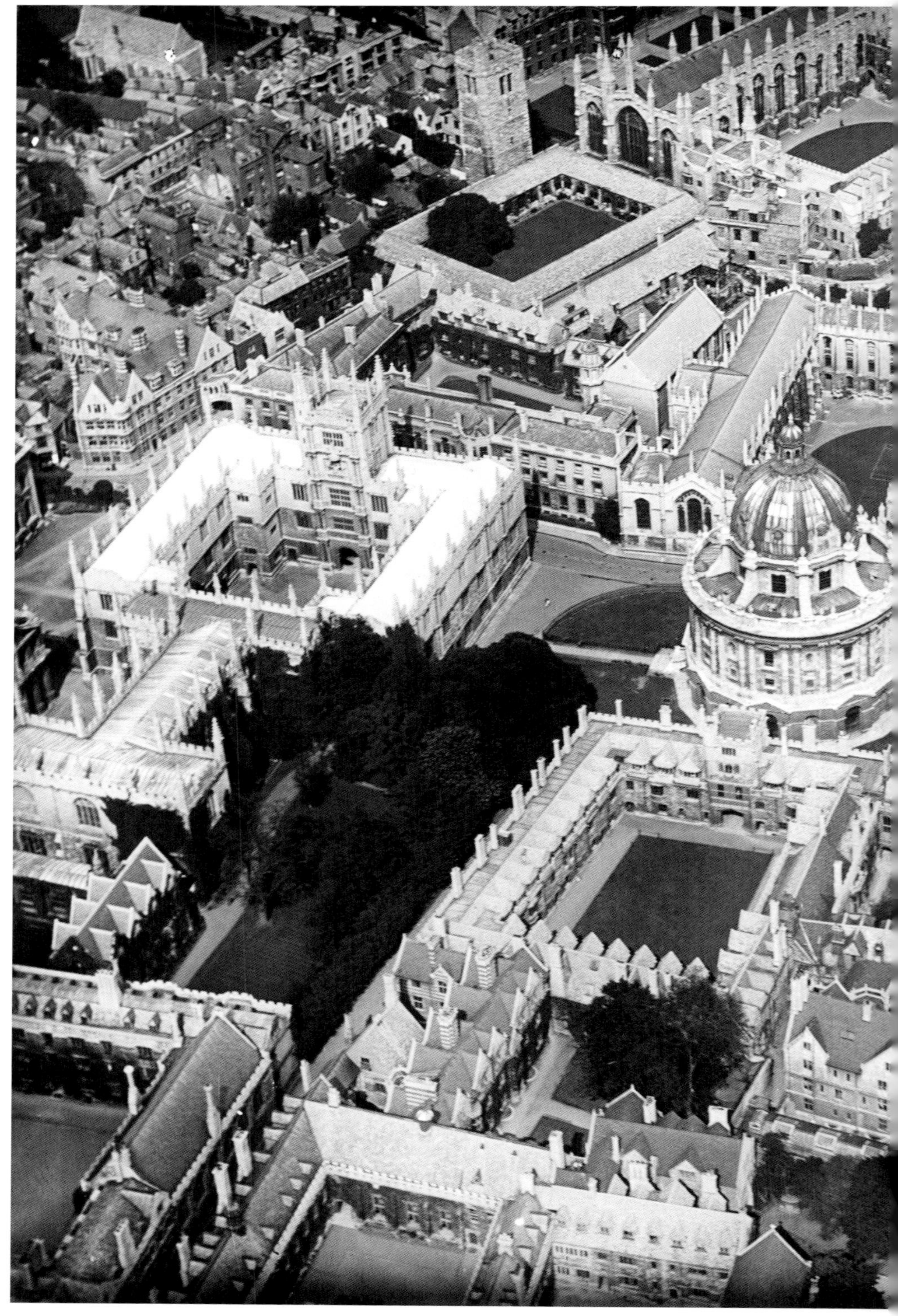

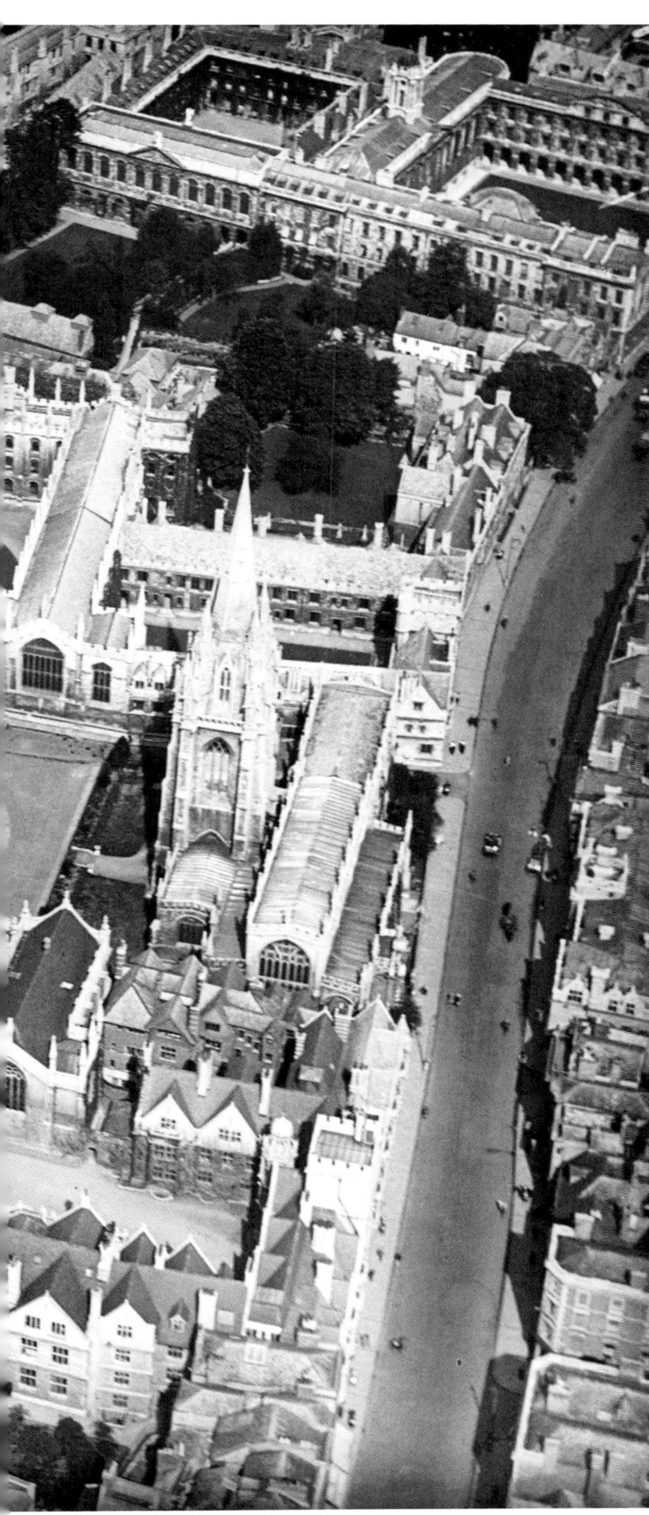

Aerial Photograph
This aerial view of the area around the Radcliffe Camera shows St Mary's Church to the right and the buildings that comprise the 'Old Bodleian' to the left, while All Souls and Hertford colleges can be seen to the east. Brasenose and Lincoln colleges feature in the foreground.

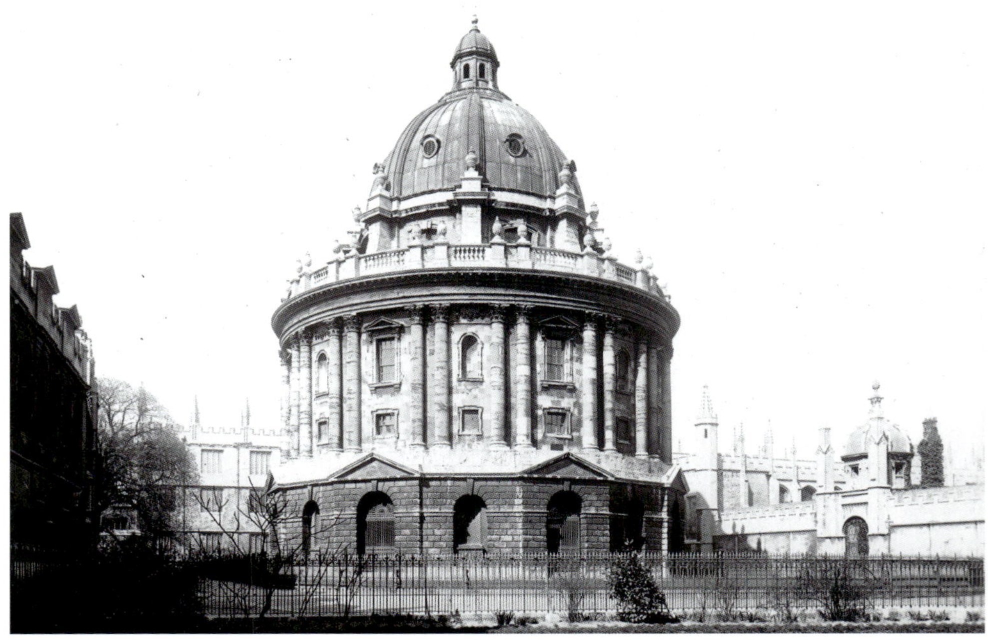

The Radcliffe Camera

Completed in 1749, the Radcliffe Camera derives its name from Dr John Radcliffe (1650–1714), who left £40,000 to erect a new 'Physic Library', and a further sum to pay the salary of a librarian. The architect was James Gibbs (1681–1754). The building has been used by the Bodleian as a reading room since 1860. This iconic Oxford building is sited in Radcliffe Square, to the south of the Divinity School. The upper photograph was taken by the prolific Henry Taunt in 1901, whereas the colour view was taken in June 2012.

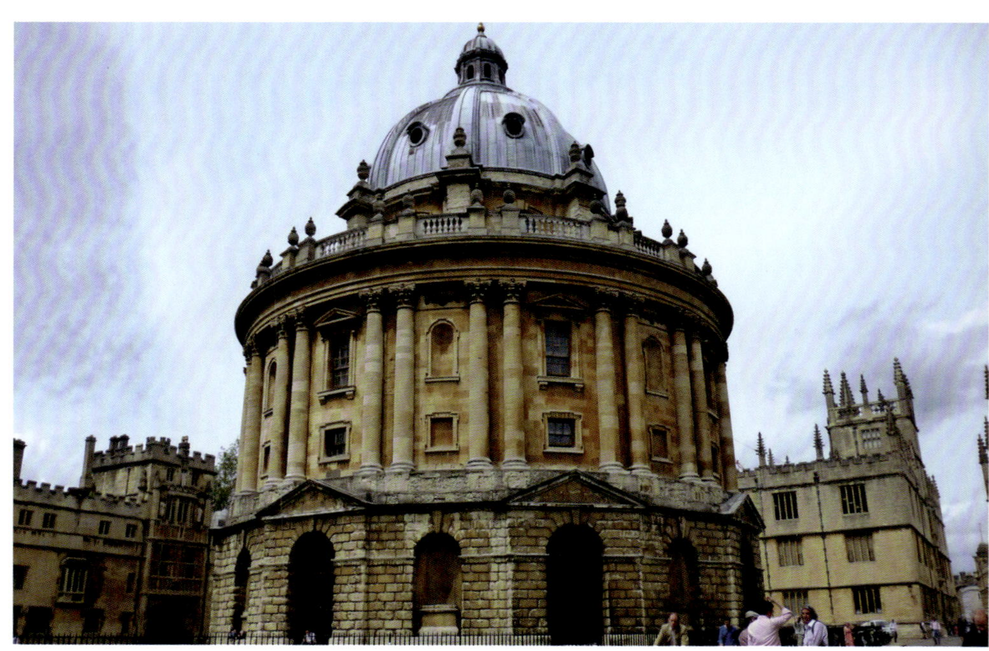

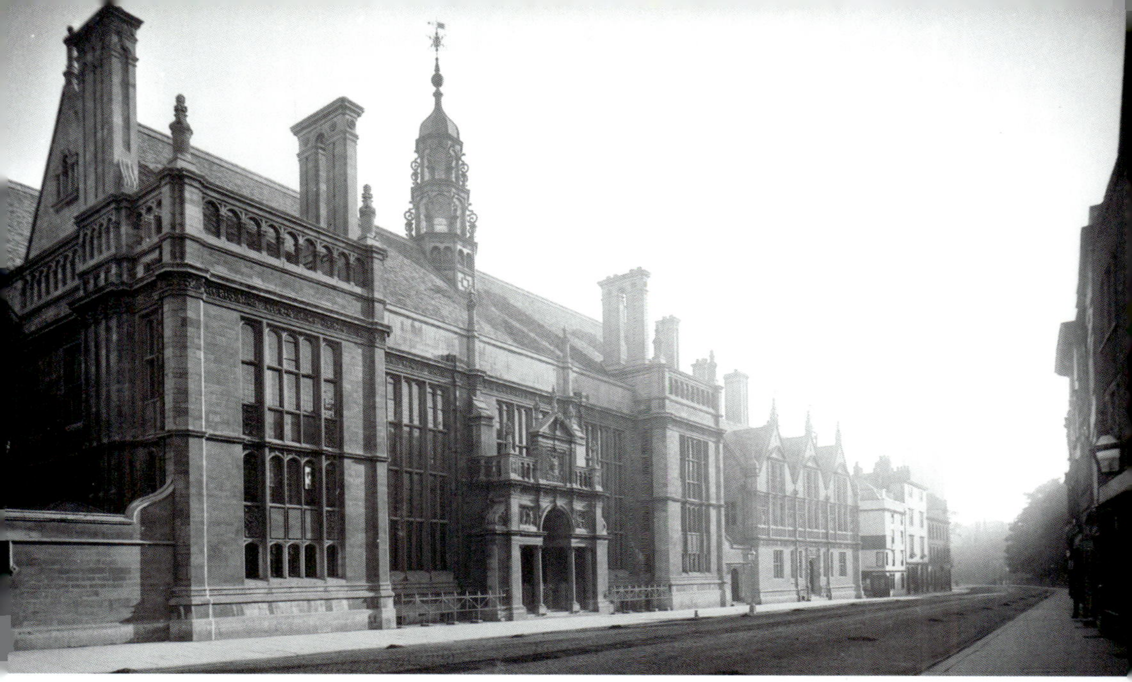

The Examination Schools

The Examination Schools, on the south side of the High Street, are of comparatively recent construction, having been designed by Sir Thomas Jackson and opened in 1882. This impressive, Jacobean-style building was pressed into military service during the First World War when it became the headquarters of the 3rd Southern General Hospital – its capacious interior being filled with hospital beds. These two photographs were both taken during the early years of the twentieth century.

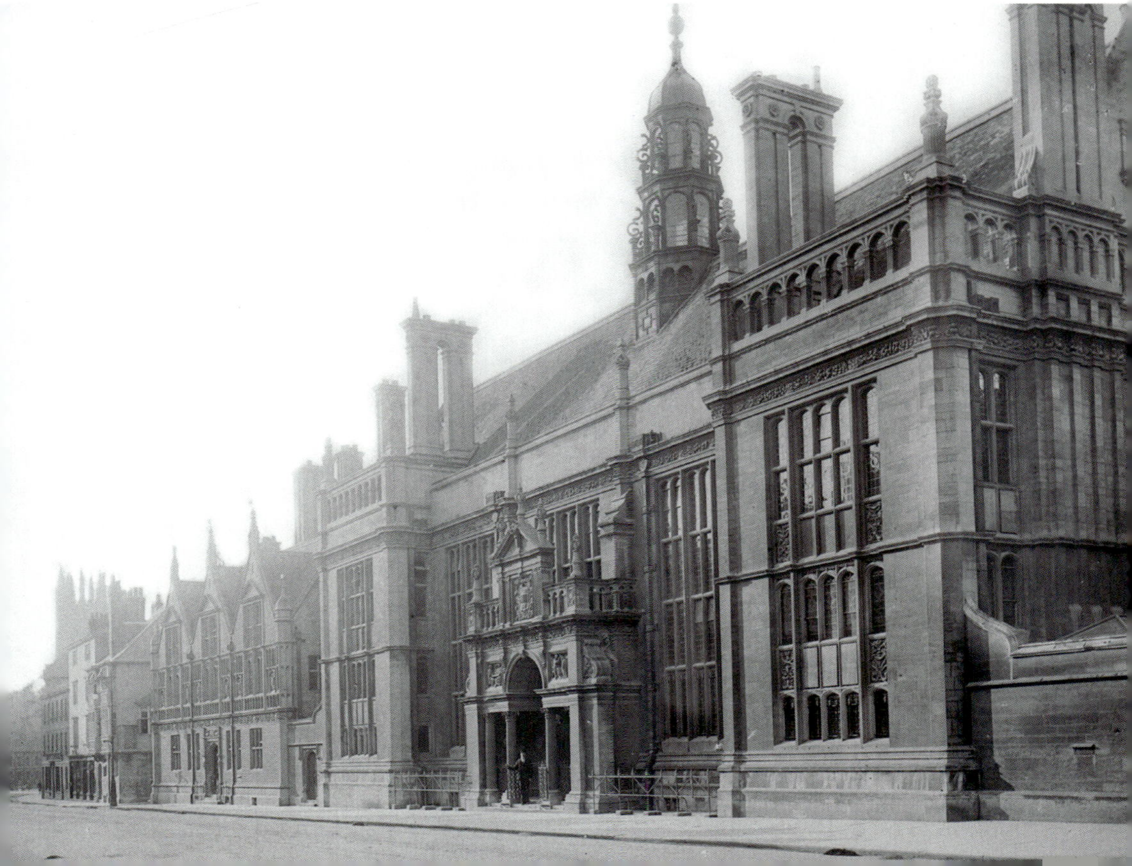

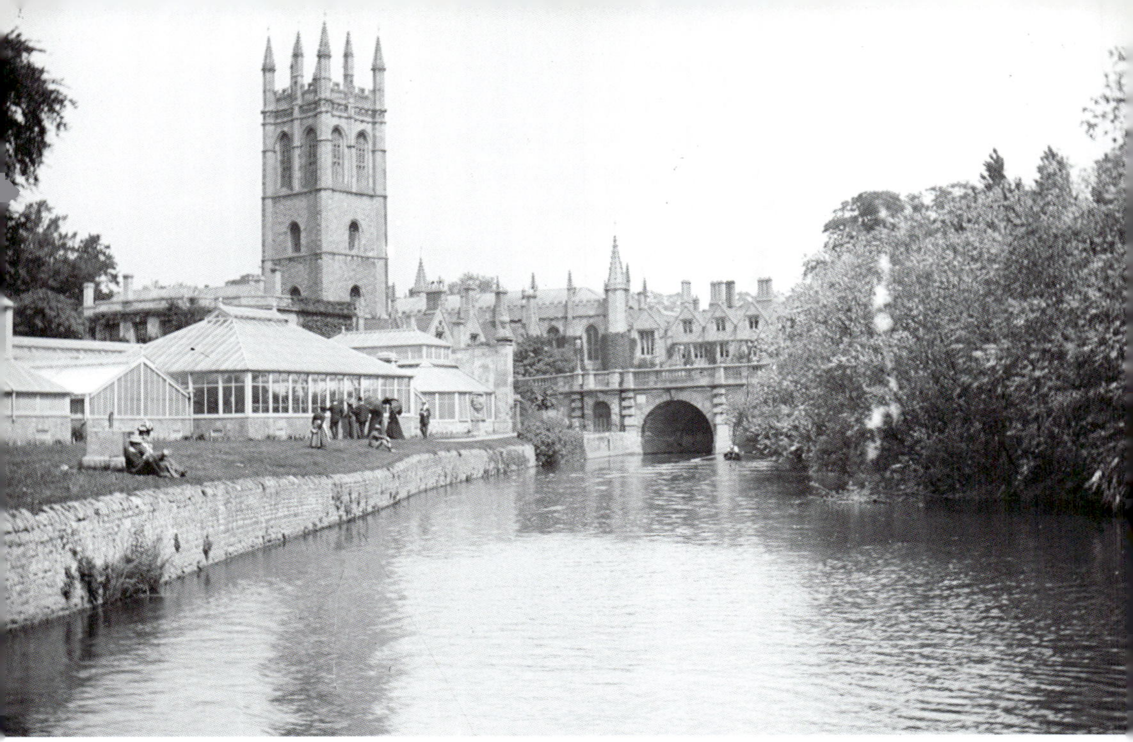

The Botanic Gardens

Sited on the west bank of the Cherwell, on the opposite side of the road from Magdalen College, the Botanic Gardens (above) were founded in 1621 by Henry Danvers, Earl of Danby (1573–1644), and they are the oldest gardens of their kind in England. The gardens have three gateways designed by Nicholas Stone, the main entrance, known as the Danby Gate (below) being a particularly exuberant baroque structure; the statues represent Charles I, Charles II and the Earl.

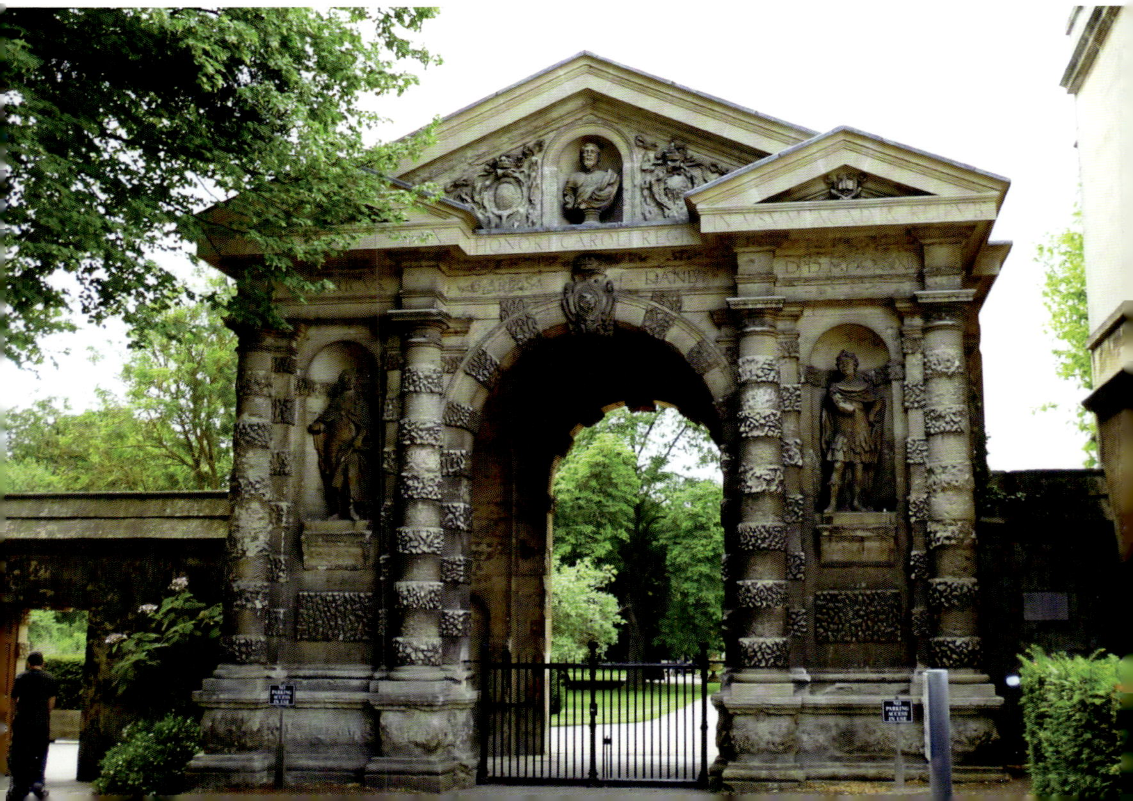

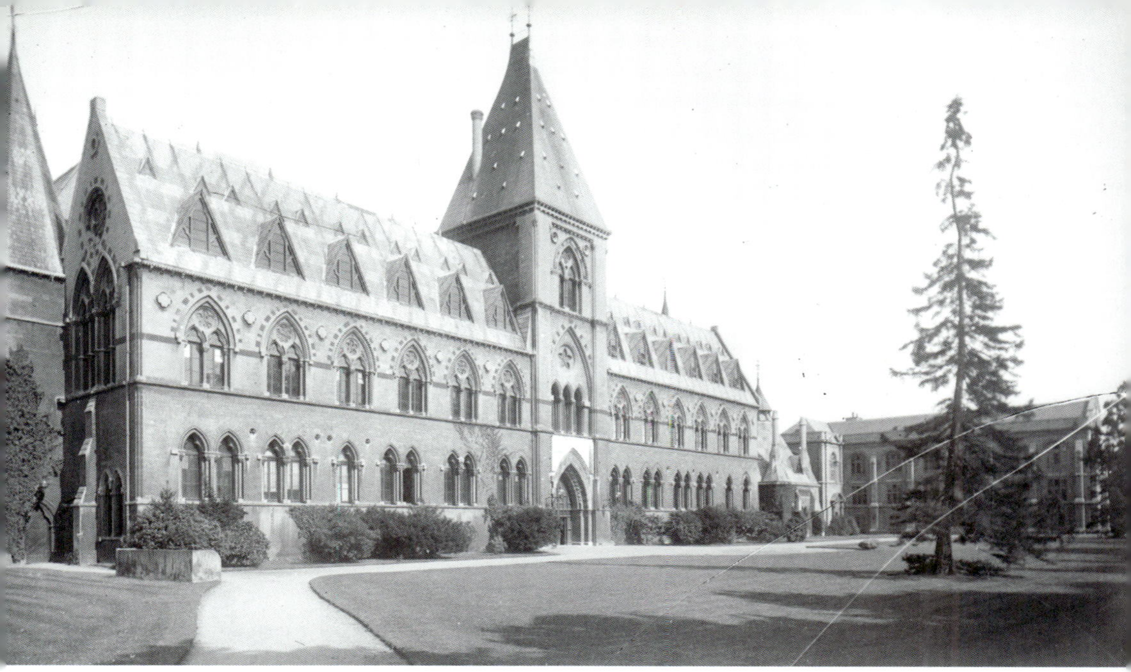

The University Museum

In 1847 Dr Henry Acland suggested that the university should establish a centre for the study of natural history, and the University Museum was duly constructed in 1855–60, the architects being Sir Thomas Newenham Deane (1828–99) and Benjamin Woodward (1816–61) of Dublin. The museum building, which features a large central gallery with a glass-and-iron roof, was extended in 1885–86 when the Pitt Rivers Museum was constructed, but the main frontage, seen here in 1915 (above) and in 2012 (below), remains more or less unchanged.

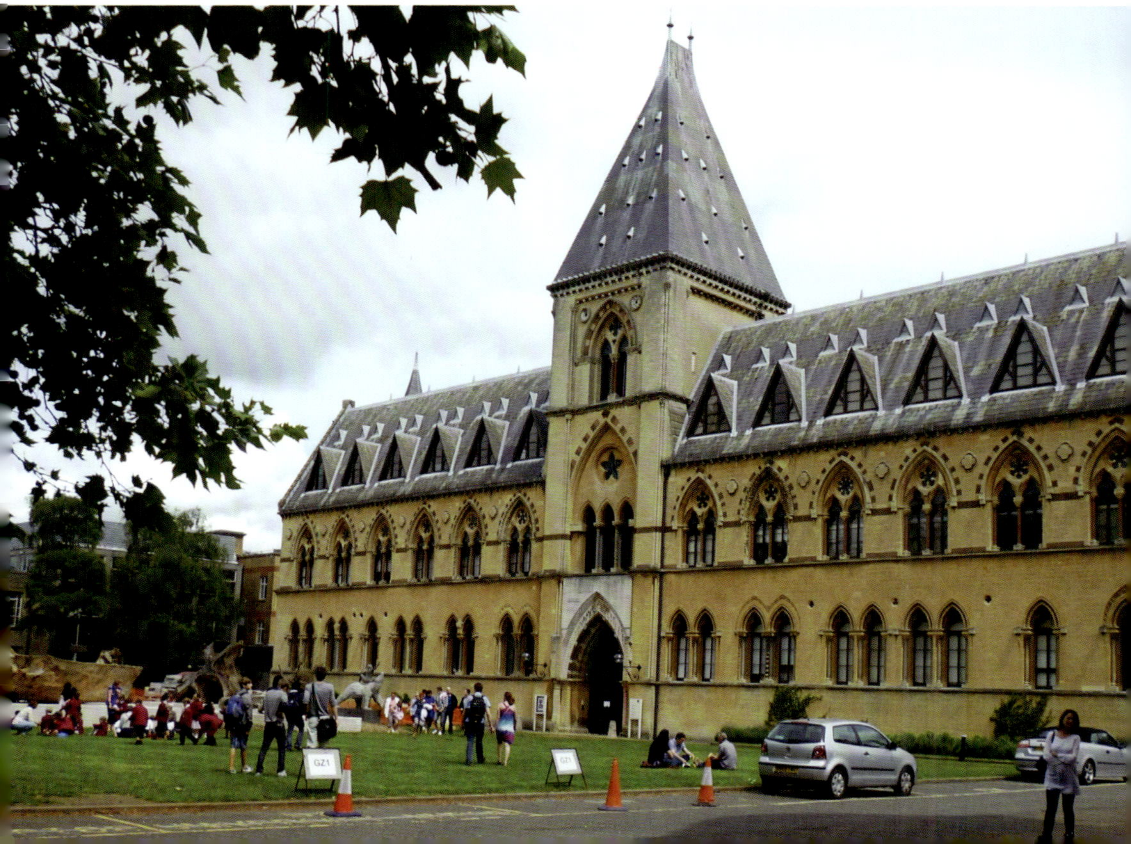

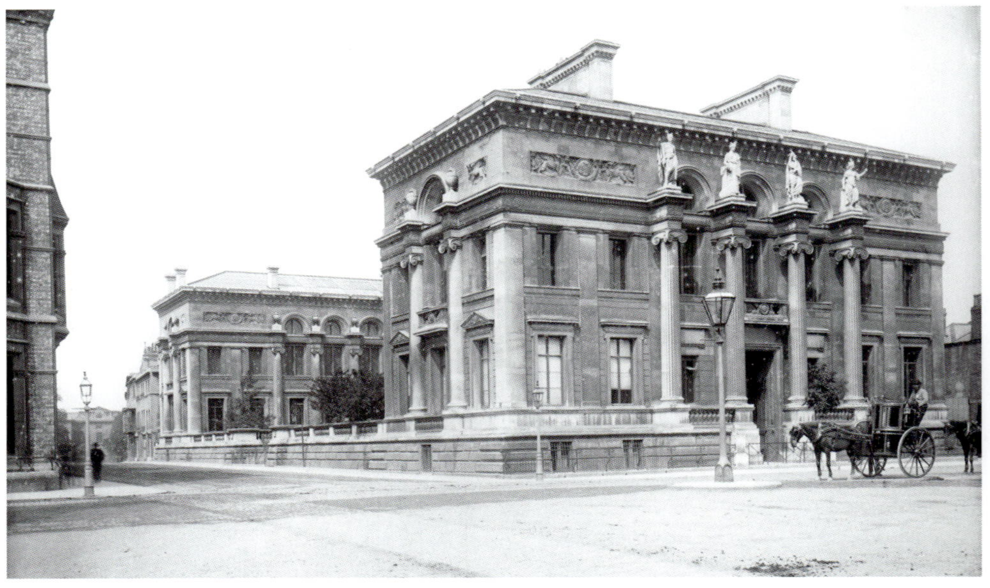

The Ashmolean Museum and Taylorian Institute

Founded by Elias Ashmole (1617–92), the Ashmolean Museum is the oldest museum in the British Isles, although the present building in Beaumont Street was not built until 1841–45. The architect was Charles Robert Cockerell (1788–1863). The eastern wing, shown in the upper view, faces St Giles' and houses the Taylorian Institute, which was endowed by Sir Robert Taylor in 1788 for the study of modern languages. The lower photograph shows the main façade in Beaumont Street.

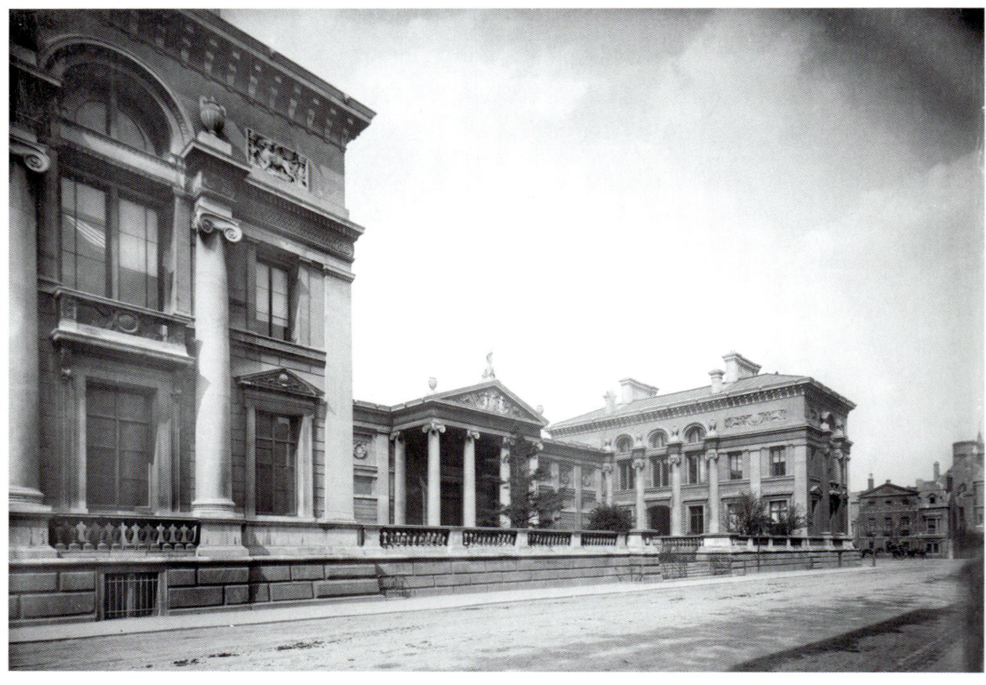

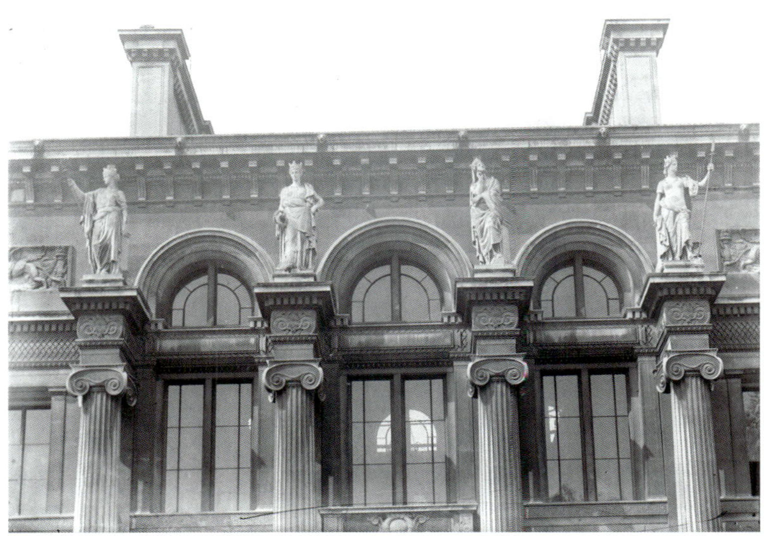

The Ashmolean Museum and Taylorian Institute

Above: A detailed view showing the figures that stand sentinel on top of the four detached Ionic columns of the Taylorian Institute, which represent France, Italy, Germany and Spain.

Below: The interior of the Ashmolean, as it appeared in the 1890s. The museum houses historical, archaeological and fine art collections of international interest and importance, including 'Old Masters' from Italy and the Low Countries, and a notable collection of Victorian and Pre-Raphaelite paintings.

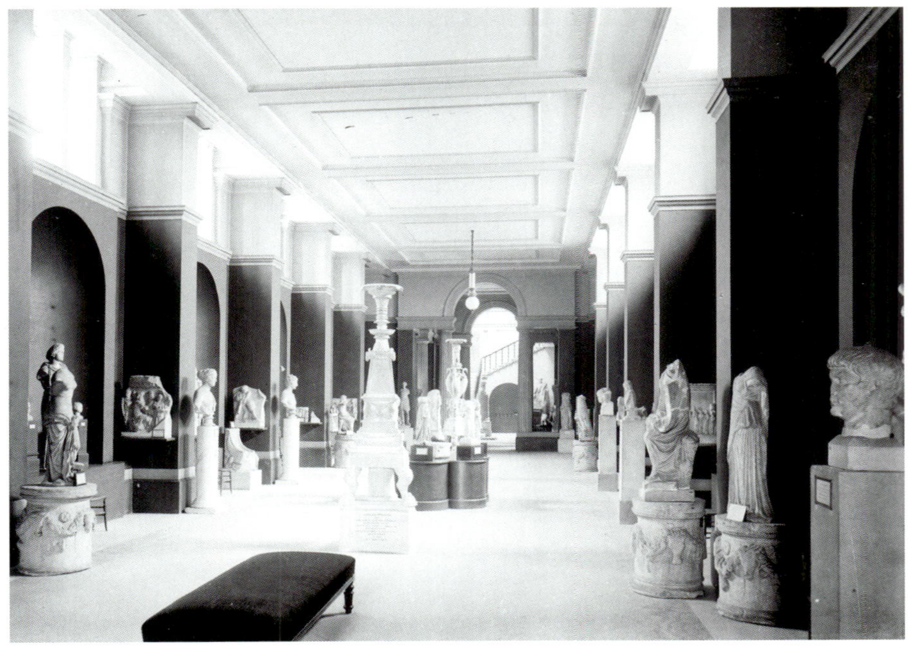

Some Places of Worship

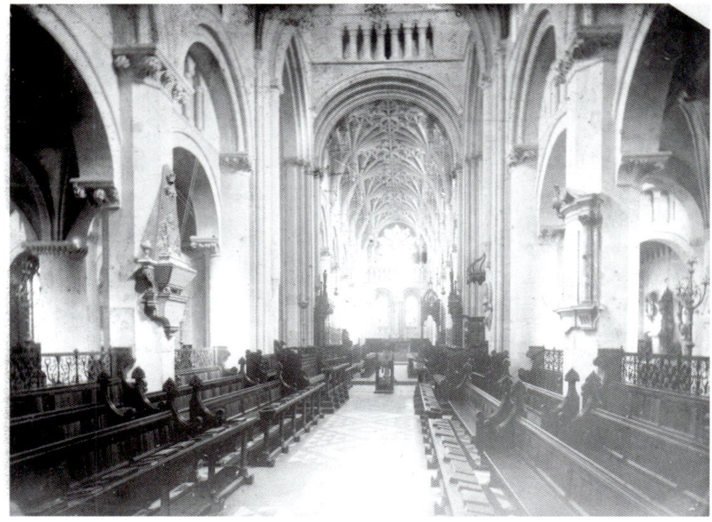

Christ Church Cathedral

Cardinal Wolsey had intended to demolish St Frideswide's Priory Church and replace it with a new college chapel on the north side of Tom Quad. According to the seventeenth-century antiquary Anthony Wood (1632–95), the cardinal pulled down the west end of the nave, 'containing almost half the body of the church, intending that the remaining part should serve only for private prayers'. At the time of the Dissolution of the Monasteries Henry VIII created six new sees, one of these being the diocese of Oxford, and in 1546 the truncated Church of St Frideswide became Oxford Cathedral. These two Victorian views show the interior of the cathedral, which contains a fine display of Romanesque stonework.

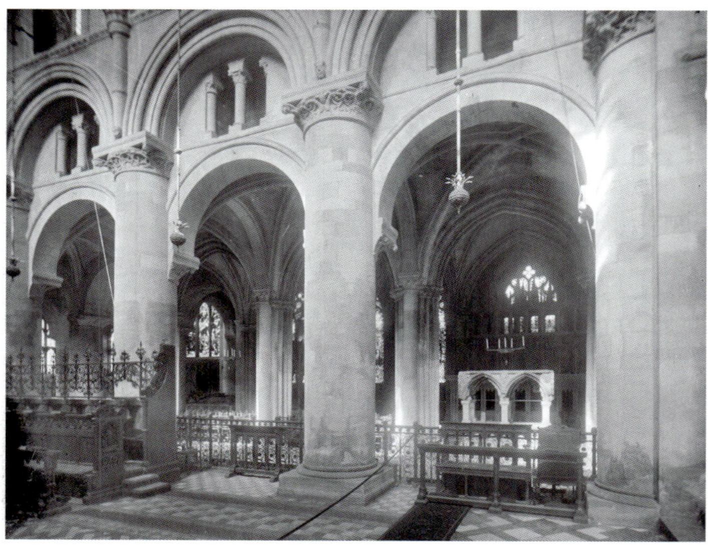

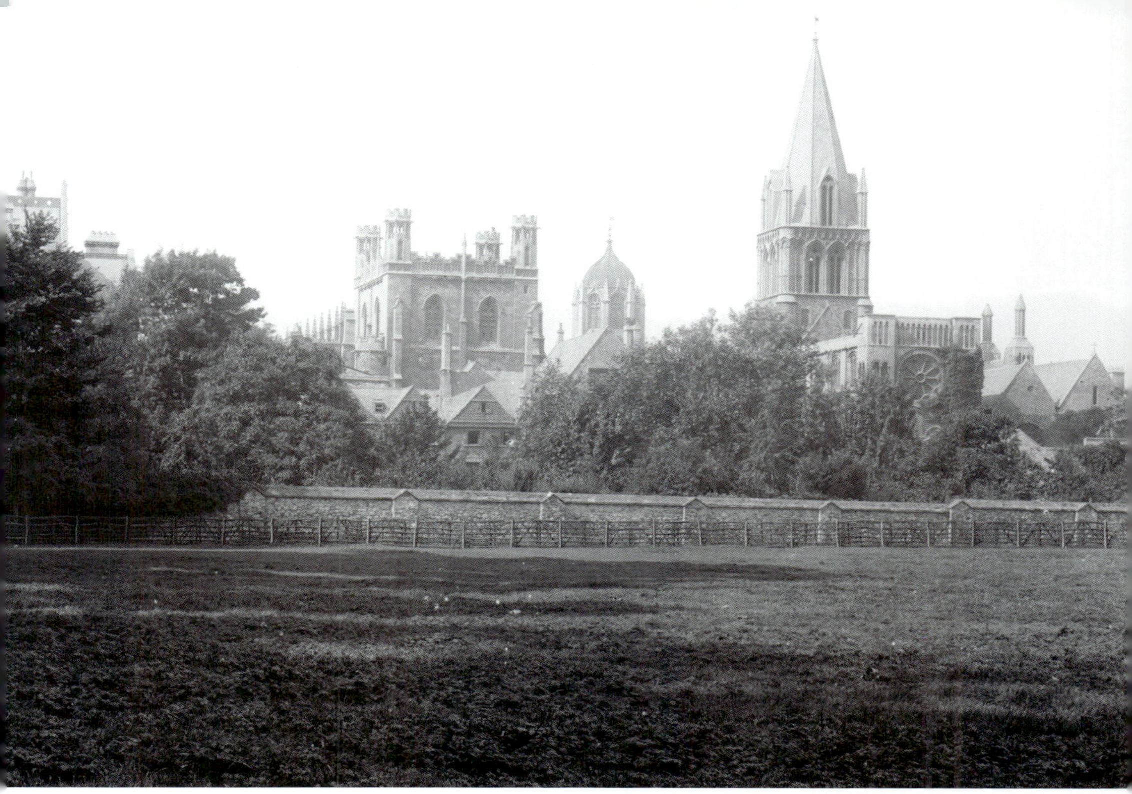

The cathedral, which also serves as the college chapel, forms an integral part of the collegiate buildings, and it is, in consequence, difficult to obtain external photographs of this Anglo-Norman structure, although the eastern end can be glimpsed from the college gardens and Christ Church Meadows, as shown in these two photographs, one of which was taken in 1896, while the other shows the east end of the cathedral in August 2012. The lower part of the tower dates from the Norman period, but the upper part, with its corner pinnacles and octagonal Early English spire, was added during the thirteenth century. The prominent rose window was inserted by the Victorian architect Sir George Gilbert Scott (1811–78), who carried out a major restoration in 1870–76.

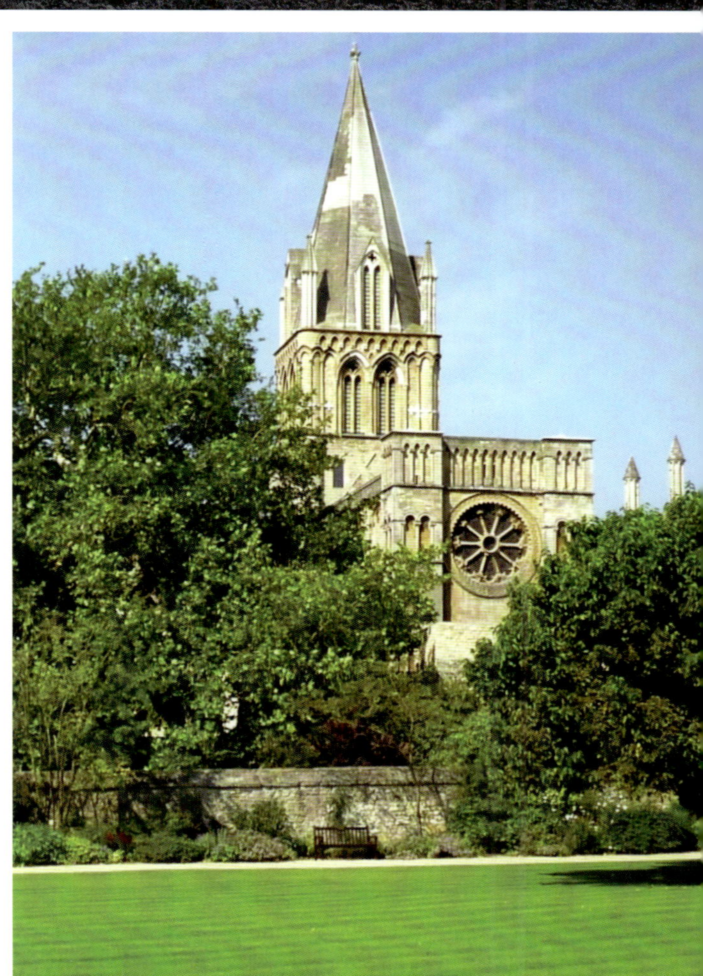

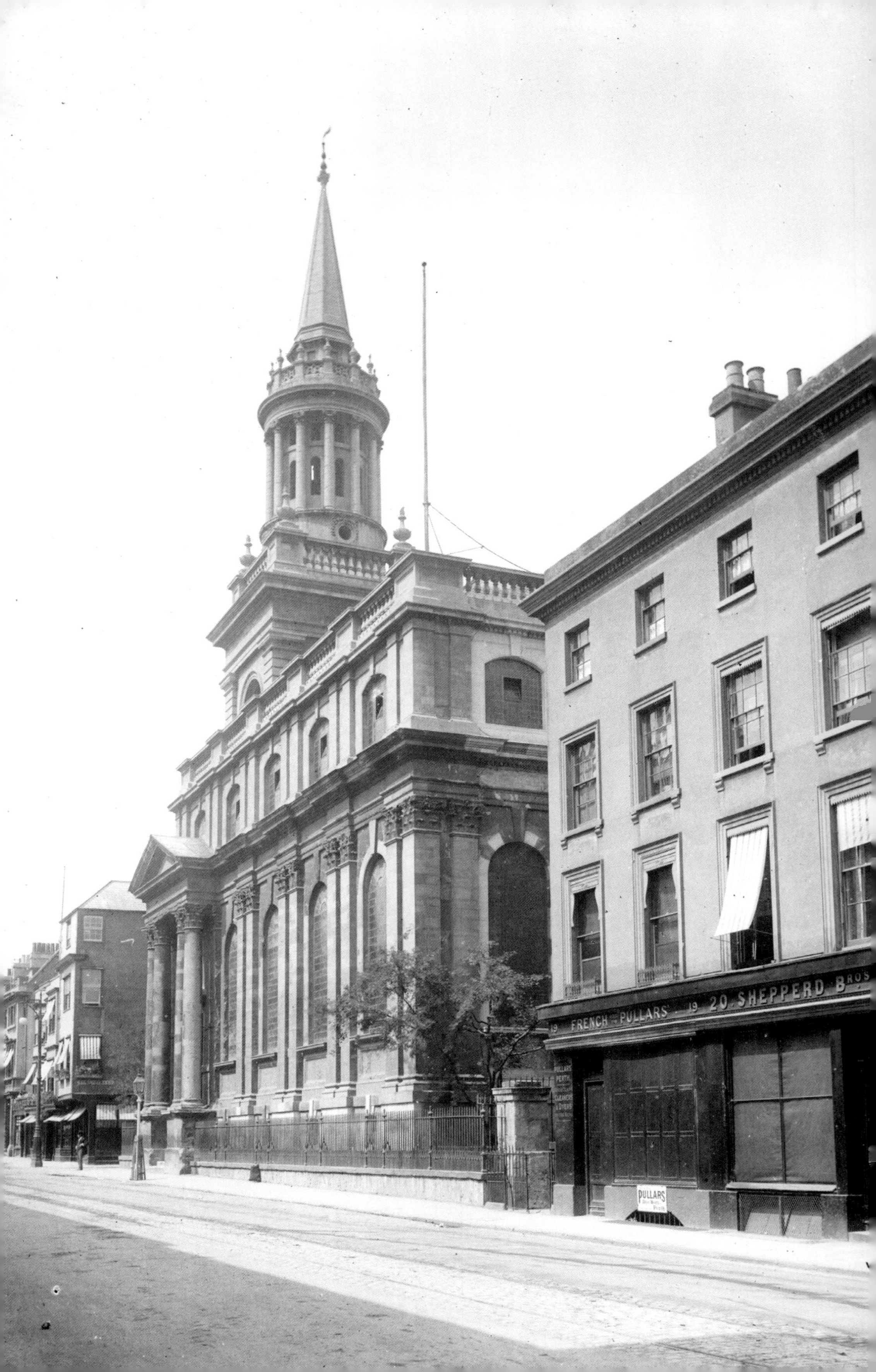
19 FRENCH ~ PULLARS ~ 19 20 SHEPPERD BROS
PULLARS

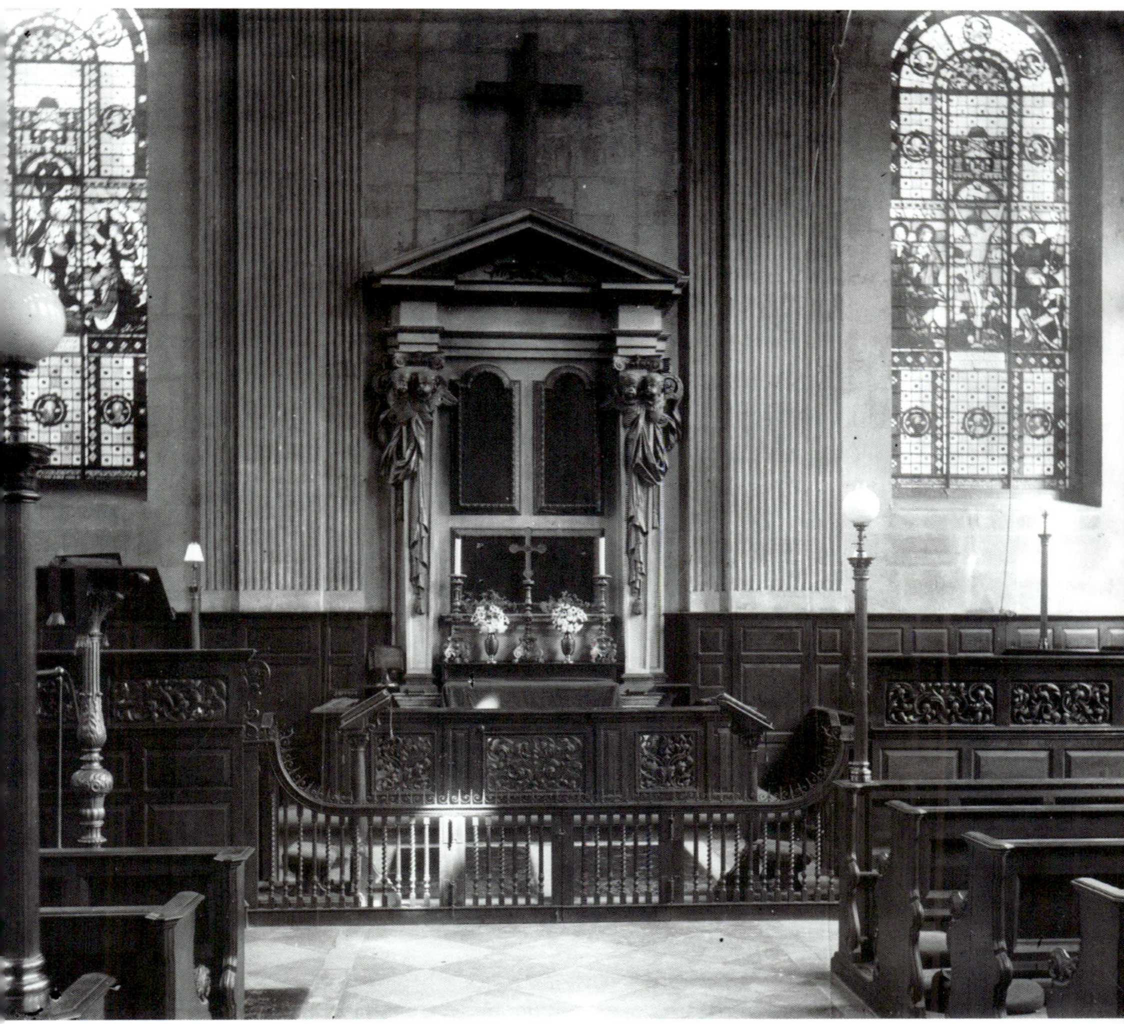

All Saints Church, High Street

All Saints Church was erected in 1706–08 to replace an earlier medieval church that had been badly damaged by the collapse of its spire in 1699. The church has no aisles or chancel, the interior being, in effect, one great open nave. The external walls are enlivened by Corinthian pilasters, while the tiered 'wedding cake'-style tower incorporates a ring of Corinthian columns. The architect is unknown, although it is known that Nicholas Hawksmoor was consulted during the final stages of construction. This fine baroque building is now used as a library by Lincoln College.

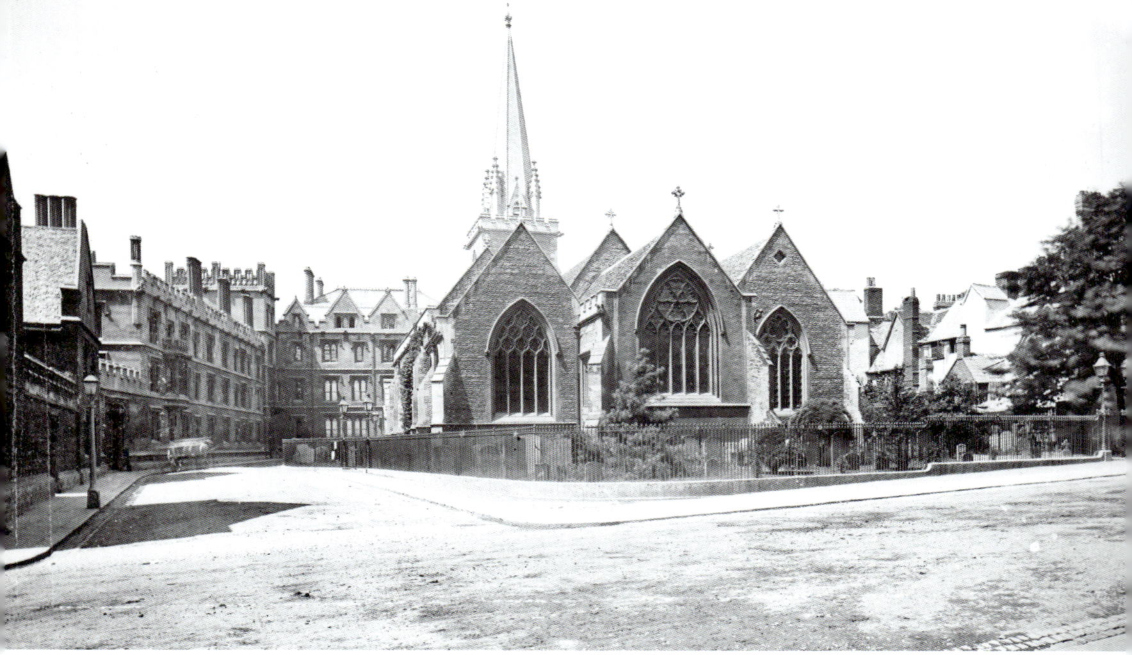

St Aldates Church

This much-restored church is said to be of Saxon origin, although little early stonework remains apart from some Norman arcading in the north chapel. This church, which faces Christ Church and is next door to Pembroke College, had, prior to the Restoration, been vested jointly in the Abbey of Abingdon and St Frideswide's Priory. The fifteenth-century font, shown in the lower view, has a frieze of angel heads, and lions around its base.

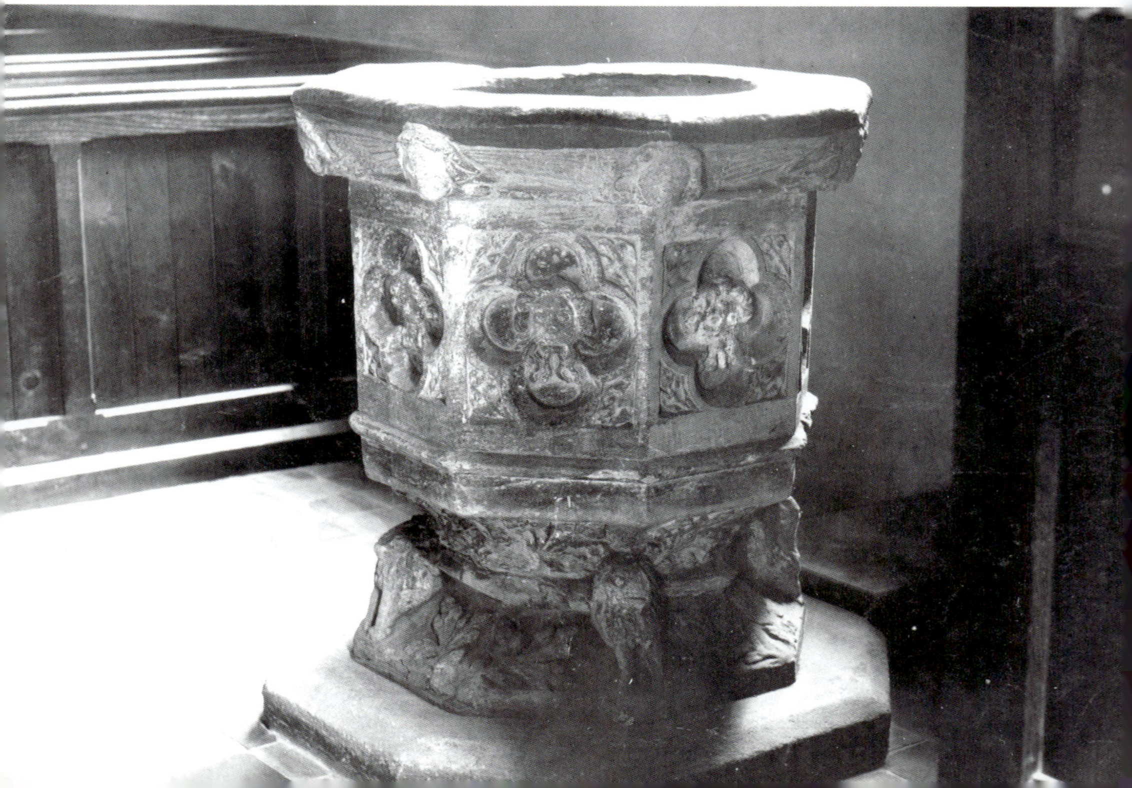

St Aloysius Roman Catholic Church, Woodstock Road

St Aloysius Roman Catholic Church was designed by Joseph Aloysius Hansom (1803–82), the inventor of the Hansom cab. It is constructed of yellow brick, and incorporates a nave, aisles, an apsidal chancel and several side chapels. The church, which was consecrated in 1875, is associated with the Jesuit poet Gerald Manley Hopkins (1844–89), who served as curate here for a period of ten months in 1878. The two views show the interior of the church around 1906. The church is dedicated to Aloysius Gonzaga (1568–91), an Italian nobleman who became a Jesuit and died of fever while attending to the sick during an outbreak of the plague. The unusual reredos, which was completed in 1887, has sixty-two statues, the upper tier representing English saints and martyrs, while the lower tier represents the rest of the Catholic Church.

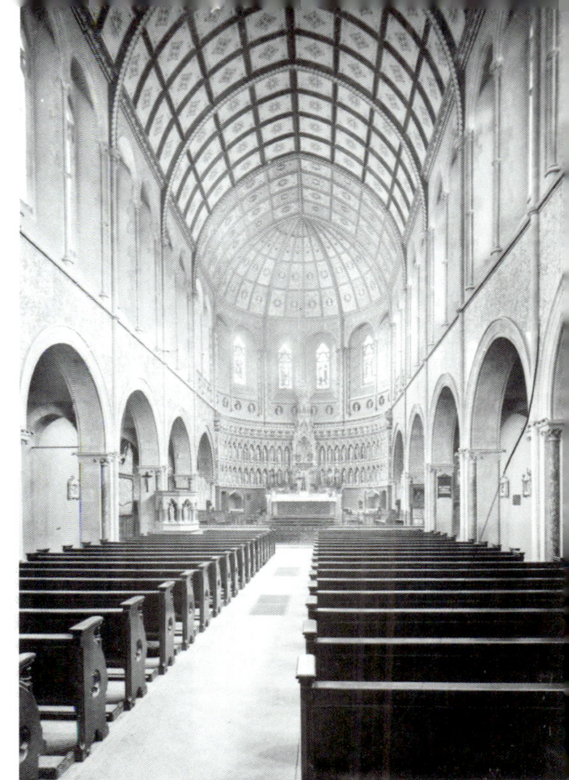

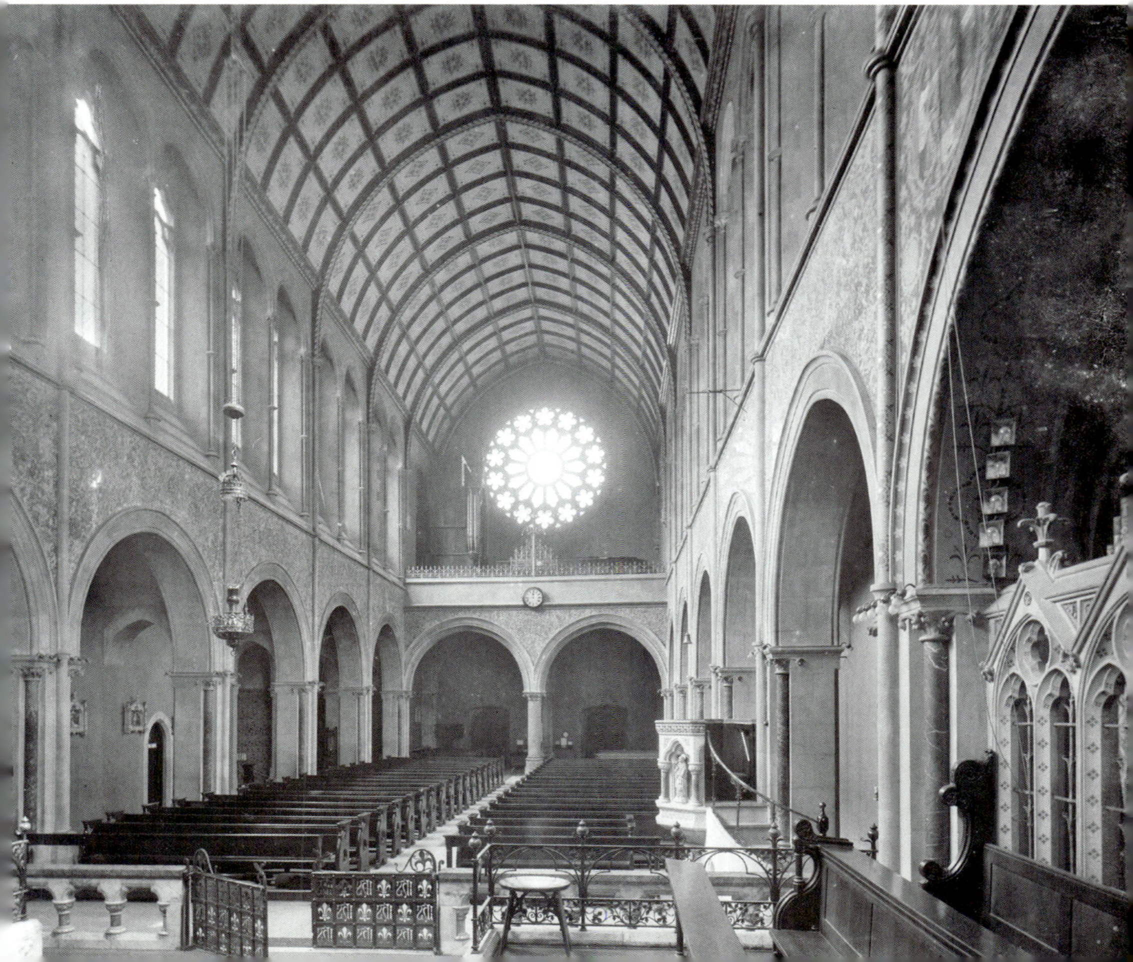

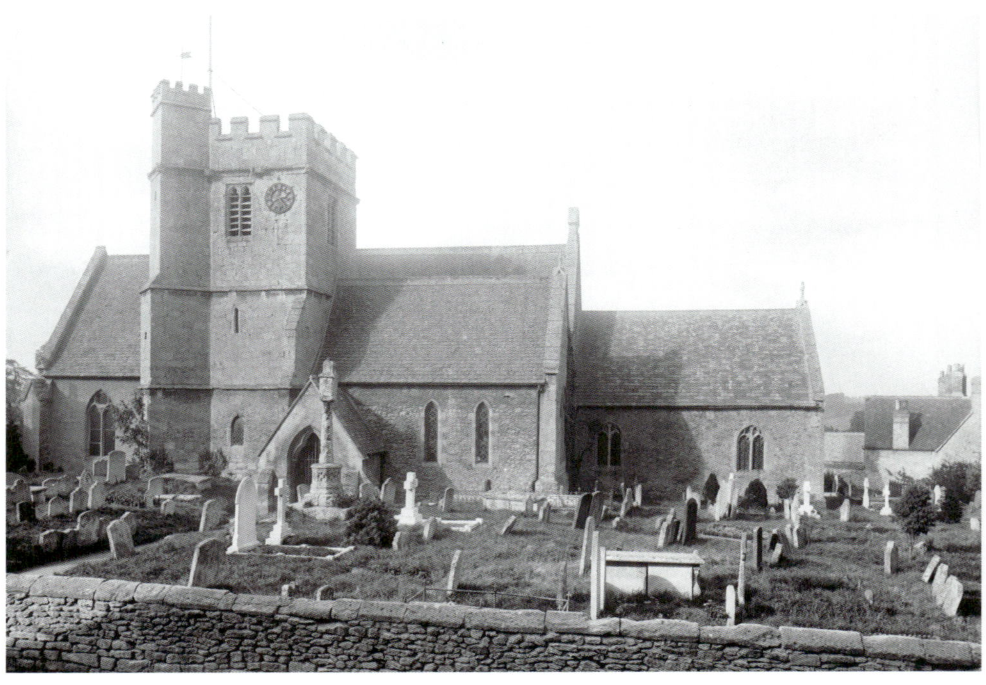

St Andrew's Church, Old Headington

Old Headington, which is linked to New Headington by Old High Street and Ostler Road, retains the atmosphere of a rural village, in spite of suburban encroachments during the nineteenth and twentieth centuries. The parish church, originally a Norman structure, was enlarged at various times, and in its present form the building incorporates a nave, aisles, chancel, south porch and an embattled west tower. The upper view shows the church around 1887, while the colour photograph was taken in June 2013.

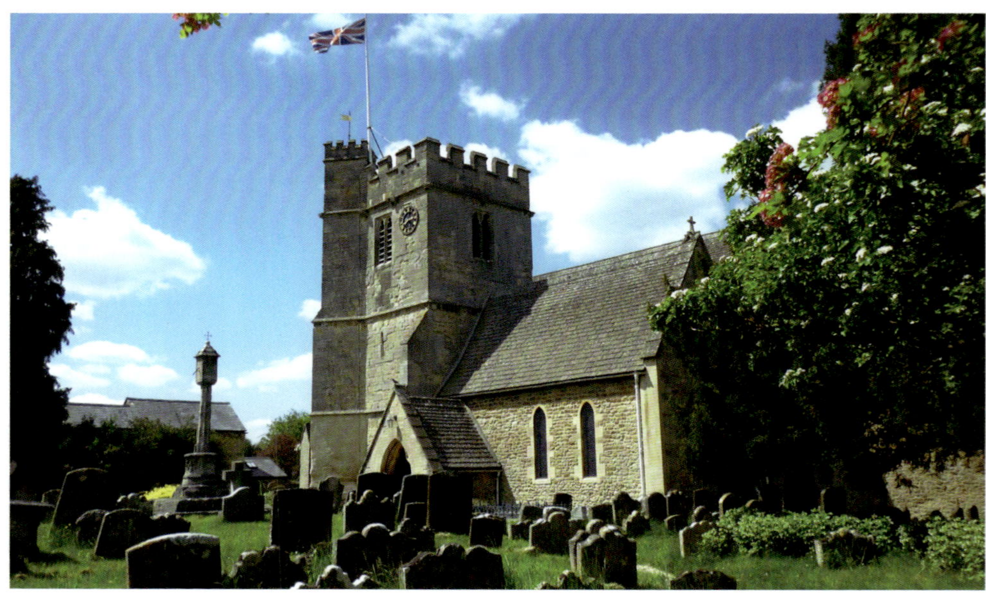

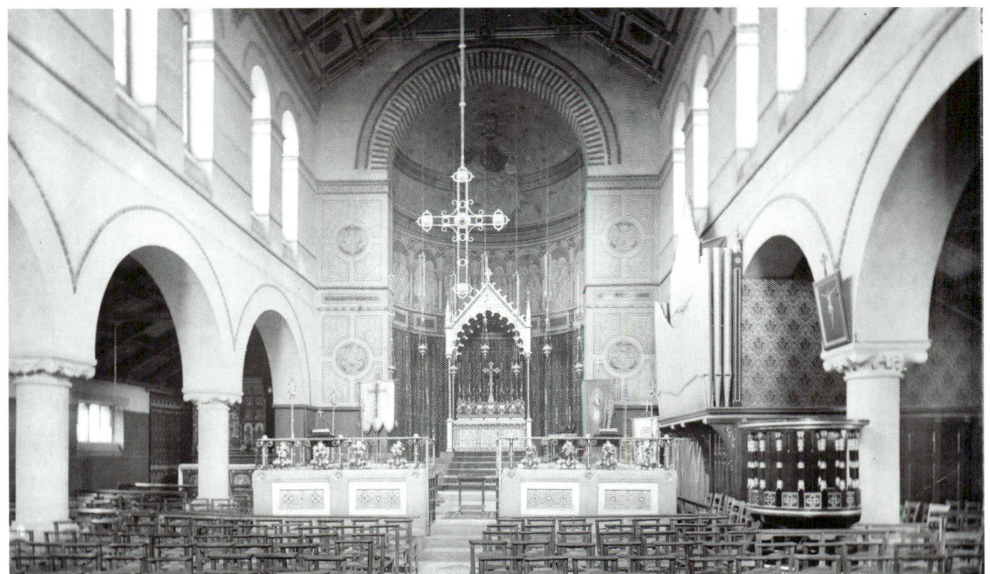

St Barnabas Church, Cardigan Street

The suburb of Jericho is an area of closely spaced Victorian terraced houses that once housed manual workers employed in local industries such as the Oxford University Press and the Eagle Ironworks. St Barnabas Church was built to serve this populous community. Designed by Sir Arthur Blomfield (1829–99), this remarkable Victorian church was consecrated by the Bishop of Oxford on 19 October 1869. The building is constructed of cement-rendered rubble walling, the overall effect being, in many ways, reminiscent of the late Roman or Byzantine style.

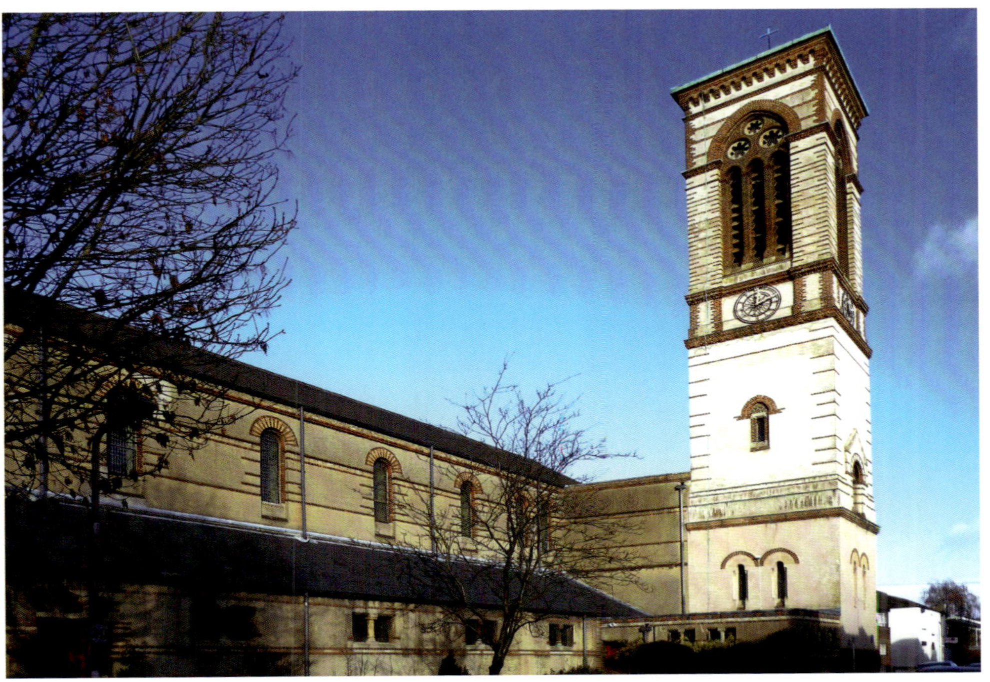

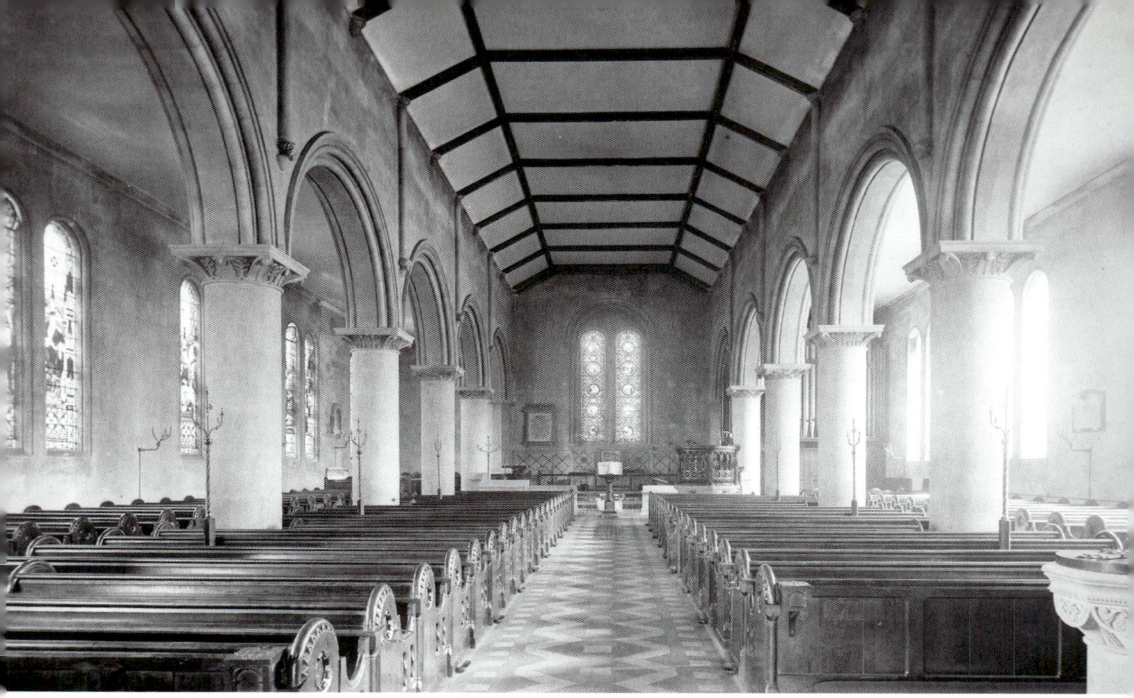

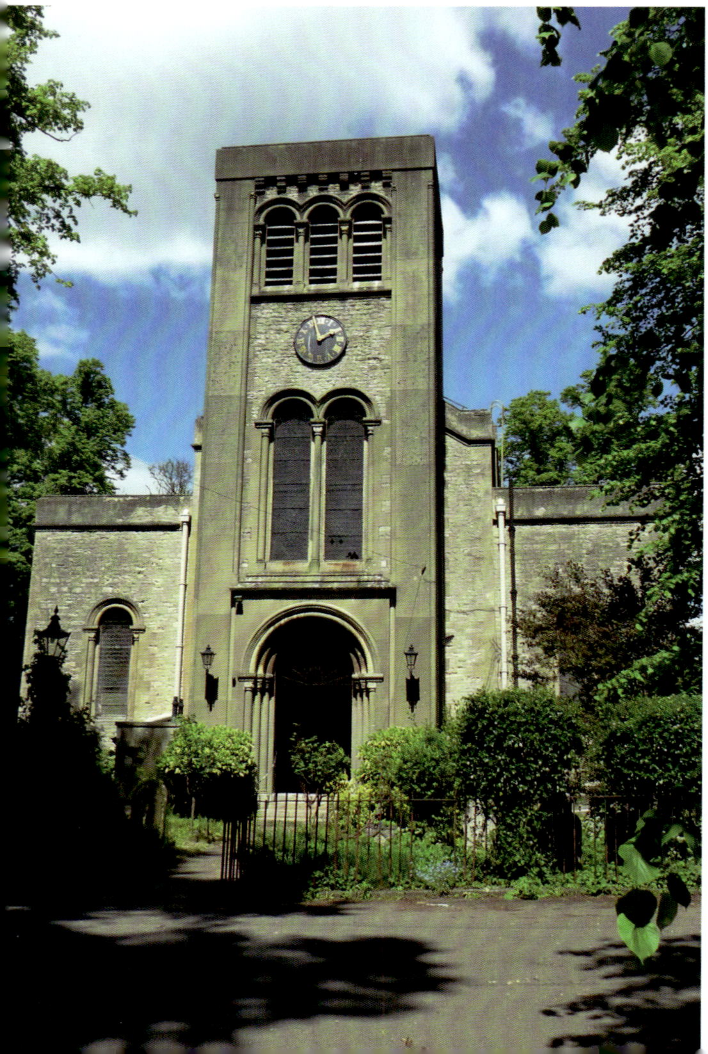

St Clements Church, Marston Road

The present St Clements Church in Marston Road was designed by Daniel Robertson and consecrated on 14 June 1828. It replaced a much earlier church that had been sited near Magdalen Bridge. The site was donated by Sir Joseph Locke, and the church, which consists of a nave, side aisles and west tower, was paid for by public subscription. The upper image shows the interior of the church during the early years of the twentieth century. Although the building is supposedly a 'Norman-style' structure, its symmetrical appearance reflects Georgian ideas of 'taste'

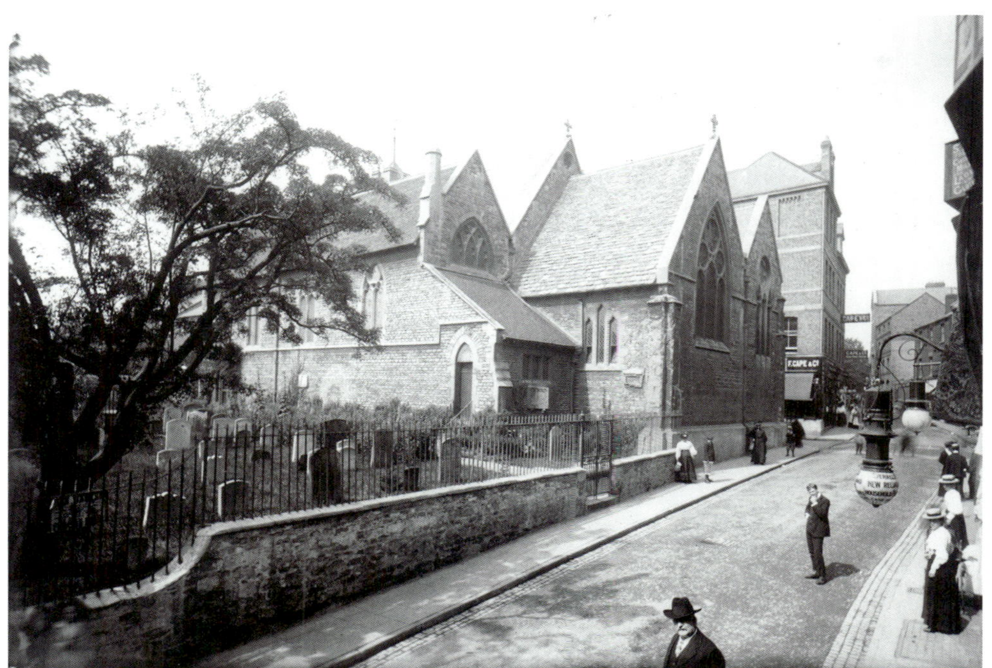

St Ebbe's Church, St Ebbe's Street

Dedicated to St Ebba, the daughter of a king of Northumbria, this church is a very ancient foundation, although few historic features remain, the church having been rebuilt in 1814–16, and again by G. E. Street in the 1860s. The lower part of the tower, however, incorporates thirteenth-century work, and a Norman doorway has been preserved at the west end of the building. The main photographs were taken by Henry Taunt in 1907.

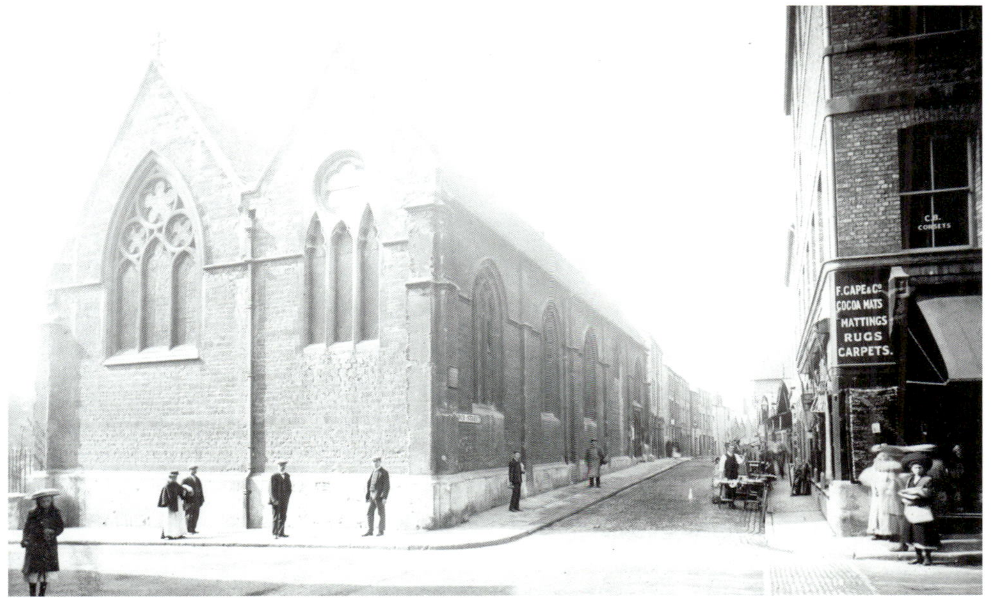

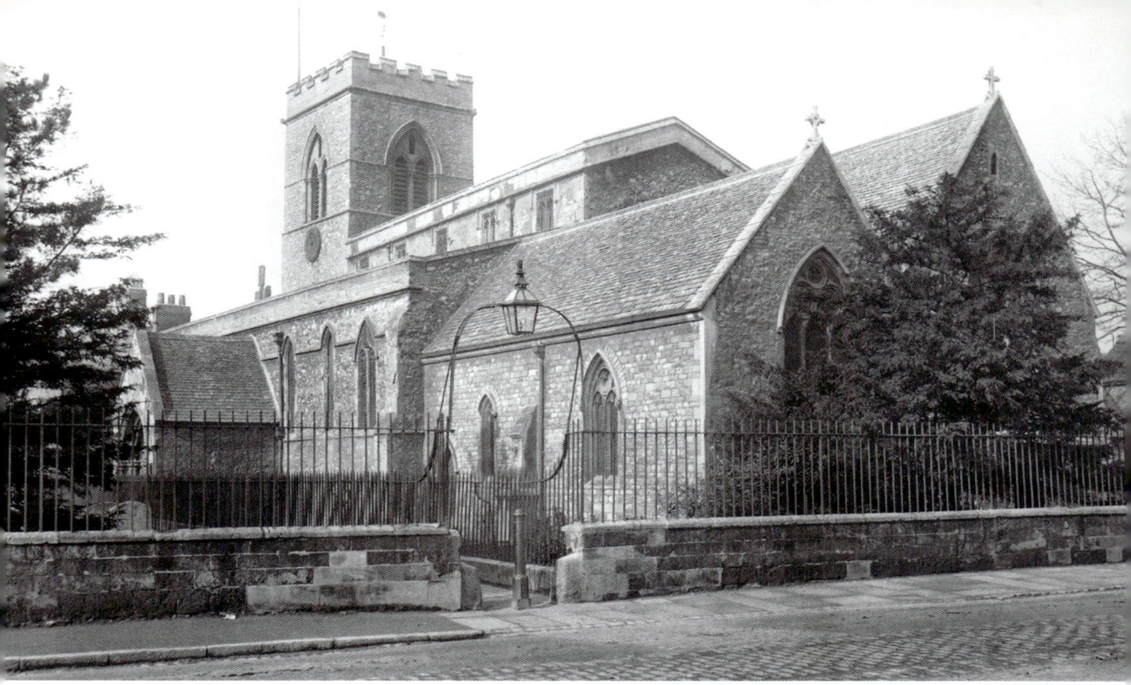

Nestling in the 'V' of the diverging Woodstock and Banbury roads, St Giles' Church retains much of the atmosphere of a rural church that it once was. The building, which consists of a nave, aisles, chancel, west tower and south porch, dates mainly from the thirteenth century, although blocked Norman windows can be seen in the nave. The upper photograph shows the church from the south-east during the early 1900s, while the colour view was taken in May 2013.

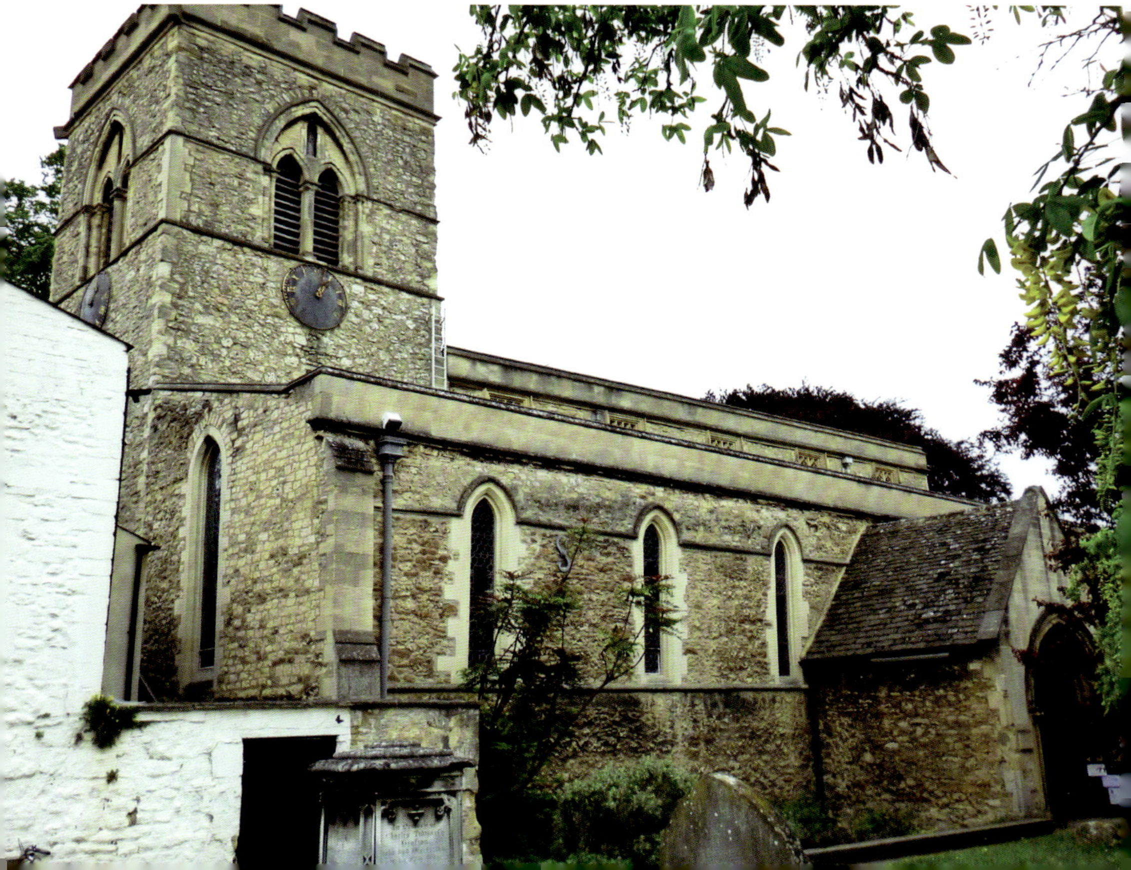

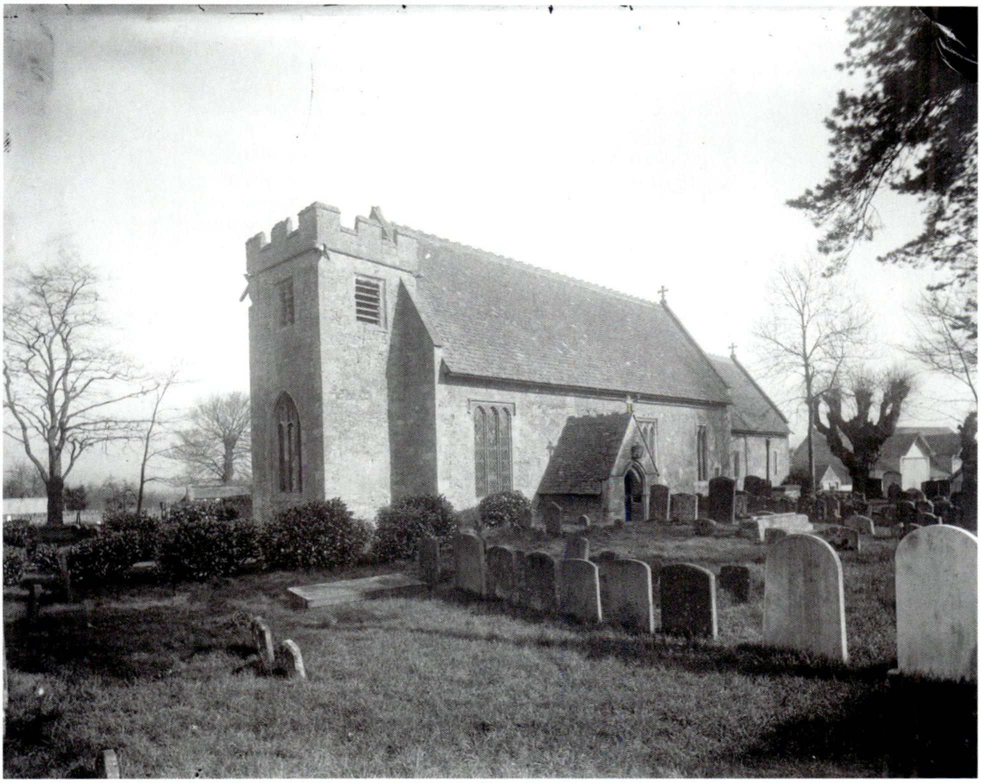

St James Church, Cowley

Although now regarded as a sprawling outer suburb of Oxford, Cowley originally comprised the villages of Temple Cowley and Church Cowley. The Church of St James, in Church Cowley, was rebuilt by G. E. Street during the 1860s – the most significant modification carried out at that time being the addition of a much-enlarged nave, which now dwarfs the rather stubby west tower. A detailed view of the Norman south doorway is shown on the right.

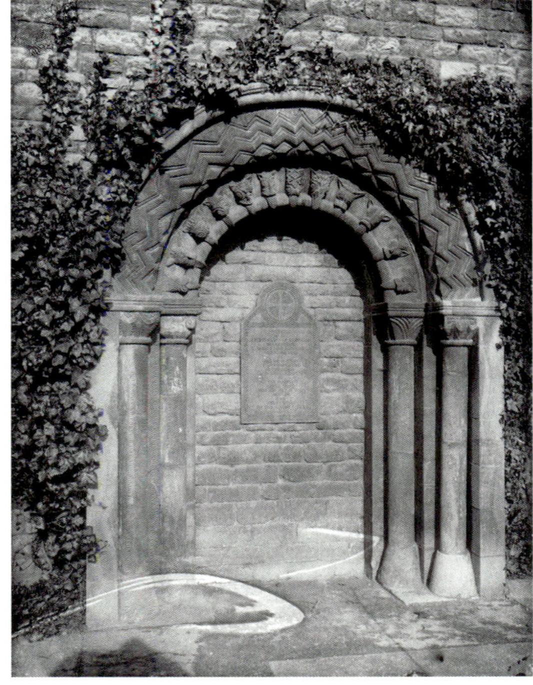

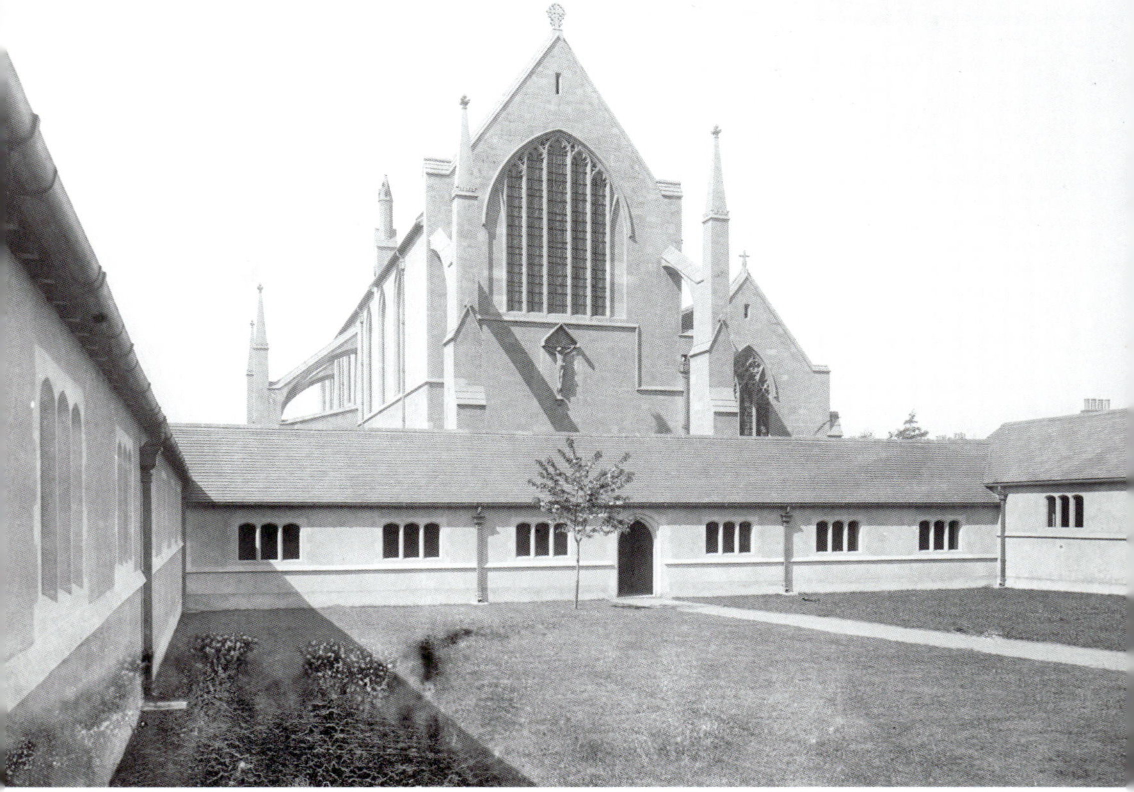

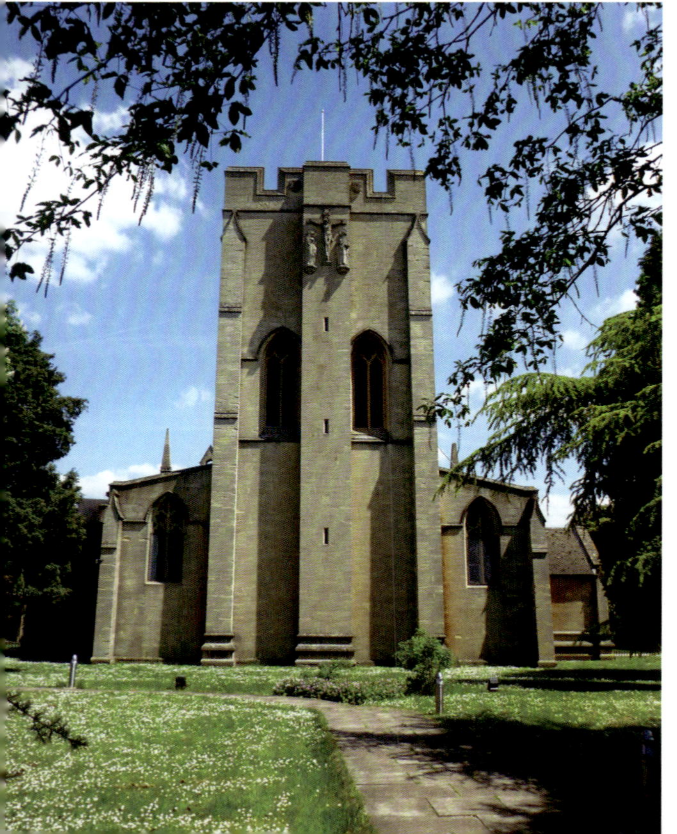

The Church of St John the Evangelist in Iffley Road was built as a chapel for the Society of St John the Evangelist, an Anglican religious order that had been founded by Richard Meux Benson (1824–1915), the vicar of Cowley, in 1865. This impressive Victorian church was completed in 1896, the architect being George Frederick Bodley (1827–1907), although the west tower was not added until 1902. The church is now part of an Anglican theological college known as St Stephen's House. The upper photograph provides a view of the cloister, while the colour view is a detailed study of the west tower, which features three tall buttresses – the massive centre buttress being adorned with a small relief carving of the Crucifixion.

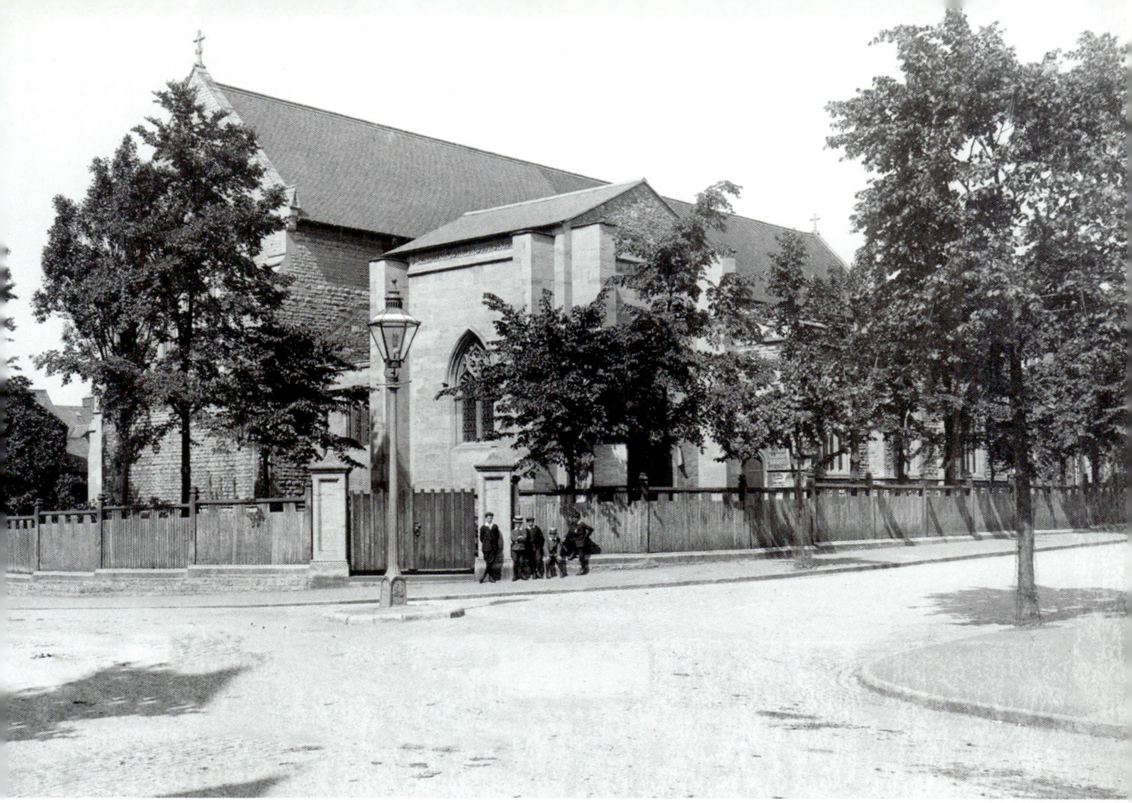

Situated in St Margaret's Road, St Margaret's Church was designed by Harry Drinkwater (1844–95). The foundation stone was laid on 8 May 1883, but construction was a protracted business, and although plans for a tower porch were drawn up by George Frederick Bodley (1827–1907), the tower was never completed. The church was, at first, a chapel of ease within the parish of St Philip and St James, but it became a separate parish in 1896. The photographs show the church in 1911.

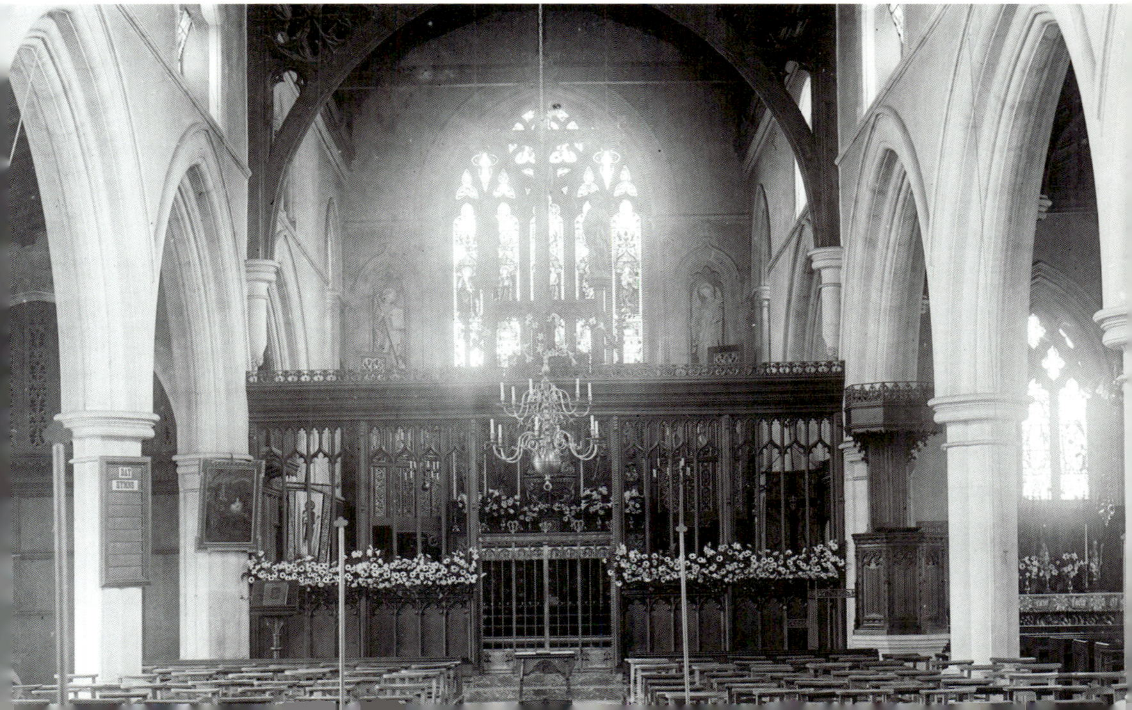

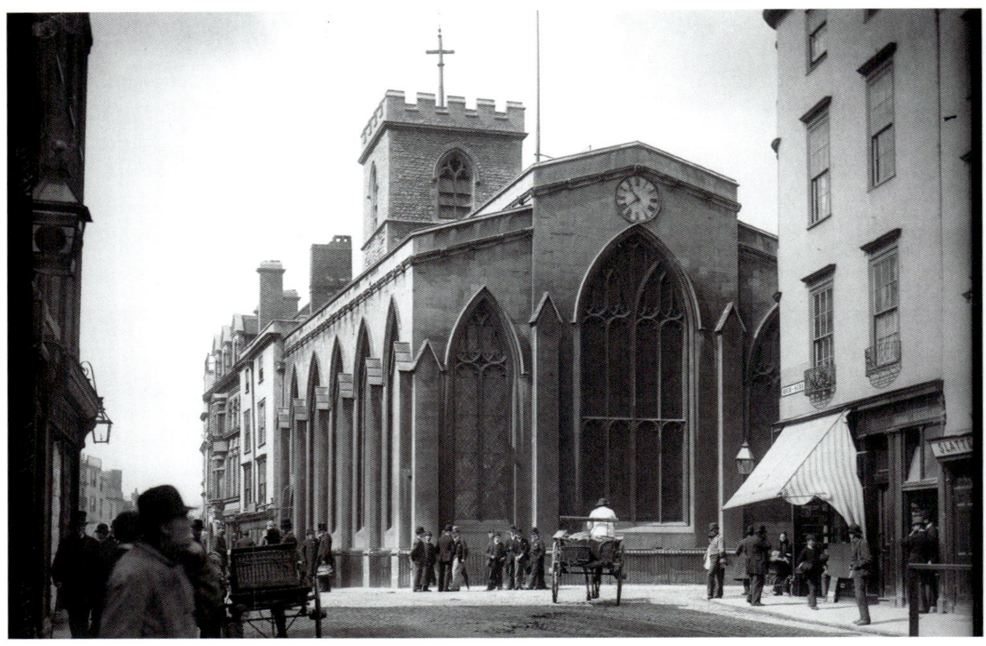

St Martin's Church, Carfax

The upper view provides a glimpse of St Martin's Church, which formerly stood on the corner of Queen Street and Cornmarket. In April 1895 *Jackson's Oxford Journal* reported that the old church would be 'pulled down and removed with the exception of the tower', which was considered to 'mark a historic site of local and general interest'. Demolition commenced in March 1896, the font and monuments being moved to All Saints – the two parishes having been combined. The lower view shows 'Carfax Tower'.

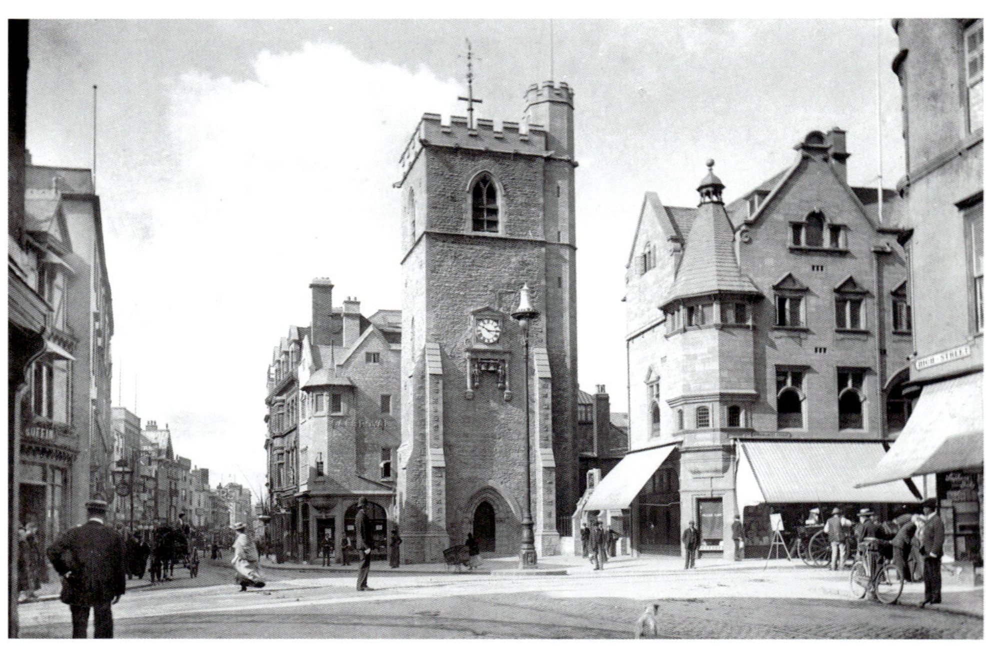

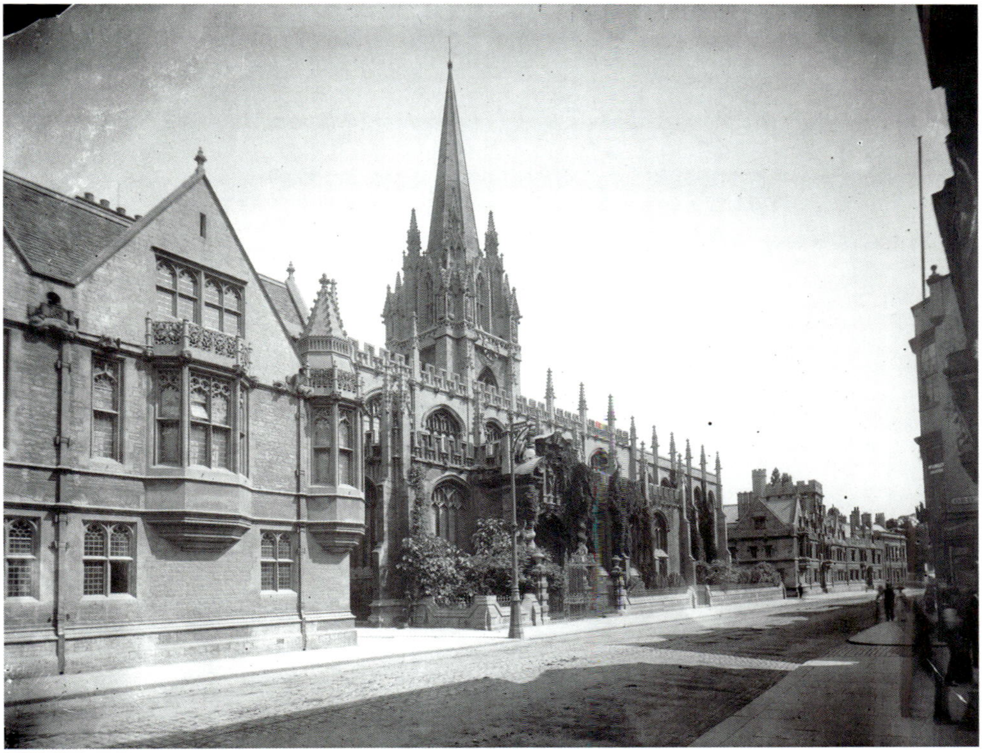

St Mary the Virgin Church, High Street

Situated on the north side of the High Street, St Mary's is the university church and, as such, it has been the setting for many historic events – notably the 'show trials' of the Oxford martyrs Cranmer, Latimer and Ridley, which took place in 1554. Although the tower is thought to date from around 1320, much of the building dates from the fifteenth century, its architectural details being in the Perpendicular style. Above is a general view of the church, with part of Brasenose College visible to theleft. The image below shows the unashamedly baroque south porch, with its curious helical columns, which was added in 1637, the architect being Nicholas Stone (*c.* 1585–1647), the son of a Devon quarryman who became a master mason and an accomplished sculptor.

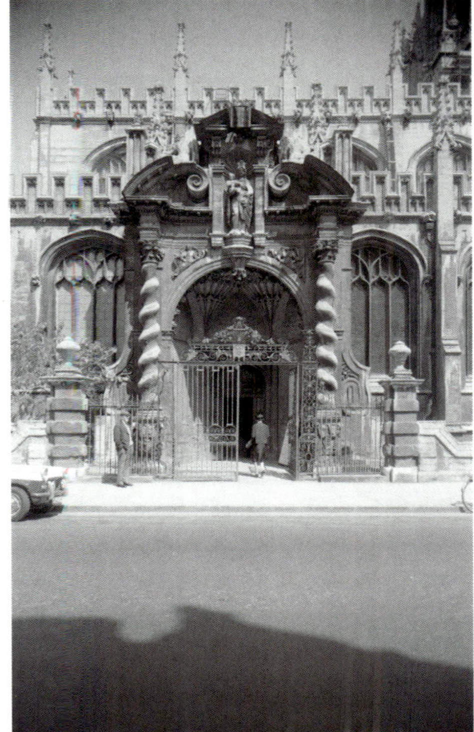

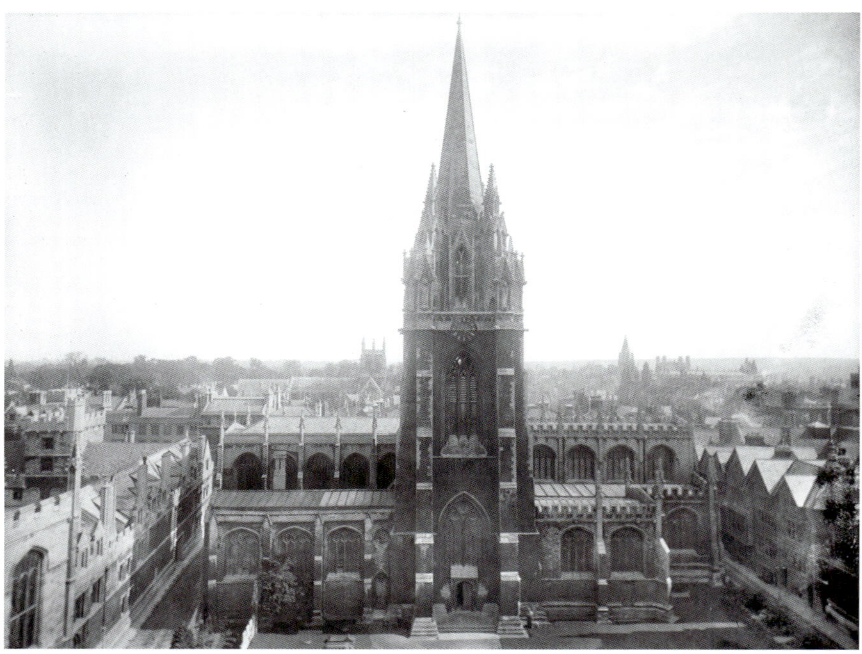

St Mary the Virgin

Above: An unusual view, showing the north side of the church from the nearby Radcliffe Camera in 1915. The nave, to the right of the tower, has six bays, while the chancel, to the left, is almost as long, with five bays; the total length of the building from east to west is around 165 feet.

Below: A detailed view of the south side of the building in 2012. The gabled building on the right is part of neighbouring All Souls College.

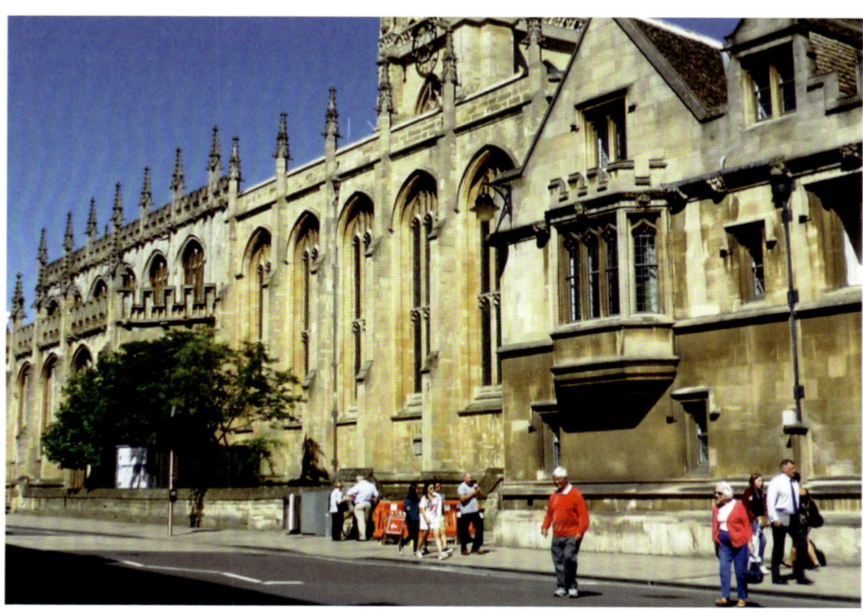

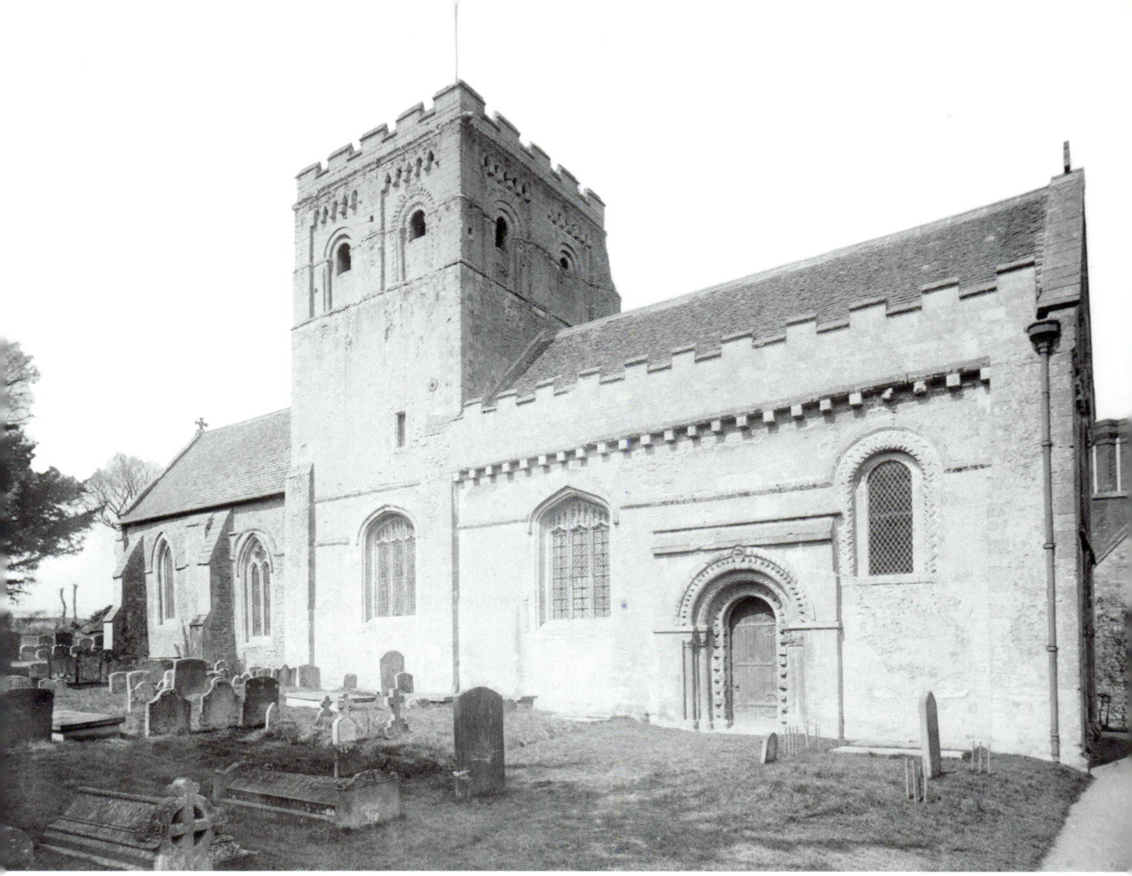

St Mary's Church, Iffley

Iffley parish church is generally considered to be one of the finest Norman churches in England. It was probably built between 1170 and 1180, and the building retains its original 'axial' plan, with an aisle-less nave and chancel separated by a central tower. The upper view shows this interesting old church from the south, probably around 1912. The chancel is to the right, while the nave is to the left of the picture. The eastern bay of the chancel was rebuilt during the thirteenth century and some of the windows are later additions but, otherwise, the church is a near-perfect example of late-Norman architecture, with a wealth of beakheads, chevrons and other carvings. The colour photograph shows the west end of the church, with its restored rose window and well-preserved Romanesque doorway.

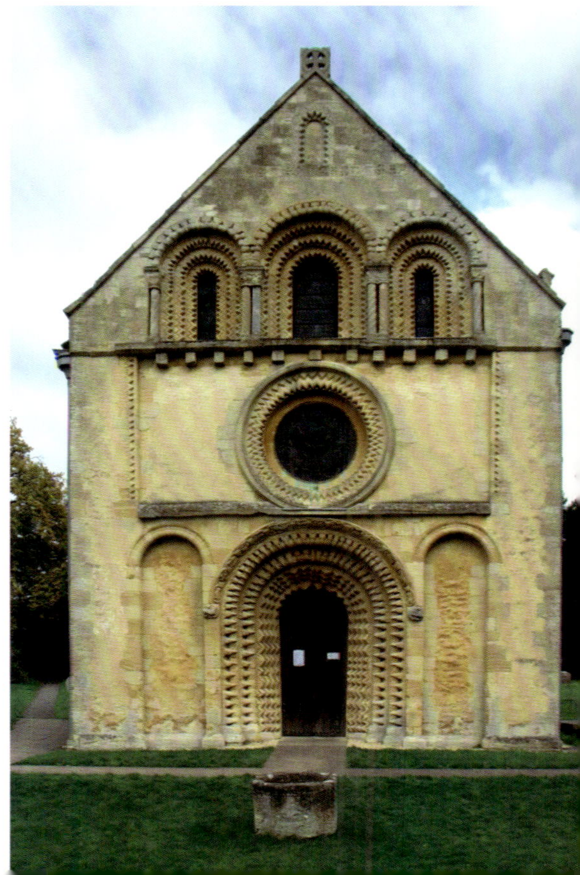

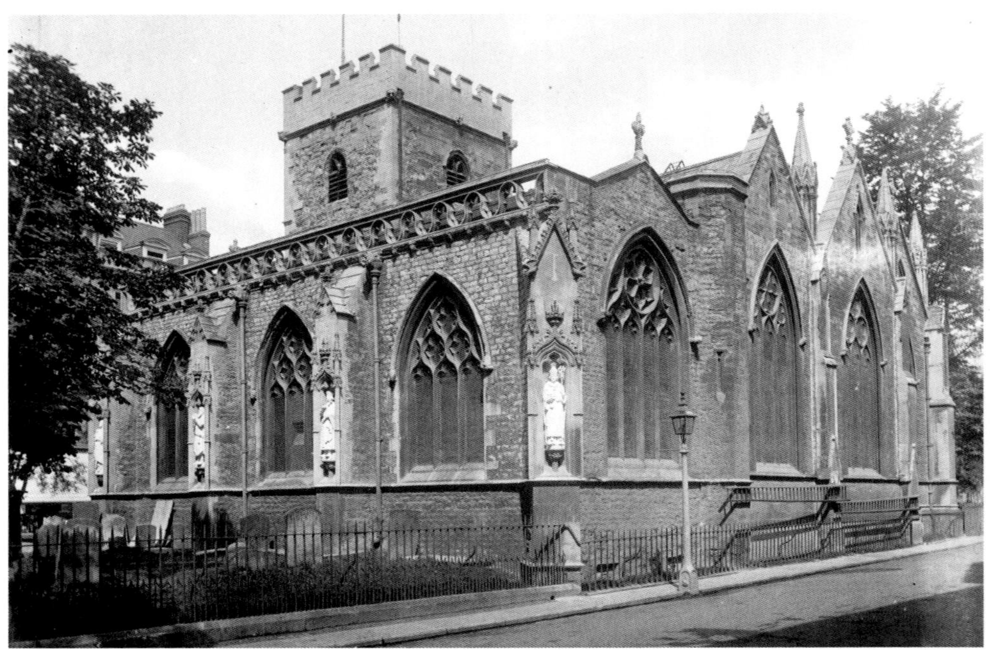

St Mary Magdalen Church, Magdalen Street
This city centre church originated in Saxon times, but the building was modified and reconstructed at various times, and it now incorporates a nave, chancel, north and south aisles and a south chapel, together with a south porch and an outer south aisle. The north aisle, known as 'The Martyrs' Aisle', was rebuilt in 1841 as an adjunct to the nearby Martyrs' Memorial. The upper photograph shows the church from the south-east in 1914, while the interior view is looking east towards the altar in 1919.

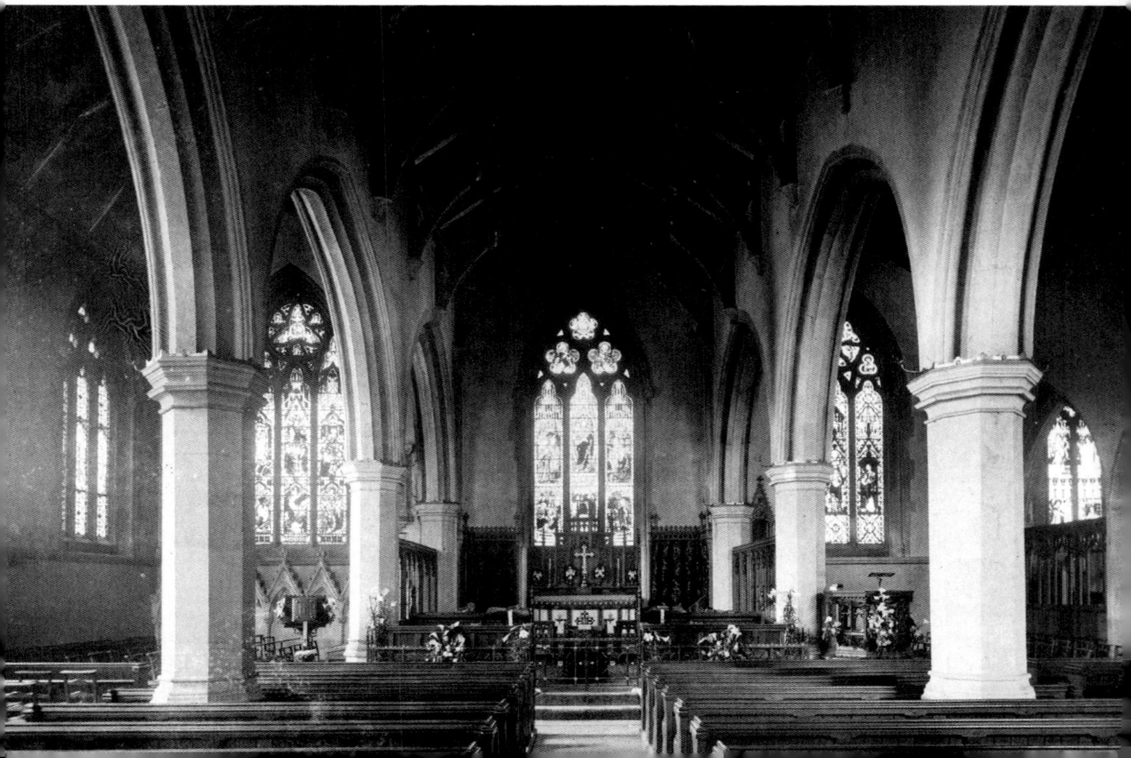

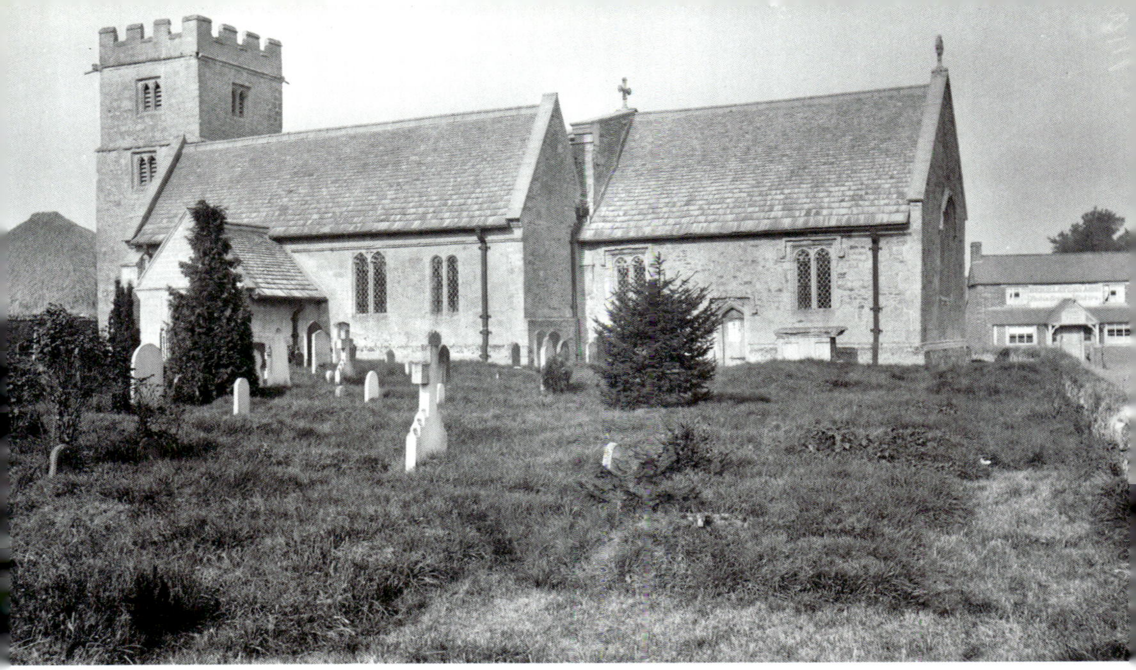

St Nicholas Church, Old Marston

Marston, to the north-west of Headington, consists of the suburb of New Marston and the original Old Marston village, which were absorbed into Oxford in 1929 and 1991 respectively. The view here (from 1885) shows Old Marston parish church, which consists of a nave, aisles, chancel, south porch and west tower. Although the exterior details of the church reflect the Perpendicular style, the nave arcades and chancel arch are Early English. The photographs were taken around 1885 and in June 2013.

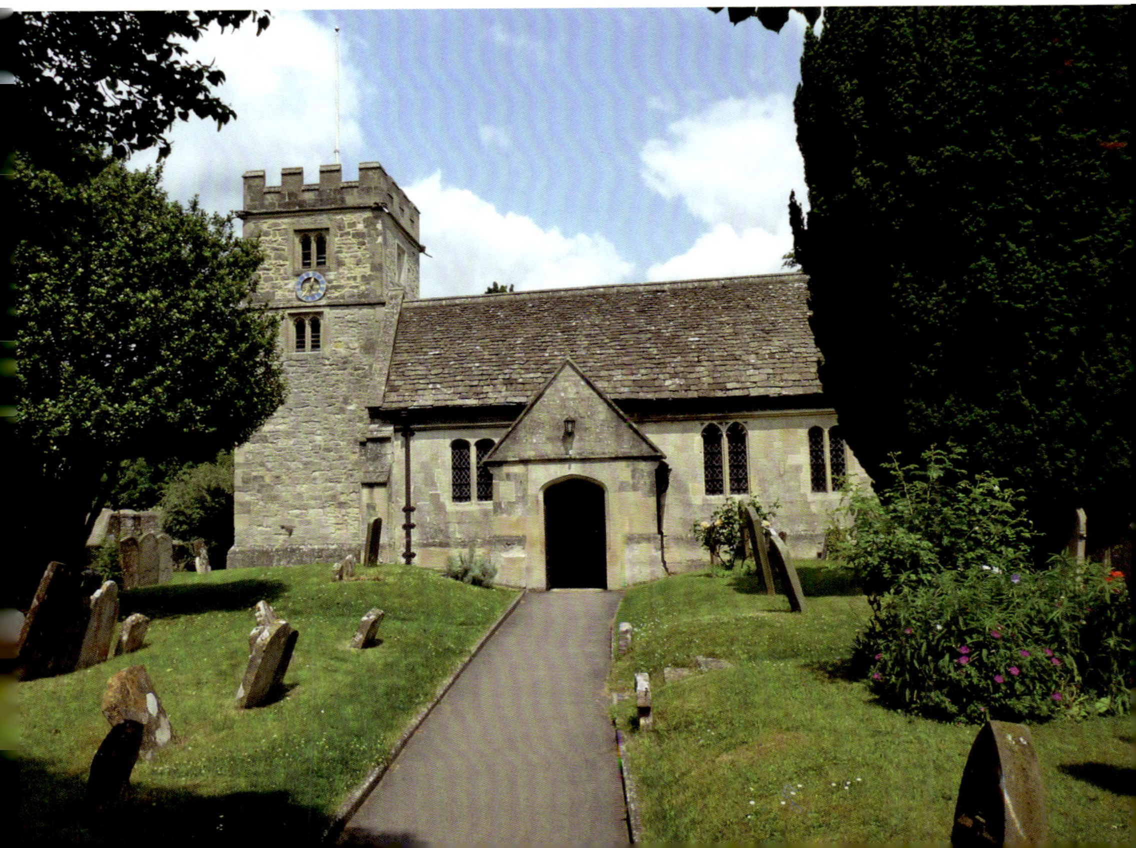

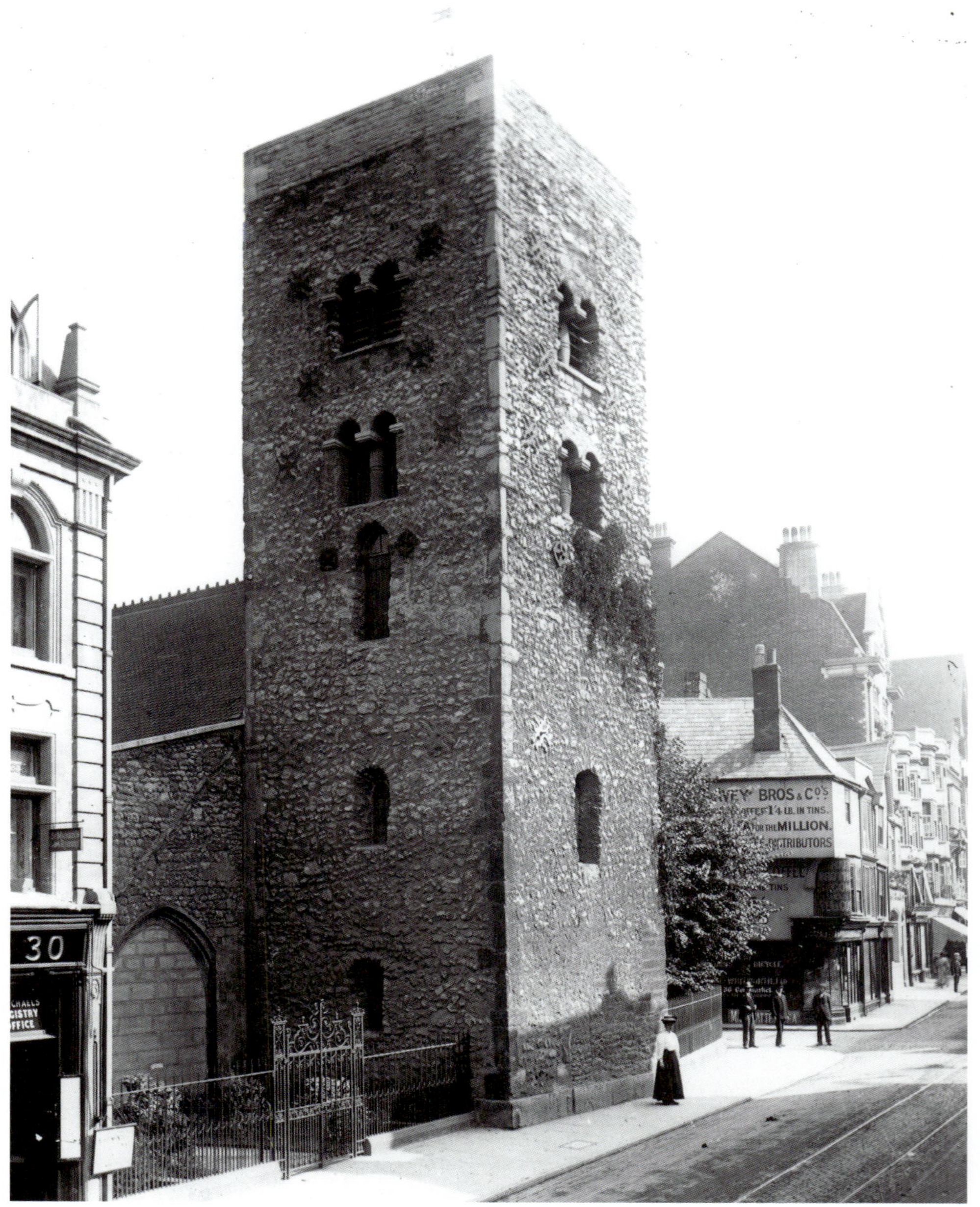

St Michael at the Northgate, Cornmarket

In historical terms, St Michael at the Northgate Church, at the north end of Cornmarket, is of particular importance, as its five-storey Anglo-Saxon tower is thought to have served as a defensive tower beside the north gate of the Saxon burh and, as such, it is the oldest building in Oxford. This *c.* 1907 view shows the tower from Cornmarket, and provides a detailed study of the north and west sides of this historic structure. A blocked doorway on the second floor must have given access to the wall walk at the top of the city wall.

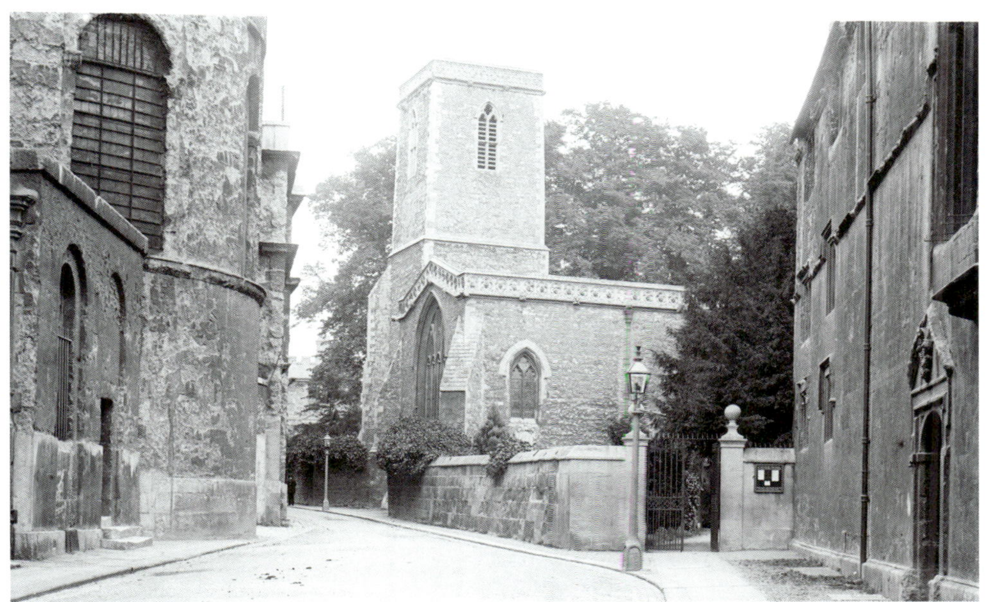

St Peter-in-the-East Church, Queen's Lane

Hidden away in Queen's Lane, near St Edmund Hall, this interesting church dates mainly from the Norman period, the chancel arch and south doorway being of obvious Norman origin. There are a number of Norman features throughout the building, but the most remarkable feature is the twelfth-century crypt beneath the chancel, which contains eight round columns with a variety of Romanesque carvings on their capitals. The church is now used as a library by St Edmund Hall.

Below: A detailed view showing the modest entrance to St Edmund Hall, which is situated next to St Peter-in-the-East Church in Queen's Lane. The church is now, in effect, an integral part of the college. (Photograph contributed by Ingram Murray)

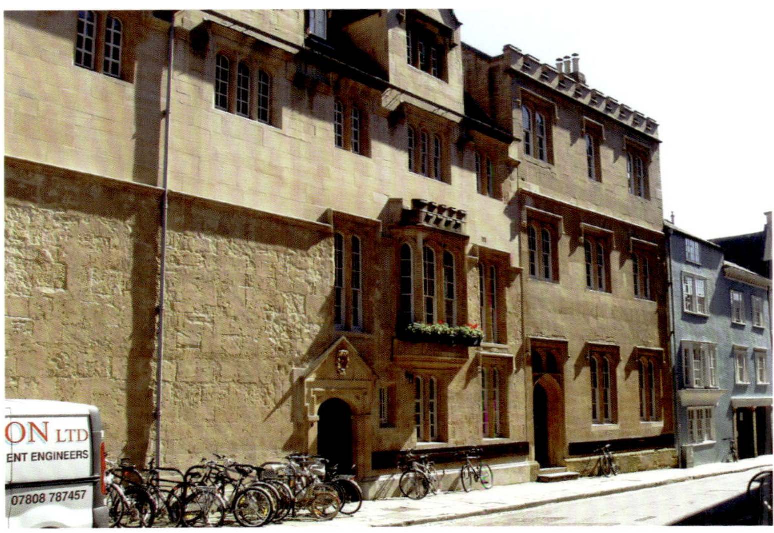

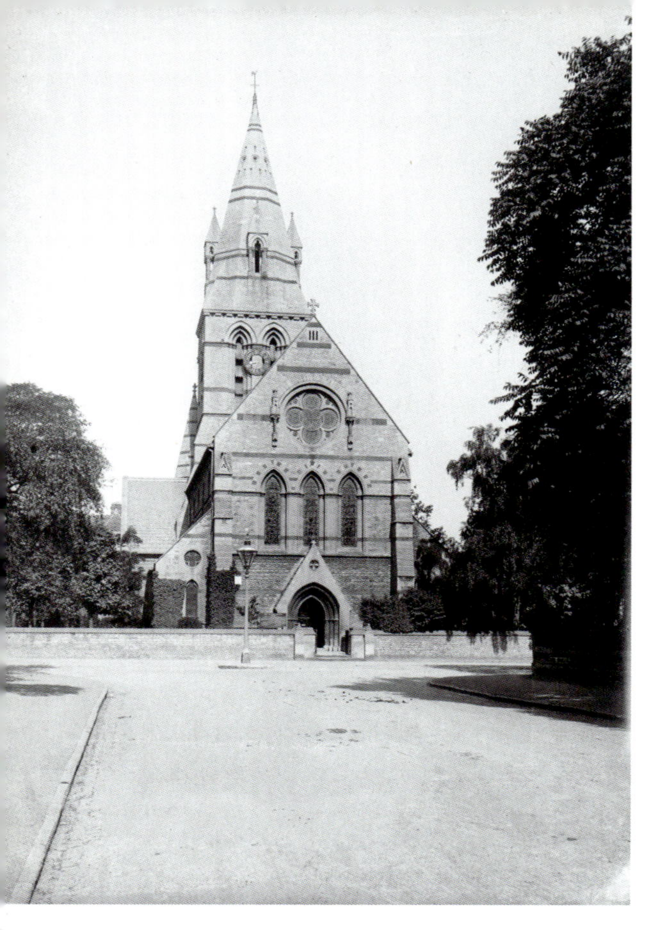

The Church of St Philip and St James, Woodstock Road

Designed by George Edmund Street (1824–81), the diocesan architect, this substantially built Victorian church was intended to serve as the parish church for the inhabitants of rapidly expanding north Oxford. The foundation stone was laid on 1 May 1860 and the church was consecrated by the Bishop of Oxford on 8 May 1862. The parish of St Philip and St James was reunited with the parish of St Margaret in 1976, and the Church of St Philip and St James was finally declared redundant in April 1982. It is now the home of the Oxford Centre for Mission Studies.

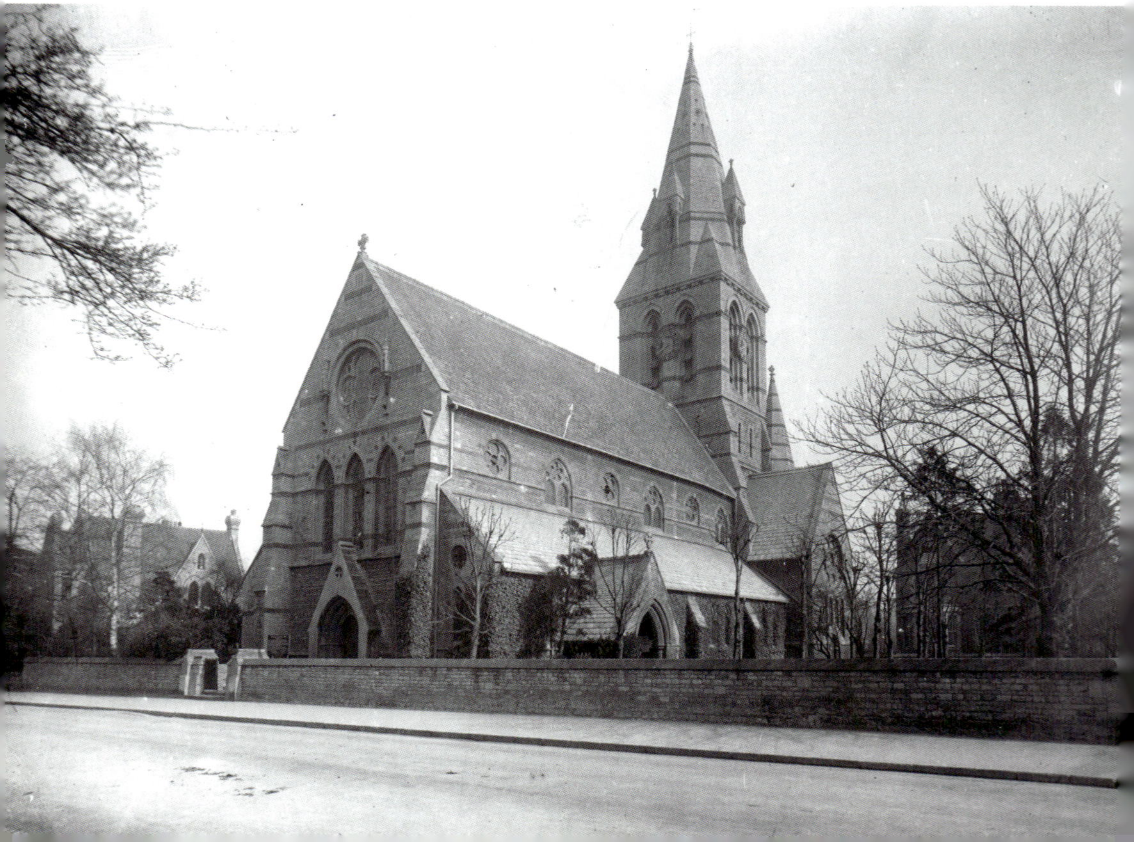

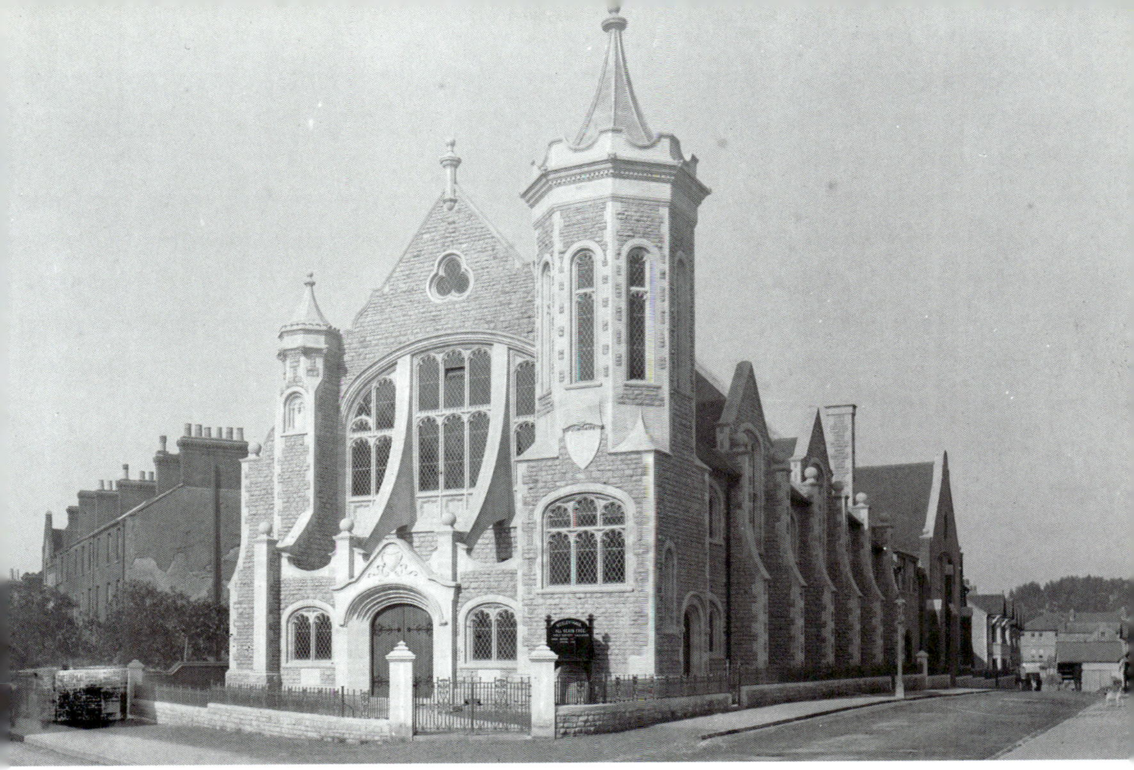

Wesleyan Chapel, Cowley Road

Opened in 1904, the Cowley Road Methodist chapel was designed by Stephen Salter and built by Messrs Kingerlee & Sons of Oxford. It was able to seat 700 worshippers, while the adjacent school could accommodate 500 pupils. With its curious turrets and boldly curved buttresses, the building is unexpectedly flamboyant for a Nonconformist chapel. The upper view shows building shortly after its completion, while the colour photograph was taken in June 2013.

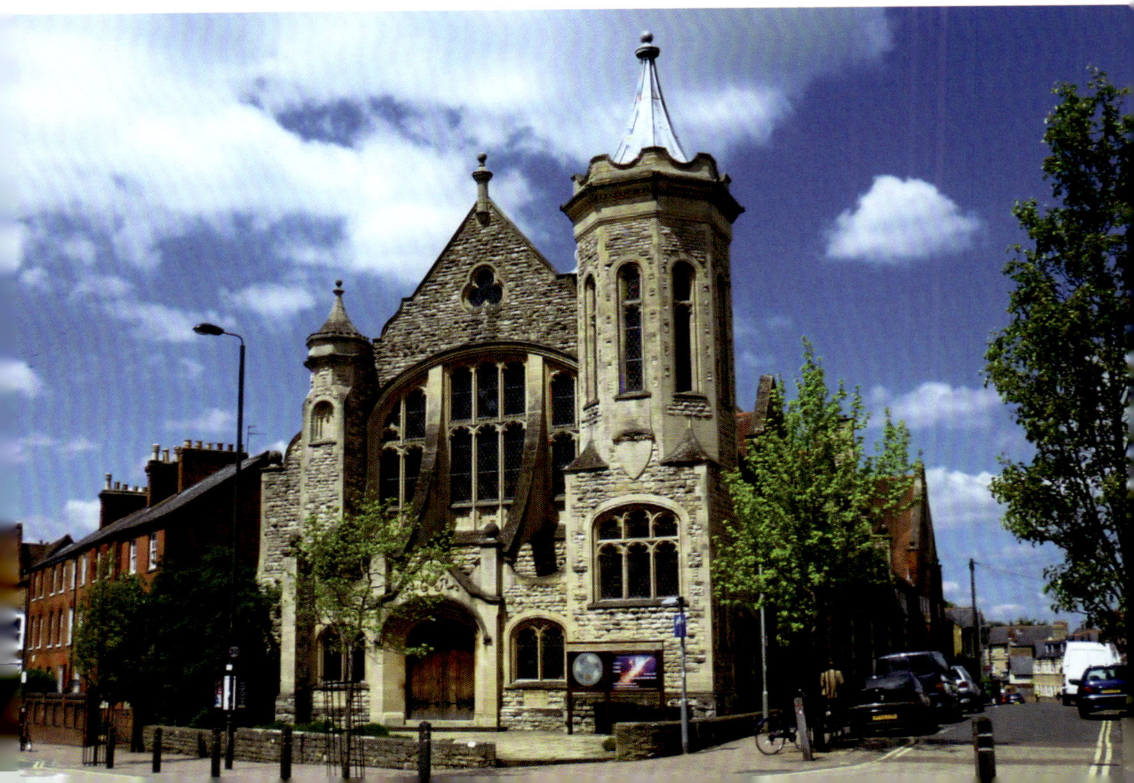

Miscellaneous

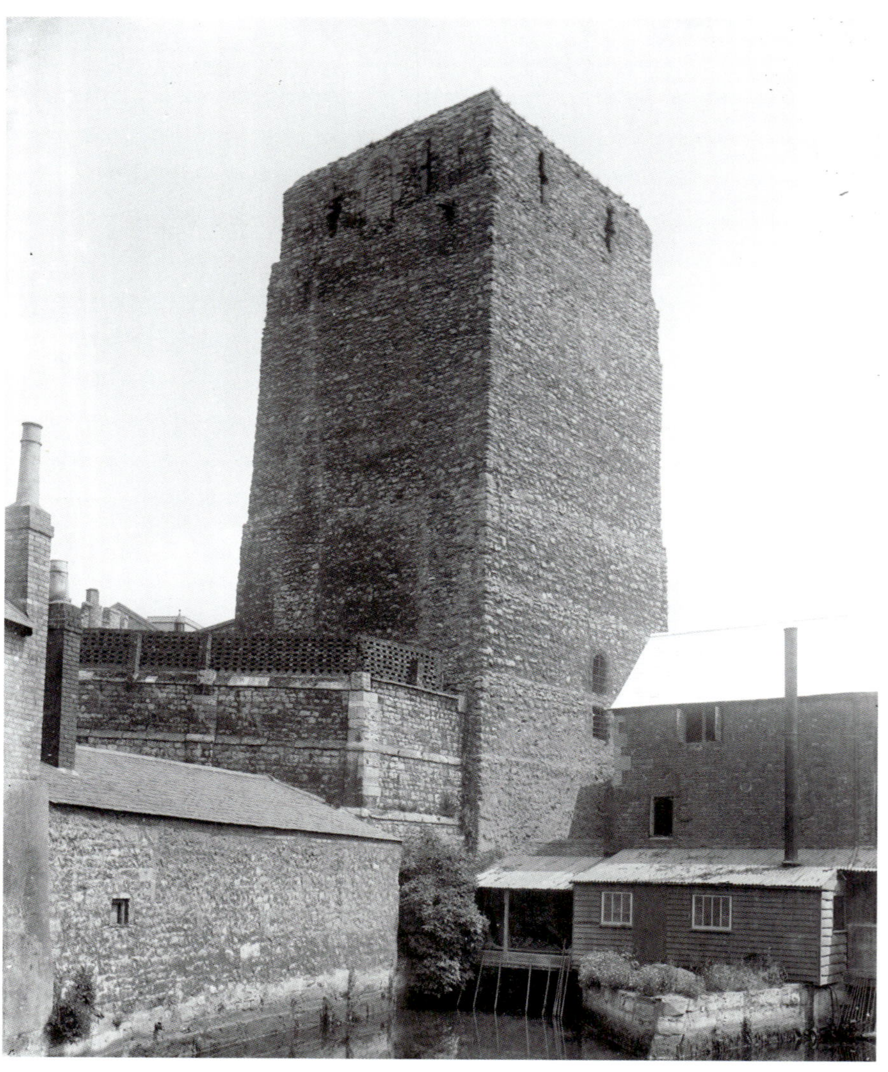

Oxford Castle – St George's Tower

Oxford Castle was founded shortly after the Norman Conquest by Robert d'Oyly, who erected a motte-and-bailey castle with timber buildings, which were later replaced by permanent stone-built structures, including a tall keep on top of the Castle Mound. Most of the castle was dismantled after the Civil War, but a prison and county court were built on the site during the 1840s. Five of the castle's six mural towers have been destroyed, but St George's Tower remains extant. It is thought that this grim-looking tower may have been erected during the eleventh century to serve as a rudimentary keep, because the earth of the newly raised motte was unable to bear the immense weight of a stone building. Although clearly of military origin, the tower also functioned as the bell tower of the long-demolished castle chapel.

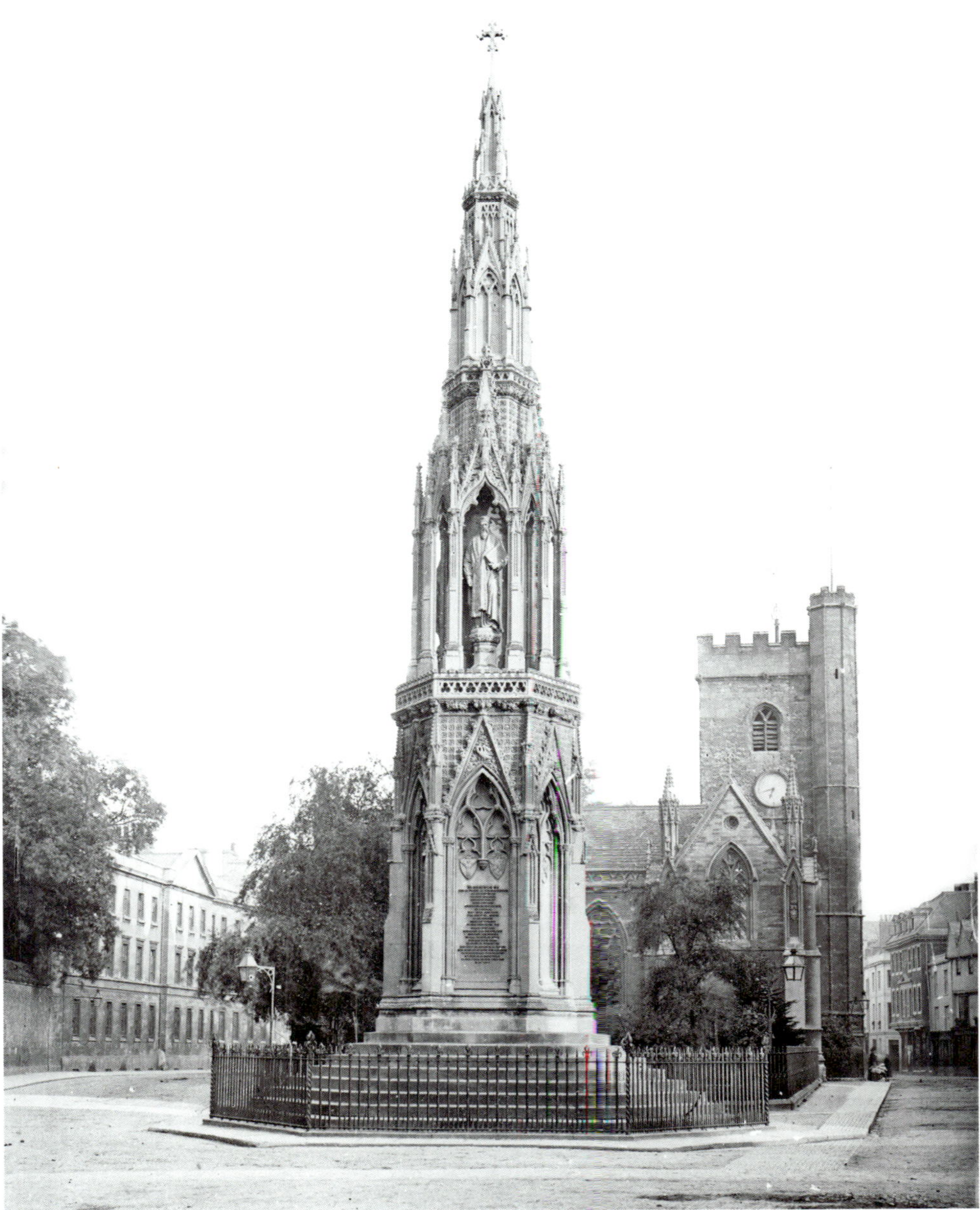

The Martyrs' Memorial

Designed by Sir George Gilbert Scott, the Martyrs' Memorial was erected in 1841–43 to commemorate the three Protestant bishops – Thomas Cranmer (1489–1556), Hugh Latimer (*c.* 1485–1555 and Nicholas Ridley (*c.* 1502–55) – who were burned to death during the reign of Queen Mary. Archbishop Cranmer, who had been persuaded to sign a recantation renouncing the Protestant faith, famously held his right hand in the flames and watched it burn, saying 'this hand hath offended'. His final words are said to have been: 'Lord Jesus, receive my spirit … I see the heavens open and Jesus standing at the right hand of God.'

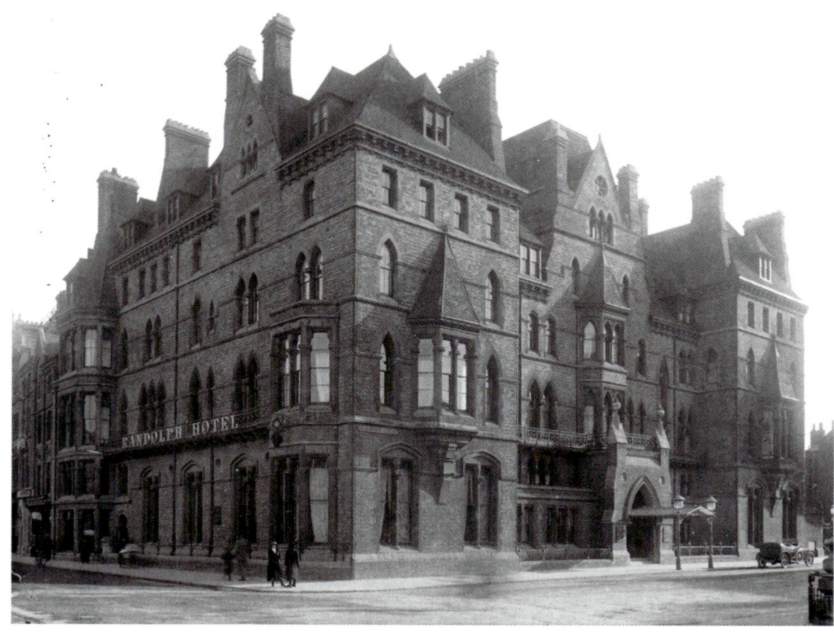

The Randolph Hotel

Designed by the Witney architect William Wilkinson (1819–1901), the Randolph is an archetypal Victorian 'grand hotel' in the Gothic style, with its main entrance in Beaumont Street. It is of yellow-brick construction with stone dressings and a steeply pitched hip roof. The hotel was completed in 1864 and an extension was added in 1952. The hotel narrowly escape destruction on the night of 15 December 1874 when a huge fire broke out in a neighbouring carriage maker's works, resulting in the destruction of several shops and business premises. The black-and-white view shows the hotel in 1915, and the colour photograph was taken in 2012.

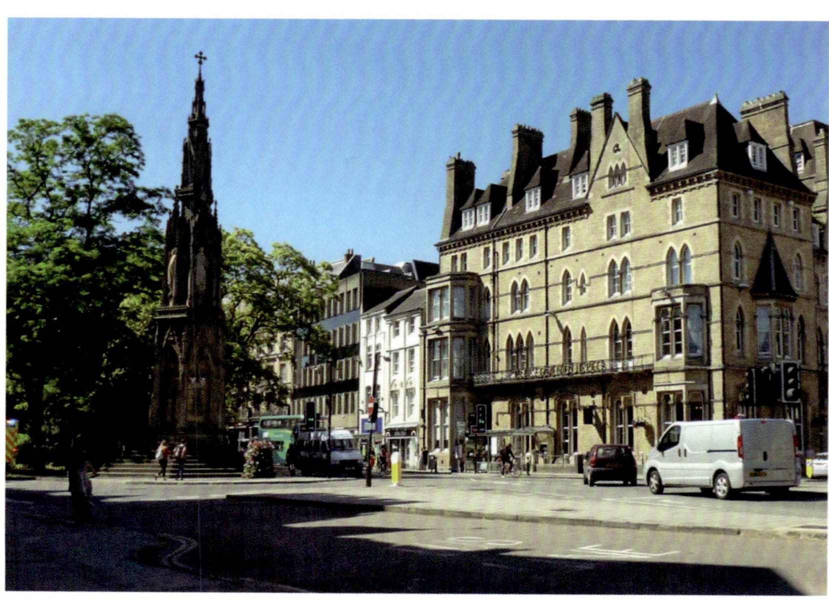

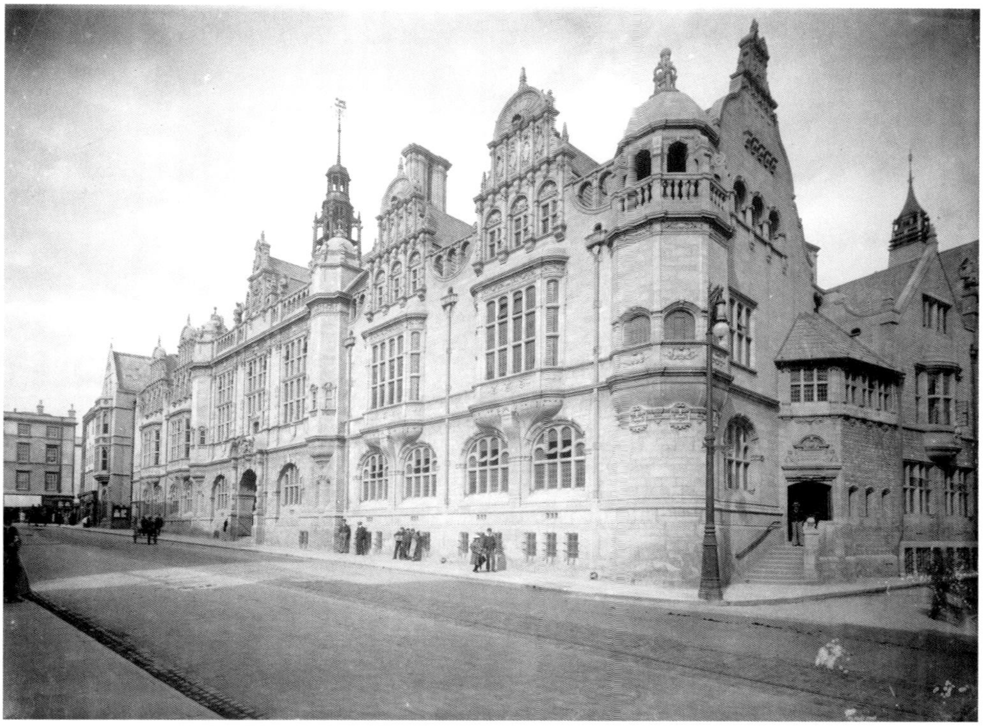

Oxford Town Hall
Constructed during the 1890s, the Town Hall, in St Aldates, was obviously intended to emphasise civic pride in a city that had been dominated by the university for centuries. Designed by Henry T. Hare (1861–1921) in the English Renaissance style, the building is lavishly decorated – the Council Chamber and Mayor's Parlour being richly panelled. The main assembly hall contains an organ made by Henry 'Father' Willis (1821–1901), the celebrated Victorian organ builder who built over 2,000 organs during his lengthy career, including the one in the Albert Hall.

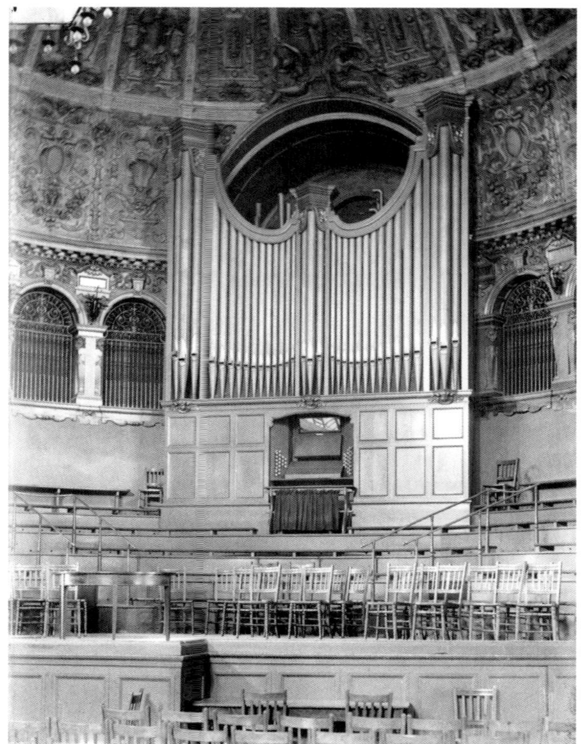

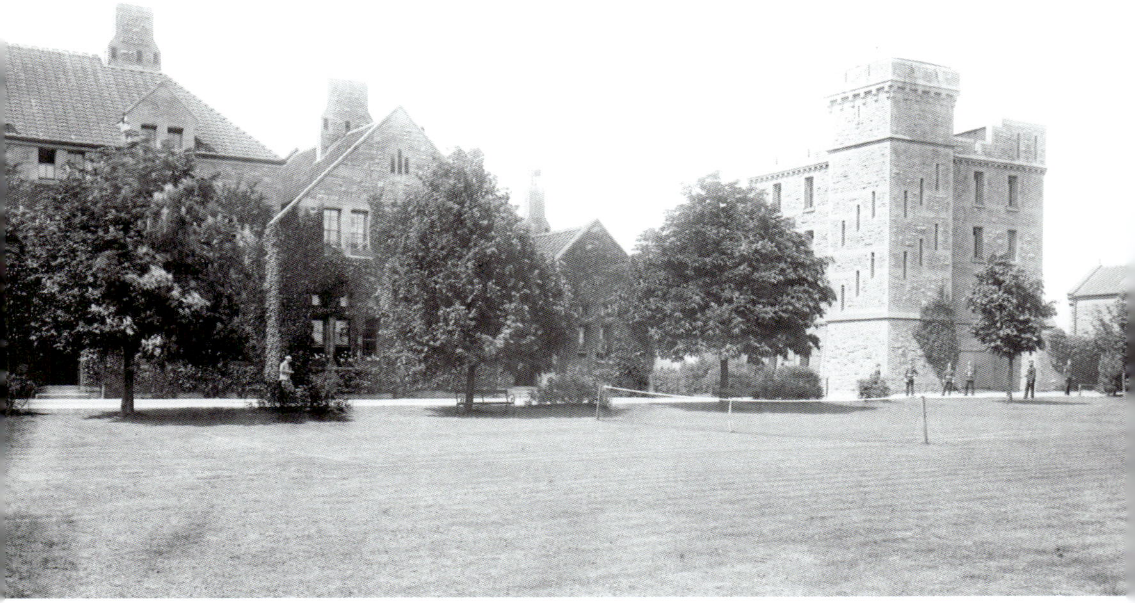

Cowley Barracks

Cowley Barracks was built in connection with the army reforms which were implemented between 1869 and 1871 by Edward Cardwell (1813–86), the Secretary of State for War. It was decided that a network of regional military 'depots' would be established, and in 1873 *The Times* reported that the War Office purchased 20 acres of land in what was then open countryside, around 2 miles south-east of Oxford. Despite protests from Oxford University, the construction of the barracks proceeded apace between 1874 and 1876, most of the building work being carried out by Messrs Downs & Co. of Southwark at a contract price of £45,000. The depot was opened on 7 June 1876, the first units to occupy the site being the 52nd (Oxfordshire) Light Infantry and the 85th (Bucks Volunteers) Regiment. The upper view shows the barracks around 1907, while the lower photograph shows part of the site in 2007.

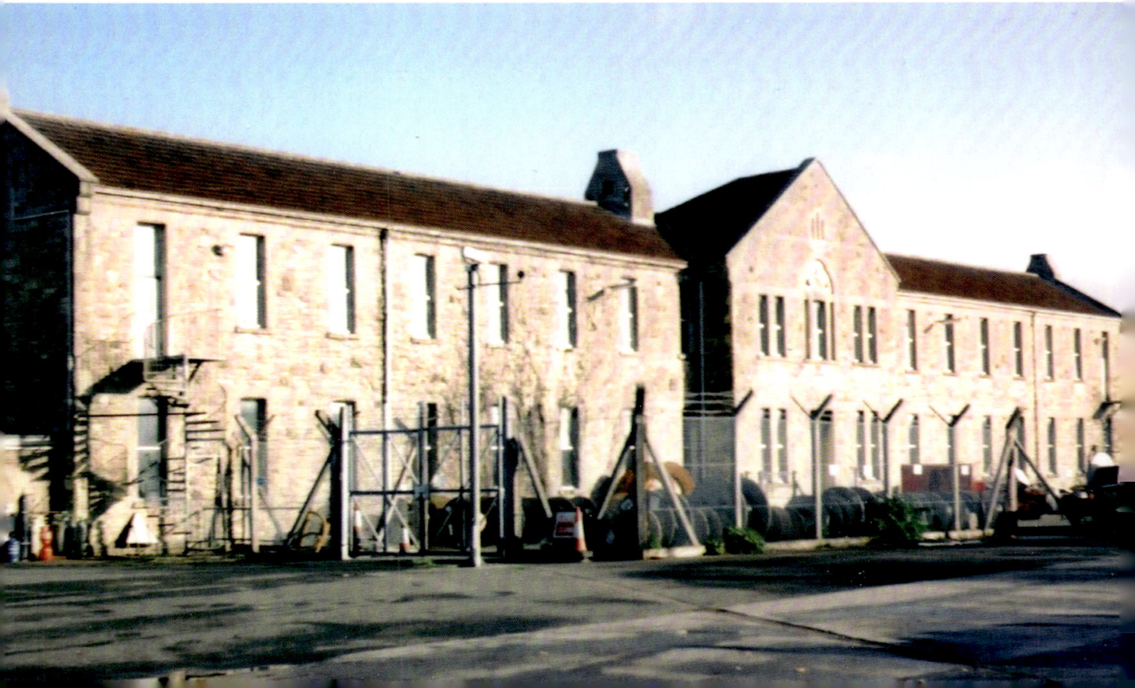

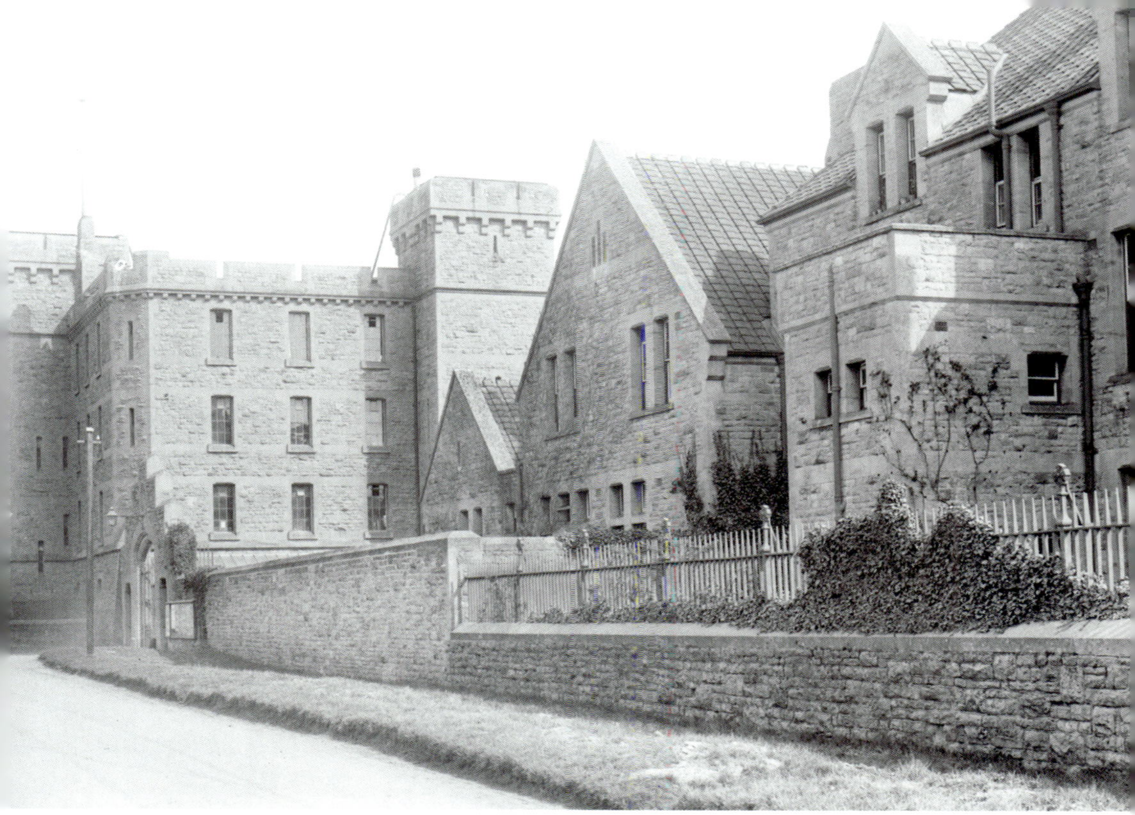

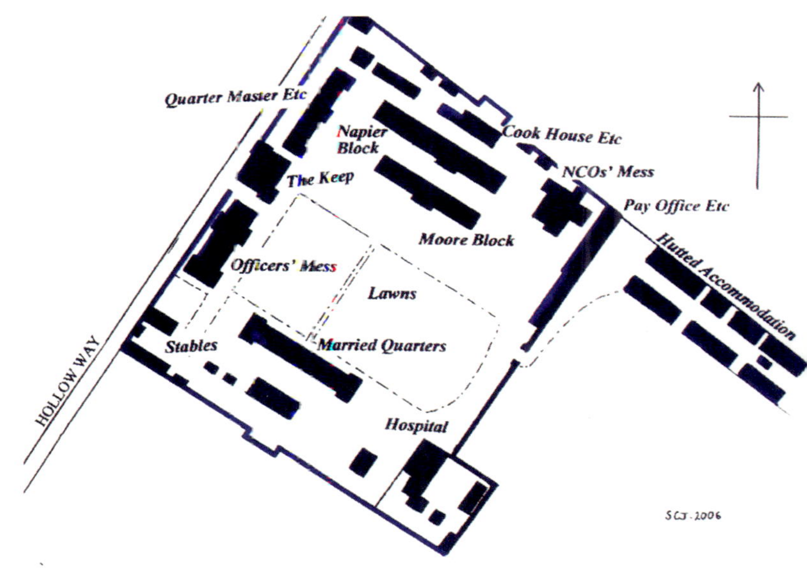

Cowley Barracks

Above: The most obvious feature of the barracks was a tall castle-like building known as 'The Keep'. This distinctive structure incorporated four full stories, together with two tall stair towers at the north-western and south-eastern corners of the building. The Officers' Mess, in the foreground, was also of 'medieval' appearance. The barracks contained a range of accommodation including offices, mess rooms, an armoury, stores, married quarters, a guardroom, cook house and stables, as well as a hospital.

Right: A sketch plan showing the layout of Cowley Barracks.

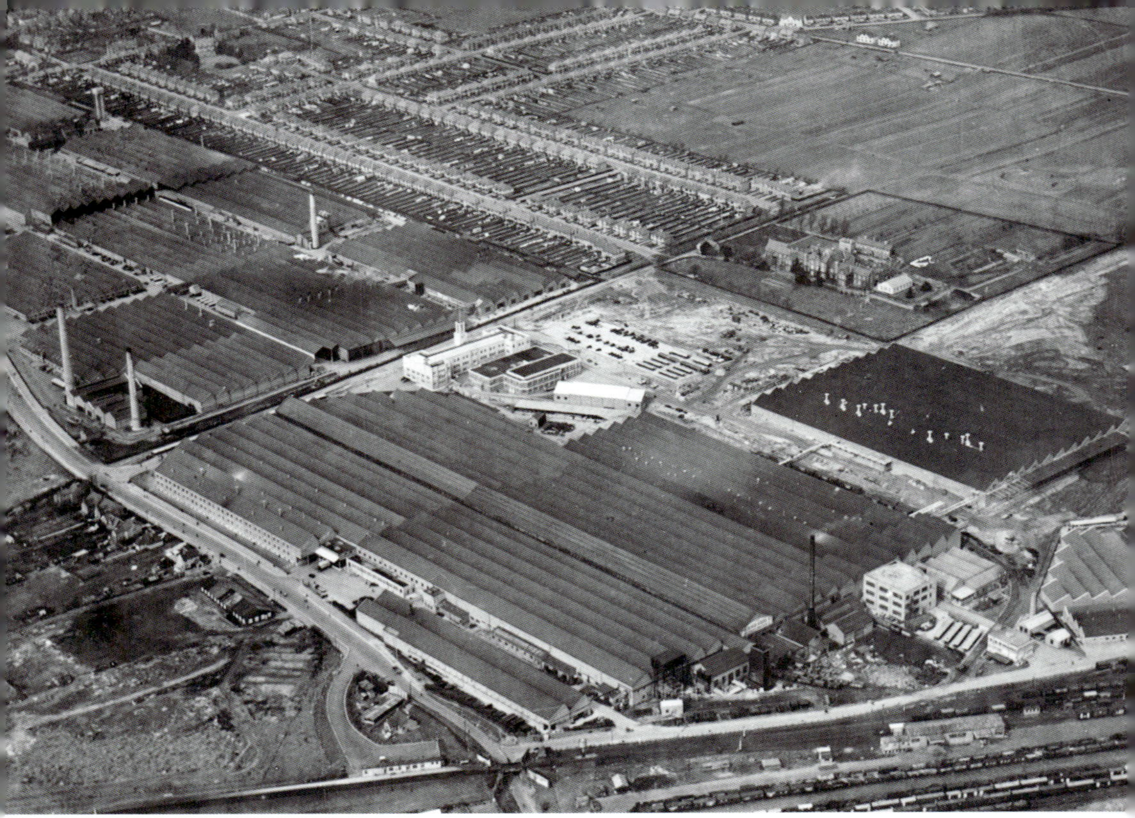

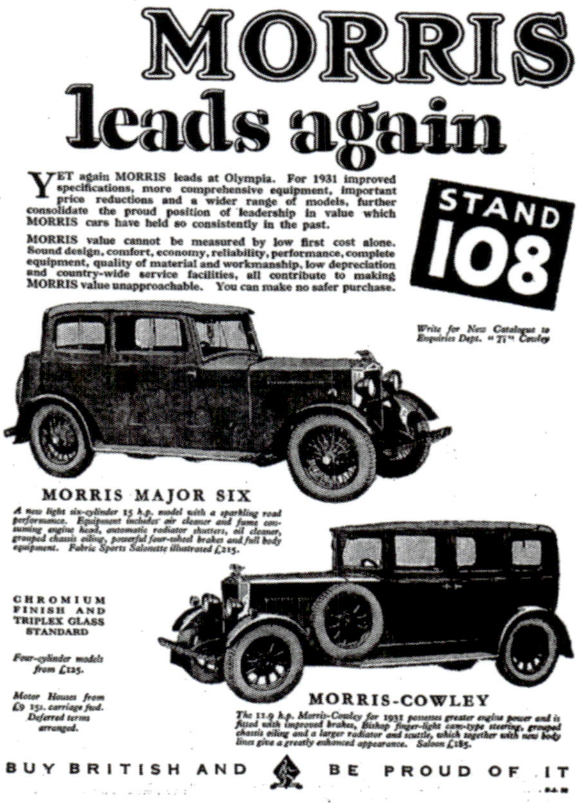

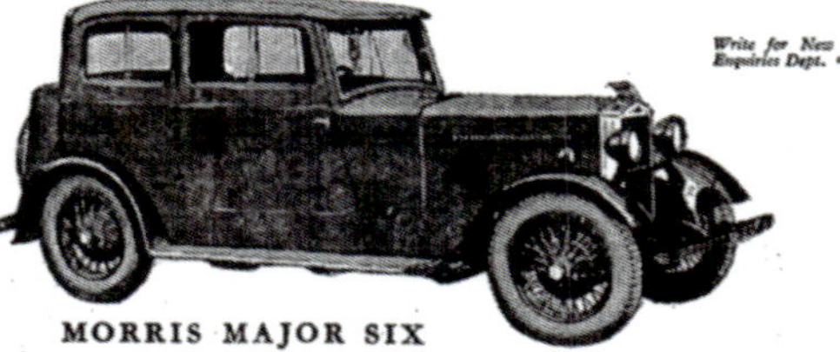

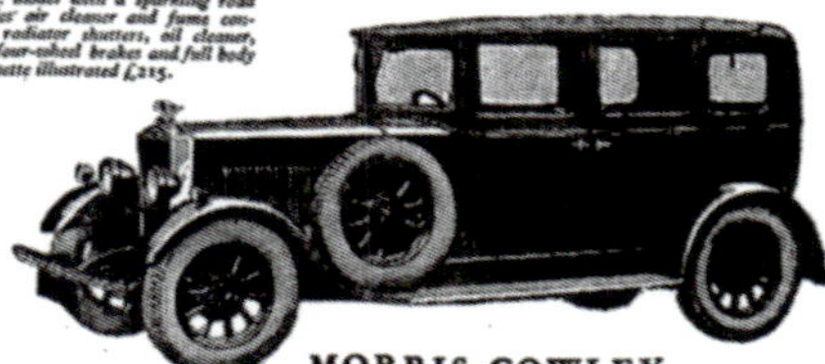

MORRIS
leads again

YET again MORRIS leads at Olympia. For 1931 improved specifications, more comprehensive equipment, important price reductions and a wider range of models, further consolidate the proud position of leadership in value which MORRIS cars have held so consistently in the past.

MORRIS value cannot be measured by low first cost alone. Sound design, comfort, economy, reliability, performance, complete equipment, quality of material and workmanship, low depreciation and country-wide service facilities, all contribute to making MORRIS value unapproachable.   You can make no safer purchase.

CHROMIUM
FINISH AND
TRIPLEX GLASS
STANDARD

Four-cylinder models
from £125.

Motor Houses from
£9 15s. carriage paid.
Deferred terms
arranged.

BUY BRITISH AND  BE PROUD OF IT

Lord Nuffield and Cowley Works

Born in Worcester, William Morris (1877–1963) attended Cowley village school until the age of fifteen, and having been apprenticed for a short time to an Oxford bicycle maker, he set up his own business at the age of just sixteen. The new venture prospered, and in 1913 Morris produced his first motor car – the two-seater Morris Oxford. In 1912, Morris rented a former school at Cowley know as the Military College, which he adapted for use as a car factory. An additional building known as the 'Old Tin Shed' was built to the north of the school, while 'B Block' and the main production lines were added in the 1920s and 1930s respectively. By 1939 the car plant employed over 2,000 people. The upper view shows part of the Cowley complex from the air, while the illustration on the left depicts a Morris advertisement from 1931.

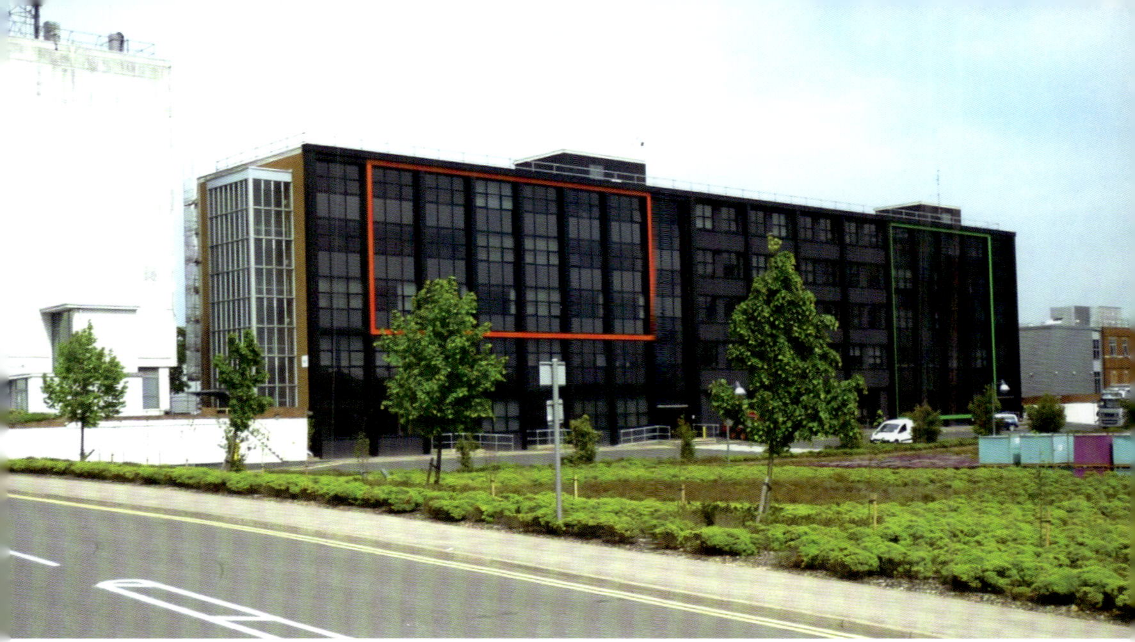

Lord Nuffield and Cowley Works

In 1926 Morris opened the Pressed Steel body plant as a joint venture with the Budd Company of America and J. Henry Schroder, a merchant bank. Morris and the Budd Company subsequently withdrew, leaving Pressed Steel as an independent concern, and there were thus two factories at Cowley – although both eventually became part of the British Motor Corporation (later British Leyland). After many vicissitudes, the factories were acquired by BMW. The North and South Morris works were demolished, but the former Pressed Steel site was modernised and re-equipped so that it could produce an all-new version of the highly successful MINI. The photographs show the MINI plant in 2013; over 20,000 people worked at Cowley in the 1970s, whereas today the workforce is around 3,700.

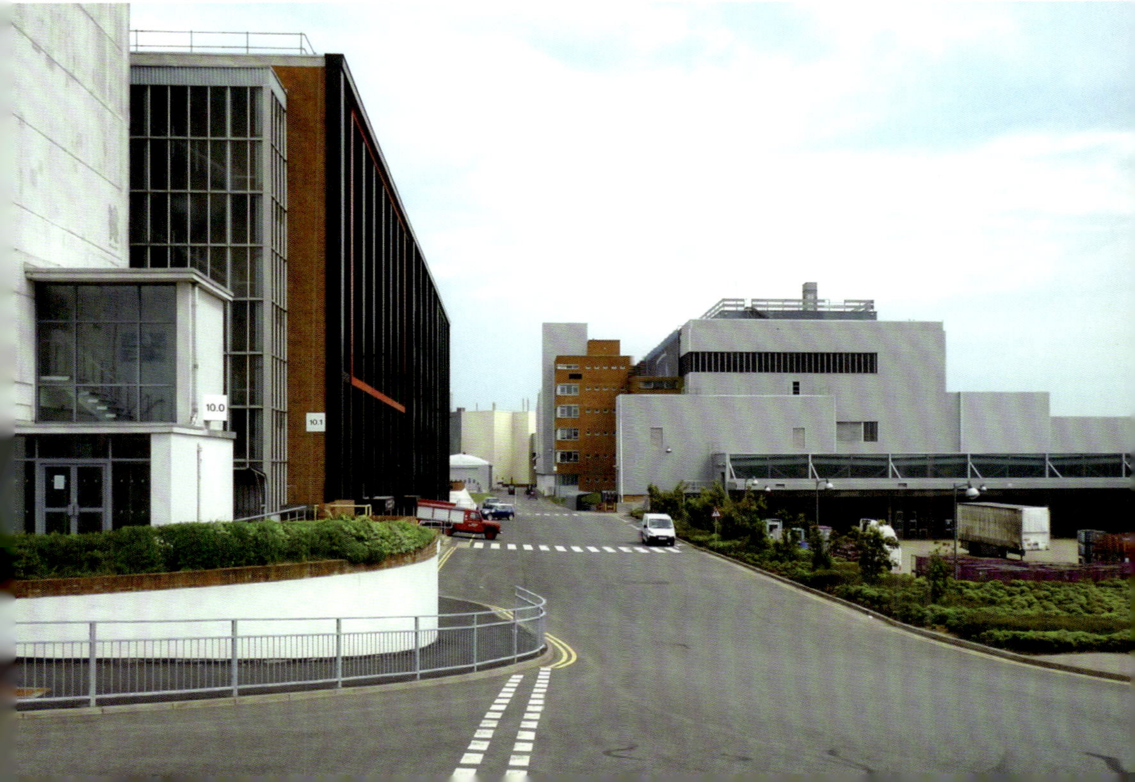

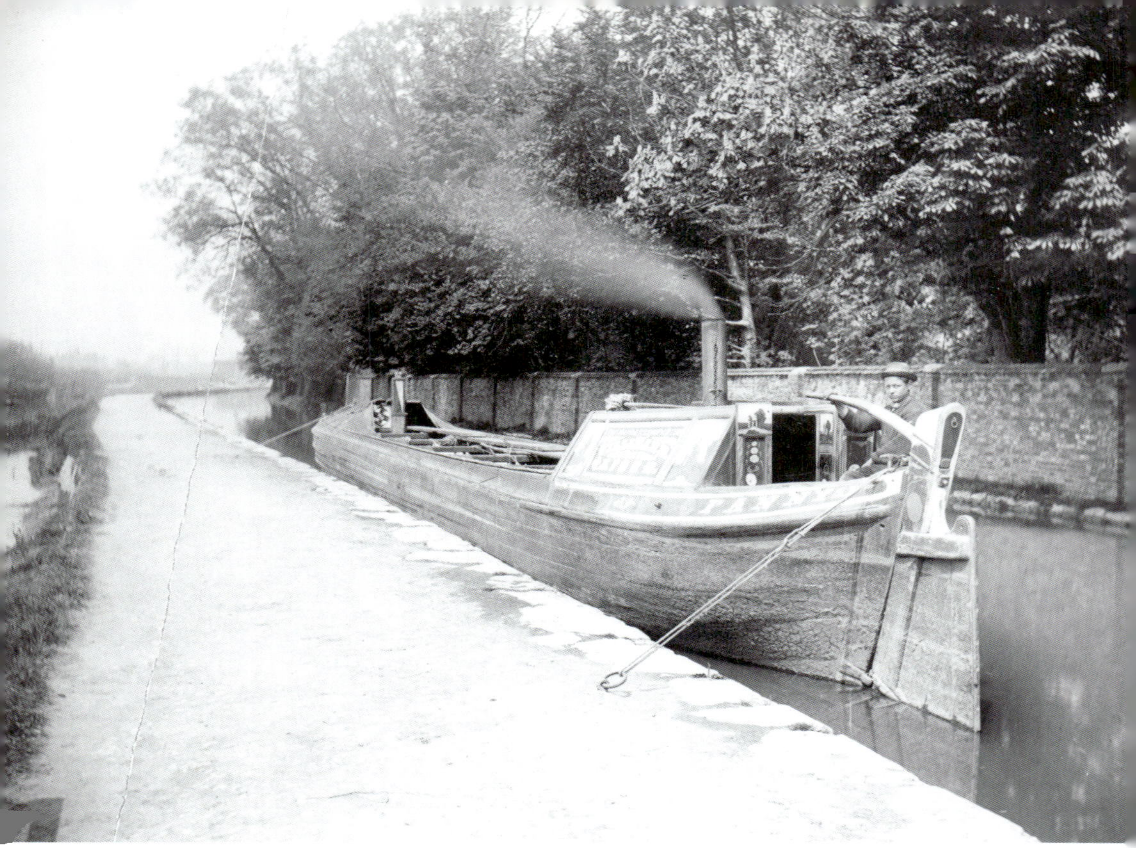

As mentioned earlier, the Oxford Canal was completed throughout to Oxford in 1790, but the waterway went into decline after the opening of the railways. The upper photograph was taken by Henry Taunt in 1890, and it shows the horse-drawn narrowboat *Fanny* moored alongside the canal in Oxford. The colour view, taken over a century later, shows the motor boat *Towy* on the same stretch of the canal. The distinctive tower of St Barnabas Church is visible in the background.

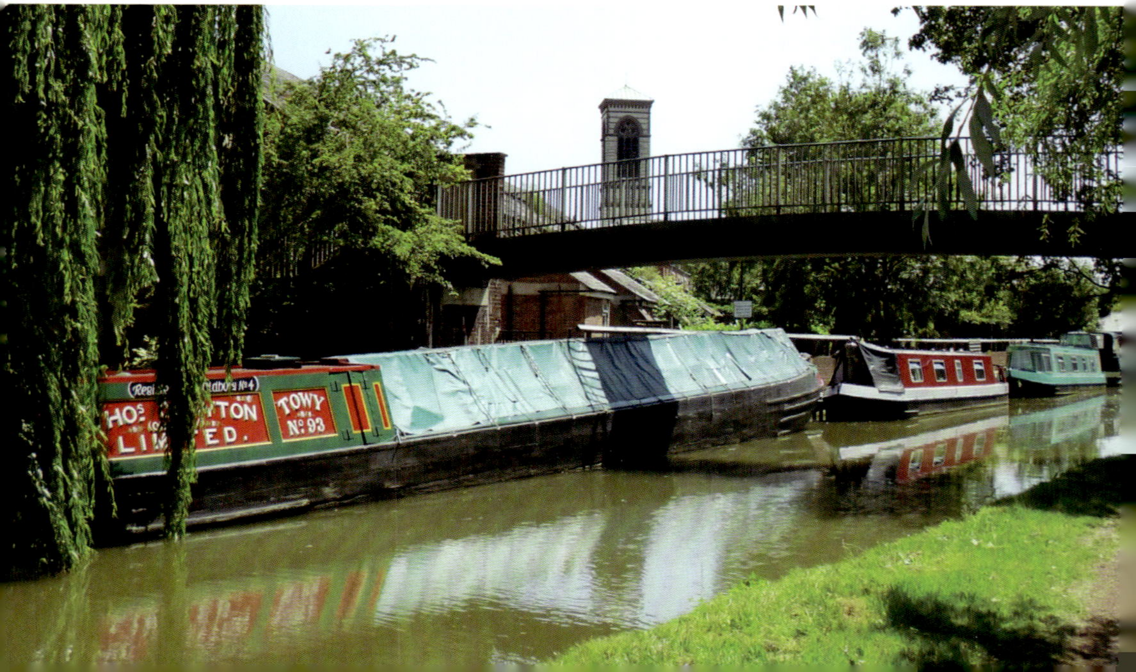

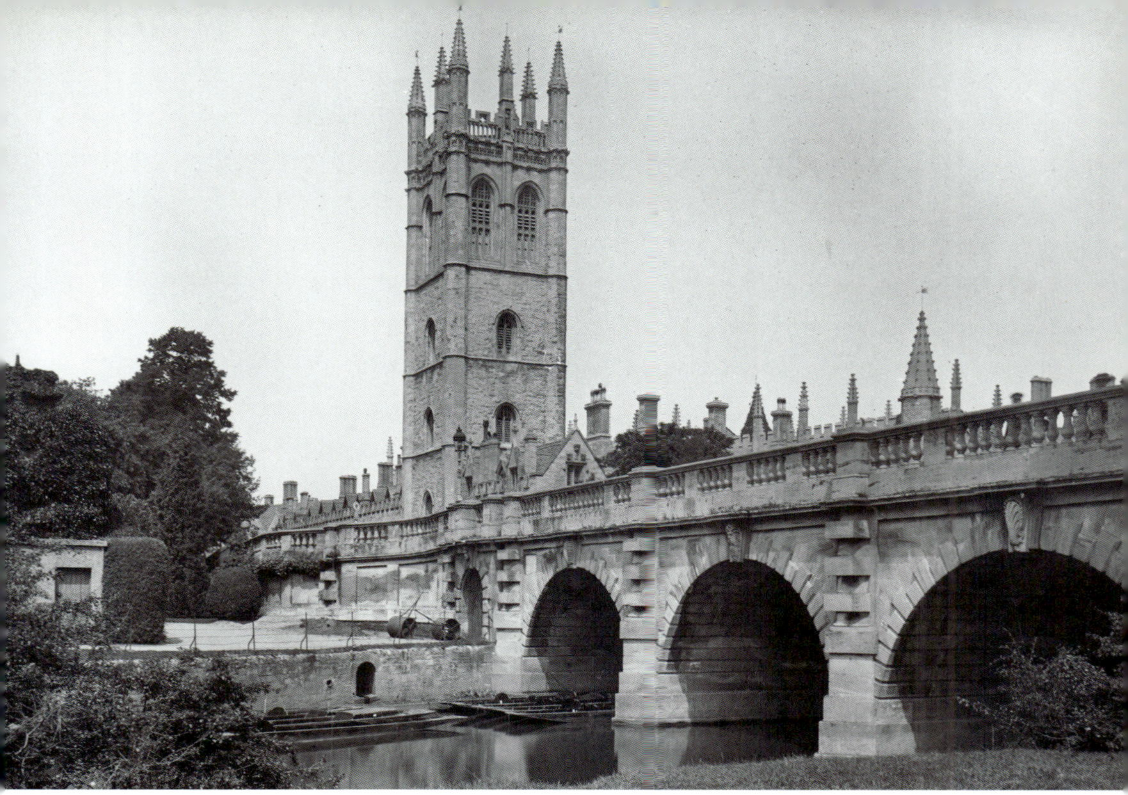

Magdalen Bridge

The present Magdalen Bridge was built in 1772–78, although further work was carried out in the 1790s. The bridge, which has eleven arched spans of varying dimensions, was widened in 1882 to provide sufficient room for the Oxford & District Tramway Co.'s 4-foot gauge tram line, which was opened from the railway stations to Cowley Road on 1 December 1881 and abandoned in 1914. The upper photograph shows the bridge in 1920, while the lower view dates from the 1880s.

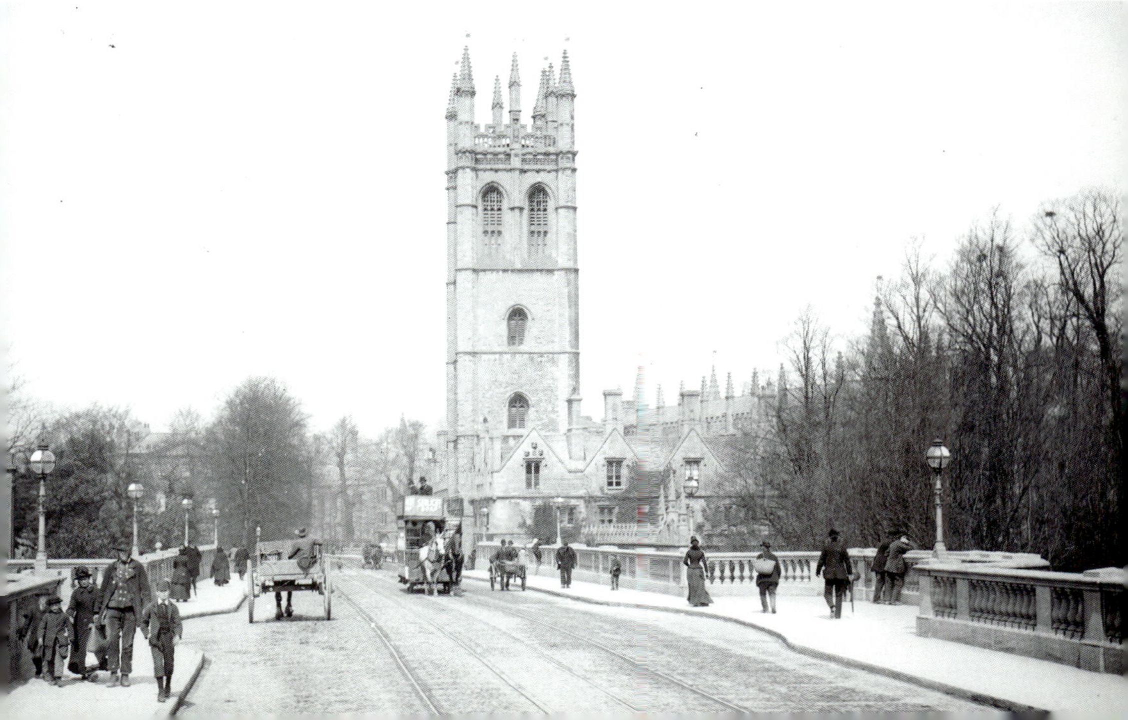

About the Archive

Many of the images in this volume come from the Historic England Archive, which holds over 12 million photographs, drawings, plans and documents covering England's archaeology, architecture, social and local history.

The photographic collections include prints from the earliest days of photography to today's high-resolution digital images. Subjects range from Neolithic flint mines and medieval churches to art deco cinemas and 1980s shopping centres. The collection is a vivid record both of buildings that are still part of everyday life – places of work, leisure and worship – and those lost long ago, surviving only in fragile prints or glass-plate negatives.

Six million aerial photographs offer a unique and fascinating view of the transformation of England's towns, cities, coast and countryside from 1919 onwards. Highlights include the pioneering photography of Aerofilms, and the comprehensive survey of England captured by the RAF after the Second World War.

Plans, drawings and reports provide further context and reconstruction artworks bring archaeological sites and historic buildings to life.

The collections are housed in a purpose-built environmentally controlled store in Swindon, which provides the best conditions to preserve archive items for future generations to enjoy. You can search our catalogue online, see and buy copies of our images, as well as visiting our public search room by appointment.

Find out more about us at HistoricEngland.org.uk/Photos
email: archive@historicengland.org.uk
tel.: 01793 414600

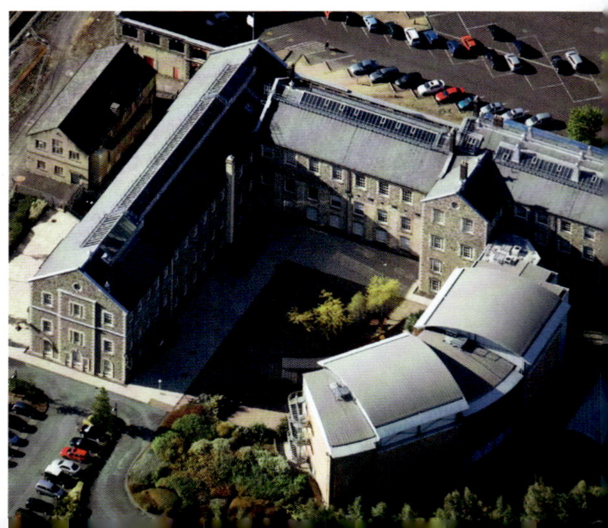

The Historic England offices and archive store in Swindon from the air, 2007.